THE
BOOK
OF NICE

THE
BOOK
OF NICE

*A Nice Book About
Nice Things for Nice People*

.

JOSH CHETWYND

Illustrations by Phil McAndrew

WORKMAN PUBLISHING · NEW YORK

Library of Congress Cataloging-in-Publication Data is available.

ISBN 978-0-7611-7294-9

Cover design by Raquel Jaramillo
Interior design by Ariana Abud
Illustrations by Phil McAndrew
Cover photo by © ZEBRAHORSE / Shutterstock

Workman books are available at special discounts when purchased in
bulk for premiums and sales promotions as well as for fund-raising or
educational use. Special editions or book excerpts can also be created
to specification. For details, contact the Special Sales Director at the
address below, or send an email to specialmarkets@workman.com.

Workman Publishing Company, Inc.
225 Varick Street
New York, NY 10014-4381
workman.com

Printed in the United States of America
First printing April 2013
10 9 8 7 6 5 4 3 2 1

*For
Jennifer,
Miller,
and Becca*

Contents

Introduction

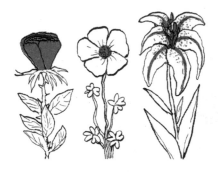

Nice just doesn't get the love. Few sentiments are so seemingly positive yet receive so much criticism.

"If you ever want to say nothing in the most efficient way possible, just say something is 'nice,'" a journalist at *Publishers Weekly* griped in 2011. "No other word ostensibly expresses contentment and acceptance while also harboring 14 (approximate) subterranean shades of doubt and pessimism."

Back in the 1980s, legendary funnyman George Carlin was more succinct in explaining his anti-nice stance on the phrase "Have a nice day." "I know what it is that bothers me about the whole thing," he said. "It's the word *nice*. It is just a weak word. It doesn't have a lot of character."

Ouch.

Nice deserves better. When nice gestures, words or images are executed with proper meaning (and accepted as such), they can be powerful shorthand for many of the virtues we consider important. If you want to convey a significant feeling like respect, love, generosity, inclusiveness or reassurance, *nice* has your back. For example, it's hard to beat a friendly hug as a (non-lusty) sign of affection—and depending on the occasion, there are numerous other options like presenting a box of chocolates, or singing "For He's a Jolly Good Fellow." If you'd like to give a little respect, you've got a hat-tip at your disposal. Then there's a wink, which can be deployed when you'd like to tell someone you're on the same page. And conjuring up the Tooth Fairy certainly takes away some of the sting of losing a tooth.

There's actually scientific proof to support the medicinal value of giving and accepting nice behavior. Studies have shown hand-holding—even clasping a stranger's hand—can calm an individual in a particularly stressful moment. A well-received compliment stimulates the brain in a positive way and, according to some studies, slurping up a bowl of chicken noodle soup from Grandma does indeed make a difference in your health.

And, lest you think *nice guys finish last,* consider this: One of America's first great department store magnates, J. C. Penney, believed treating others nicely was so important, he named his original shop (and the thirty-three that would follow it) the Golden Rule Store. If you want something a little more empirical, a group of researchers at the University of North Carolina once calculated that not being nice (i.e., acting rude) in the workplace costs companies a lot of money (in some cases, billions of dollars) annually in, among other things, lost productivity.

But at the same time *nice* isn't a naive concept. It's complicated. Let's start with the word itself. The term wasn't always a good thing. *Nice* originally stemmed from the Latin word *nescius,* meaning "ignorant," and in early French and English cultures *acting nice* meant "being foolish." It eventually morphed into meaning "shy" and then "fastidious and refined" before, in the second half of the eighteenth century, it reached its current primary definition—"pleasant, agreeable, or kind." Yet some modern dictionaries have as many as seventeen different explanations for what *nice* can mean (including such options as "suitable or proper" and "finicky or fussy tastes.") All this leaves some bewildered as to what they're really saying.

Actions that are characterized as nice aren't any simpler. Many traditions discussed in this book took time to earn nice status and feature compelling twists. For instance, the phrase "bless you" was developed by a nervous Pope during an ancient plague; the saying "eat, drink, and be merry" was originally a cautionary statement; and the literary ancestors of fairy godmothers ruined a person's future as often as they granted his or her wishes. Even the story behind slapping hands up top (aka the *high five*) is full of disagreement and heartbreak.

These complexities sometimes make it hard to identify *nice*. Nice deeds can often move on or off the list based on shifts in popular culture. Take opening a door for a lady. In polite society, it was a no-brainer a couple of generations ago. Now there are those who find it sexist and believe that rather than nice, it's a patronizing action. On the other hand, a few decades ago hand writing a letter to a friend wouldn't have been seen as nice—it was simply a way in which we interacted. But before long—if not already—email, texting, social media, and other more advanced forms of communication will make the handwritten letter more of a quaint nicety than a necessary task. (It didn't make it into this book, but if there's a sequel it might be a good candidate.)

Another problem *nice* faces is cynicism. A key component of nice behavior is sincerity. If you're told you look beautiful, the impact of that statement hinges on whether the speaker truly means it (or the recipient, genuinely believes it); If the words are sincere then it's a compliment, but if they're not, it's hollow flattery or, worse, a form of ridicule. A wink suffers from the same uncertainty. It can be a sweet gesture or it can come off as lecherous. It all depends on context and intentions.

> A KEY COMPONENT OF NICE BEHAVIOR IS SINCERITY.

There are many who like to tweak what would normally be nice behavior in negative ways (like offering a healthy serving of sarcasm with a "thank-you" or mockingly applauding another). Those disingenuous moments leave some ill-equipped to assume the best in others. Alternatively, nice behavior is often considered synonymous with *manners,* which are perceived as something you go through the motions doing without any real meaning. (Applied properly, the intention of manners has long been to give legitimate signs of regard or deference to others.) The upshot is many folks recoil at seemingly nice acts, turned off by the uncertainty of it all.

MANY FOLKS RECOIL AT SEEMINGLY NICE ACTS, TURNED OFF BY THE UNCERTAINTY OF IT ALL.

If I've done my job well, you'll discover examples and discussion of these themes embedded in the following pages and, maybe, this book will even cut through some of the vagueness at the root of *nice.* But, more than anything, my hope is you'll find this a fun read featuring the colorful origins and backgrounds of what we identify as all things nice.

While this book aims to be comprehensive, it isn't exhaustive. There were some things on the edge of *nice* that just didn't have enough unanimity to make the cut here. Moreover, *nice* is driven by local traditions. For example, in Japan bowing has very different rules and connotations than in the U.S. Recognizing that, this book primarily focuses on the niceties of the Western world (and even more specifically those of English-speaking folks) because I wanted to highlight what would be most relevant to the majority of this volume's readers. Nevertheless, where appropriate I've pointed out contrasts or similarities from elsewhere around the globe.

Finally, I must admit I've got a soft side. So if in the end, learning the history of charity, smiling, or saying "please" (or any other nice moves) leads to a little more fondness for the concept or inspires you to put a bit of *nice* into practice, well then, all the better.

Nice Handiwork

Applause

Humans have smacked their hands together for a variety of reasons since the dawn of time (I can just see Grog clapping loudly to get the attention of his clan as a herd of woolly mammoths stampedes toward them). But the Romans were among the first in the Western world to use the gesture to convey appreciation. The word *applause*, which appears in the writings of philosophers from Horace to Seneca the Elder, comes from the Latin *applaudere*, which effectively means "to clap in approval." Applause was just one rung in a hierarchy of public approval: Mild support elicited finger snapping, true appreciation called for clapping, while the highest form of praise involved waving a loose end of your toga.

Lusty approbation was so valued in the first century that the extravagant and thoroughly self-absorbed Emperor Nero, who dabbled in musical performance, required as many as 5,000 soldiers, known as *Augustals*, to applaud his performances. Clearly, there wasn't a ton of sincere loyalty there, because Nero was eventually driven from the throne.

EARLY CHRISTIANS WOULD APPLAUD A PARTICULARLY MEANINGFUL SERMON—A PRACTICE THAT'S NOW VERBOTEN IN MOST MODERN CHURCHES.

Yet, Nero's rent-a-clap did leave a legacy. In the sixteenth century, French poet Jean Daurat, looking to drum up some support for his new works, remembered reading about Nero's efforts. Inspired, he distributed free tickets to people who could then be counted on to enthusiastically clap at the end of his plays. This organized cadre of faux fans came to be known as the *claque*.

The tradition persisted, and in the 1820s, shrewd French businessman named Monsieur

Stauton turned the process into a money-making venture. Stauton's company, *Assurance de Succès Dramatiques*, or the office for the insurance of dramatic success, would make sure (for a price) that the audience delivered the appropriate reactions throughout a performance.

The exacting operation could include as many as 300 to 500 hired hands: There were *commissaries*, who would nudge the paying patrons at key dramatic moments; *rieurs* were expected to boisterously laugh at the jokes; the *pleureurs*, usually women, would pretend to cry at the right moments; and the *bisseurs* were expected to clap emotionally. There was even a *chef de claque*, who was responsible for making sure the whole operation went according to plan.

The artificial effort became so essential in Parisian theater that scripts would include direction for the *claque* on when to clap, cry, or laugh. Actors were even known to complain to the *chef de claque* if the applause didn't meet their expectations.

Eventually, there was a *claque* backlash. In the late nineteenth century, artists as diverse as British playwright George Bernard Shaw and German composer Richard Wagner wanted patrons to play a diminished role and called for an end to applause

The Big O

We think of an **ovation** as the pinnacle of applause, but in ancient Rome an ovation was just a so-so celebration. A complete victory against a fierce foe—one that qualified for a full-blown party—was dubbed a **triumph**. But when a military commander secured a minor victory, say, without bloodshed or against a slave army (back in the day, it was much more impressive to win in gruesome fashion against a bunch of well-trained mercenaries), his return from battle was merely known as an **ovation**. He would receive a crown made of the myrtle plant instead of the more significant laurel, and travel back to Rome on horse or by foot rather than in a chariot.

(and all noise for that matter) during performances. Wagner's influence allegedly led Germany to ban clapping during all concerts and shows.

These days applause is everywhere—and often where you'd least expect it. In a move that Wagner would surely approve of, Pope Benedict XVI came out against the growing trend of applauding during Catholic Mass. One British commentator also expressed concern, pointing to the funeral processional of Princess Diana in which the departed princess's casket received applause.

Is applause "an appropriate way to offer tribute to the dead?" asked Marcel Berlins in a 2007 edition of *The Guardian* (U.K.). "It should not be seen as a mere alternative to silence. It signifies different emotions, a different state of mind. Applause is the commonplace expression of appreciation and enthusiasm for a sporting feat, an enjoyable entertainment, or a speech at a wedding. It recognises that something good has occurred."

Blowing a Kiss

Blowing a kiss is cute, but can it save your soul?

Originally reserved for the religious realm, kisses were thrown by worshippers to show dedication to their chosen deity. According to one scholar, it was known as "lifting the hand," and it was a practical solution to a specific challenge of expressing religious devotion.

While experts have difficulty pinpointing the dates, this practice likely started in Mesopotamia between 3500 and 3000 B.C. The heavily ritualized ceremonies of the time often prohibited regular folk from getting close enough to bestow respectful kisses upon altars, idols, graves, or other sacred objects. Still, it was vital to show appreciation. The answer: a long-distance smooch. Simply mimicking the puckering motion was too small a gesture, so using your hand as a launching pad for this show of religious zeal was a must.

Both the Greeks and Romans embraced the practice but not without controversy. When the Roman emperor Otho blew a kiss to the masses upon taking the throne in the year 69, critics took quill to scroll in protest. They insisted the gesture should be limited to the spiritual realm, with one describing Otho's populist move as "slavish." The kisses may have upset more than just pundits, since Otho lasted only three months in power before he was overthrown.

The religious stance on blowing a smooch persisted for centuries. Sixteenth-century archbishop Giovanni della Cassa, who penned a book on manners, wrote that blowing kisses was the domain of "those solemnities that church men do use at their Altars, and in their divine service of both to God and to his holy things." Throwing a kiss to mere mortals was wholly wrong because it treated them "as if they were holy things."

Ultimately, the archbishop had little sway. By the end of the the sixteenth century, blowing a kiss became *de rigueur* in Europe's royal courts. (Aristocrats have always been suckers for all forms of flattery.) Etiquette experts provided detailed descriptions on how to blow the perfect kiss. One writer provided a disturbingly long how-to list: The maneuver must only be done with the right hand and the hand should not touch the mouth. The wrist and hand should be bent in with the index finger coming closest to the lips. And of course, the thrown kiss must be accompanied by a bow or curtsy. The pomp surrounding the pantomimed smooch escalated to such over-the-top proportions that William Shakespeare mocked it in several plays. The literary scorn helped diminish enthusiasm for the fad, which fell out of fashion by the nineteenth century.

But it was the blown kiss's fall from grace that became its saving grace. "The secret of its survival," according to the authors of the book *Gestures: Their Origins and Distribution*, ". . . lies in its removal from the formal sphere to the informal." When blowing a kiss made its twentieth-century comeback, it was in the far-from-holy (or royal) realm of 1930s

Rubbing Noses

The **Eskimo kiss** (nuzzling noses as a sign of affection) is not really a kiss. And, technically, it has nothing to do with Eskimos. The term *Eskimo* is a catchall name for a vast group of indigenous arctic people. (It was a pejorative term used by non-Eskimos, basically meaning *eaters of raw flesh*.) What we call the Eskimo kiss is the Canadian Inuit people's way of greeting each other with the gesture, *kunik*, which involves pressing the nostrils against another's skin and taking a friendly whiff.

Betty Boop cartoons (though, in my humble opinion, Boop was outdone by another animated siren—Jessica Rabbit, in the 1988 movie *Who Framed Roger Rabbit*). Today, like Otho nearly 2,000 years ago, beautiful (real-life) starlets blow kisses to the crowds. And while these kisses won't save any souls, we can be pretty certain—though not positive—it won't lead to any actresses' downfall.

Fist Bump

Deep down, everyone wants to be just a little bit cool. And when it comes to saying hello, there's nothing hip about the traditional handshake. Enter the fist bump.

"With its restraint and hint of machismo, the fist bump sends a more ambiguous message than the handshake, let alone the loosey-goosey rapturous high-five," *The New York Times* explained in 2001. And according to a dictionary on gestures, it can also signal "an aroused emotional state, as

Cartoon Bump

Cartoon-watching kids of the 1970s might point to another possible (and significantly less hip) explanation for the fist bump's popularity. The Hanna-Barbera animated series *Super Friends* featured a pair called the Wonder Twins, who would touch fists and exclaim, "Wonder Twin powers, activate!" before shape-shifting in preparation to take on the bad guys. As a former *Super Friends* fan, I'd like to believe it, but it's probably an after-the-fact claim.

in anger, excitement, or fear." Perhaps that vaguely dangerous element helped elevate the fist bump's cool quotient.

Most believe the ritual evolved from the *dap greeting*, which started in the late 1960s during the Vietnam War or possibly even dates back to World War II. A complex series of gestures, including the knocking of knuckles, daps were developed by African American soldiers who brought them back to their hometowns.

The man credited with putting the fist bump part of the dap on the national scene (likely inspired by the dap greetings used in his Philadelphia neighborhood) was Fred Carter, who played in the NBA for eight seasons from 1969 to 1977.

"I don't claim fatherhood, but I was one of the guys in the seventies doing it," Carter said in a 2001 interview. "The high-five was for a team accomplishment, and the bump was more an individual thing. . . . You bumped when your testosterone hit a peak. It was a crescendo of success; and when we did it, it was manly."

Other athletes embraced the move, and by the 1990s it was a regular occurrence on fields, playgrounds, and in arenas. At the dawn of the millenium, it had moved beyond the sports world with a broad range of hipsters offering up fist bumps, from musician Eddie Vedder to actress Charlize Theron.

But nothing stays cool forever, and even the fist bump has begun to show signs of overuse. Prince Charles and the Dalai Lama are among the many people who have been caught on camera fist bumping. On the game show *Deal or No Deal*, Howie Mandel reportedly avoided shaking hands with contestants and went with the fist bump to avoid germs. (Decidedly uncool.)

Still, the biggest sign that the fist bump may be on the verge of becoming quaint occured when Barack Obama took the stage at the 2008

Put Your Hands in the Air

Celebrating by pumping your arms in the air with your palms pointed skyward (aka **raise the roof**) was once a house party staple. The gesture supposedly got its start in the Houston area, but went countrywide when it became a key move on comedian Sinbad's nationally syndicated show *Vibe* in 1997. A year later, rapper Luke made it bona fide fly when his song "Raise the Roof" went to number one on *Billboard*'s Hot Rap Singles chart.

Democratic National Convention. Instead of hugging his wife Michelle, the two exchanged a fist bump. *The Washington Post* called it "the fist bump heard 'round the world," and one Internet writer famously tried to politicize it, saying it was "'Hezbollah'-style fist jabbing."

The future president opted to dial down the cool in his response to the controversy. "It captures what I love about my wife," he said. "That for all the hoopla, I'm her husband and sometimes we'll do silly things."

If that isn't proof enough that the fist bump is becoming more sweet than street, consider this: Merriam-Webster added it to its dictionary in 2011, giving the term a distinctly academic feel.

Handshake

The handshake, some say, is a gesture born of distrust. According to popular folklore, it was common for a man to have a dagger at the ready in case he ran into an enemy, thief, or other form of nasty dude. To avoid a needless bloodbath, men clasped hands to prove they weren't carrying a blade and would then shake to make sure there wasn't a knife up a sleeve (grabbing each other's forearm with the nonshaking hand was further proof that you came in peace).

This story is so persuasive that during sectarian strife in Northern Ireland in the 1990s, unionist leader David Trimble used the myth to explain why he wouldn't shake the hand of his opponent, the IRA's Gerry Adams. "The origin of the handshake is to show that there is no weapon in one's hand," Trimble said before a key 1998 meeting. "I am not going to shake his hand until I am absolutely certain that he is not holding weapons in reserve."

As compelling as this yarn may be, there is little historical support for it as the genesis for the gesture. Handshakes are far more ancient. Egyptian art depicted the gods passing power to mortal rulers through locked hands. Similarly, a Babylonian ritual (circa 1800 B.C.) involved a king shaking hands with a statue of the all-powerful deity Marduk.

The Bible contains numerous references to *striking hands*, and Homer discusses the act in the *Iliad*. In these contexts, the act was generally a physical manifestation of sealing a deal. (The Greeks and Romans had their own idiomatic phrases that amounted to *let's shake on it*.) By the seventeenth century, handshakes were also used as a tool for dispute resolution. Reconciliation councils used the handshake, which in the Netherlands was often called the *hand van vriendschap* or the hand of friendship, as the final act in resolving a dispute. As sociologist Herman Roodenburg put it, the handshake was considered "a firm exhortation to burn all discord in the fire of love."

THE QUAKERS WERE EARLY ADOPTERS OF THE HANDSHAKE— THEY SAW IT AS A GESTURE OF EQUALITY.

However, extending a paw as a hello or good-bye greeting would have been an odd offering in polite culture until the nineteenth century, according to Roodenburg. And, even then, it was only permitted among peers. The rules of etiquette suggested that offering a hand to a superior was "in rather poor taste and [could] run the risk of receiving a rebuke," one manners maven wrote.

Today, the handshake is an essential part of most Western greetings and a vital symbolic tool in the political realm. John F. Kennedy was a student of the clench. It's rumored that the charismatic president commissioned a study on the art of shaking hands to make sure he'd get it just right when interacting with other global leaders. Apparently, the right grip was "firm, but not aggressive, friendly but not weak."

Kennedy was wise to take the art of the handshake seriously. In 2004, opinion polls in Australia found that Prime Minister John Howard won re-election after his more popular opponent, Mark Latham, shook Howard's hand at an event in an overly aggressive manner, turning off the electorate.

If author Gayle Westmoreland had her way, the awkward Howard-Latham interaction would never have happened. In 2007, she wrote the book *Hands: Stop Shaking Them! A Cultural Shift to End Handshaking in America.* Westmoreland saw hand-shaking and the spreading of germs as important a public health concern as smoking and safe sex. She even wrote a series of slogans, including the ever-so-catchy "Hand, hand, fingers, thumb, I don't need your germs or your scum!" to rally people to her cause. Her solution: going with a nod instead. The book was not a bestseller.

Hands Joined in Prayer

Whether clasped in prayer, contemplation, or greeting, hands joined together may be one of the world's more benign gestures, conveying warmth and spirituality. But that wasn't always the case. The Greeks, for example, believed it was the last thing you would do when offering appreciation to the heavens. According to a nineteenth-century book, *A History of Ancient Sculpture*, clasped hands were "looked upon as a hindrance to progress and good fortune, and a token of trouble." As for the Romans, when they were conquering large swaths of Europe, hands held together meant surrender (think of it as an old-school version of waving the white flag).

The Bible makes no mention of clasped hands. Instead, when it came to religious posturing, hands were supposed to be spread and raised toward the heavens. Many early civilizations, including the Greeks, gave praise in a similar fashion.

In the Middle Ages, the hands together gesture was prescribed by feudal lords, who required their serfs to demonstrate devotion and deference. It wasn't until around the ninth century that pressed palms evolved into the signature posture of Christianity, likely an offshoot of its usage in the secular world. Instead of mortal submission (à la Romans) or obedience (hello, English dukes), the gesture was a more humbling option for people of all classes—a surrender to a *much* higher power.

Nowadays, the posture isn't just for places of worship. Consider David Bowie, who, during his famed Ziggy Stardust tour in 1972 and 1973, was photographed in the pose during a moment of reflection—decked out in full makeup no less. Yoga instructors will also bust it out as a nonreligious show of respect at your local gym. And, while most

A Twisted Story

For those who like munching on **pretzels**, give praise to the fact that joining hands together was not always the universal sign for prayer. In seventh-century France and Italy, the common way to pray was with crossed arms. Legend tells us that a monk, who worked days as a baker, was looking to make use of some extra scraps of dough. Opting for a religious theme, he emulated the arms-crossed gesture and unknowingly provided the future couch potato with a fantastic go-to snack.

can't put a price tag on the gesture, one man was willing to try: In 2007, an art aficionado shelled out a staggering $25.8 million for Rembrandt's 1661 depiction of St. James the Greater with his hands together in prayer. (See illustration on page 20.)

High Five

SPN *The Magazine* described the high five as "one of the most contagious, transcendently ecstatic gesture in sports—and maybe, for that matter, in American life." It's true that going airborne in a show of slapping elation has become shorthand for happy times whether you're a geeky stockbroker or an ultracool jet fighter pilot (okay, the latter might be outdated, but when Tom Cruise did it in the 1986 film *Top Gun*, it was pretty sweet).

Yet, despite its universality, the high five was a product of a man who felt marginalized. Glenn Burke was a can't-miss prospect for baseball's Los Angeles Dodgers in the late 1970s—potentially the next Willie Mays, some said. So it wasn't surprising when he reached the Major Leagues in 1977 that he immediately showed flashes of his great athleticism and speed.

Off the field, he was outwardly exuberant and fun loving, but internally, Burke was struggling to hide the fact that he was gay. Though he wasn't out of the closet, Burke's teammates had their suspicions, which Burke said weighed heavily on him. But he resolved to stay focused on the positive.

That upbeat effort supposedly led to the first high five. On October 2, 1977, Burke's teammate and friend Dusty Baker launched his thirtieth home run of the season. The blast meant Los Angeles now had four sluggers who reached that milestone in one year—a first in baseball history. An elated Burke was next to bat, and raised his hands in joy to greet Baker after the hitter rounded the bases. The story goes that Baker, not knowing what to do, smacked Burke's raised hand and, voilà, the up-top slap was born. (*Giving skin* or the *give me five* low slap had been around since at least World War II.)

Burke's career with the Dodgers would be a short one. In the middle of the 1978 season, he was traded to the Oakland A's (Burke later suggested that his sexuality was a factor). In a frustrating turn, the Dodgers profited from Burke's creation after his departure. By 1980—the year Burke's career ended—L.A. was selling trademarked High Five T-shirts with two hands on the verge of smacking. Burke, who would die of AIDS at the age of 42 in 1995, always took great pride in what he created.

Others have offered alternative explanations for the high five's genesis. Consider Derek Smith and Wiley Brown. The two were basketball stars at the University of Louisville in the late 1970s and early 1980s. At a practice during the 1978–1979 season, Brown, in a moment of spontaneous inspiration, recommended they move a regular low five up high. "I thought, yeah, why are we staying down low? We jump so high," Brown would tell *ESPN The Magazine* decades later. From then on, Smith began regularly looking for the vertical slap—though he limited his move. Smith would only use his left hand for high fives, since his right thumb had been amputated as a child. He figured it wasn't appropriate to go up with just his four-fingered hand.

(continued on page 28)

1930

British fencer Judy Guinness was declared an Olympic champion in the foil event at the Los Angeles Games because judges didn't notice two touches her opponent Austrian Ellen Preis had landed in their finals match. Rather than accept the gold medal, Guinness alerted the judges to the mistake and took the silver instead.

 1936

American Jesse Owens was under enormous pressure when competing before the Nazi regime in the Berlin Olympic Games. The African American star was favored in the long jump, but was on the verge of being disqualified after foot-faulting in his first two attempts. His biggest rival in the event, Carl Ludwig "Luz" Long, decided to help. He counseled Owens to begin his leap earlier than normal, which would assure he wouldn't foot fault. It worked, and Owens went on to win the gold (and Long the silver).

 1956

At the 1500-meter finals at the Australian National Championships, John Landy was the favorite. During the race, nineteen-year-old Ron Clarke tripped. Landy jumped over the teen but scraped him while doing so. Rather than continuing on, Landy stopped to make sure Clarke wasn't injured. Reassured, Landy resumed running, amazingly, making up the time he lost to win the race.

 1969

The Ryder Cup, a golf tournament that pits a team of U.S. players against a team of Europeans, can be a pressure-packed event. On the final hole of the entire event, Brit Tony Jacklin, who was going head-to-head against the great American golfer Jack Nicklaus, was facing down a short putt. If he made it, the two teams would finish in a tie; if he missed, the Americans would prevail. But Nicklaus didn't want to see Jacklin potentially miss a seemingly easy shot in front of his home fans, so he simply told Jacklin that he believed the Englishman could make the putt and conceded the point to his opponent. The kind gesture tied the two teams.

The Vendée Globe yacht race is a harrowing, nonstop, around-the-world solo sailing competition. Britain's Pete Goss looked like a contender until he learned that a French opponent, Raphael Dinelli, had capsized. Instead of continuing the race, Goss turned his craft around and, battling 30-foot waves and hurricane-force winds, found Dinelli near death in a life raft. Thankfully, Dinelli survived.

Western Oregon softball player Sara Tucholsky had never hit a home run before she launched a ball over the centerfield fence against Central Washington in a key college match-up. The only problem: As she rounded the bases, she severely injured her knee. She couldn't keep running and the umpires said the rules prevented her teammates from helping her. One of Central Washington's top players, Mallory Holtman, asked if she and teammate Liz Wallace could carry Tucholsky around the bases. The umpires okayed it and Tucholsky completed her magical moment in the arms of the opposing players.

Armando Galarraga, a pitcher for the Detroit Tigers, was on the verge of pitching a perfect game (allowing no runs, no walks, and no errors). The feat had taken place only twenty times before in Major League Baseball history. With just one out to go, Galarraga induced a batter into hitting a ground ball to the first baseman—a routine play that appeared to seal the special accomplishment. Unfortunately, umpire Jim Joyce incorrectly decided the batter was safe. The media and fans went wild, vilifying Joyce. But Galarraga forgave the umpire, and the next day made a point of publicly patting Joyce on the back.

2010

As it was a time before viral videos and instant Internet sensations, it's very possible both Burke and Smith created the magical move independently. The answer as to who came first is harder to pinpoint. Highlight reels from the 1978–1979 Louisville season show Brown and Smith slapping it up top. Smith's version of the high five probably made its national TV debut when he and his Louisville teammates played in front of large broadcast audiences en route to the NCAA men's basketball title in 1980.

A journalist once claimed that he'd checked footage from the famed 1977 Dodgers game and there was no high-fiving (a Dodgers historian would later say that game wasn't televised). But there's at least one picture of Burke appearing to go in for his signature move as a member of the Dodgers. Considering he was traded to the A's before Smith's high-five campaign began, it's likely he came first. Even so, for something that has added joy to so many events (Nice dinner, Mom! High five!), let's just agree both Burke and Smith deserve hands up in the air for their contributions.

Holding Hands

When Norma and Gordon Yeager died exactly one hour apart in October 2011, the story quickly shot around the Internet. The fact they'd been married for seventy-two years and were in the same ICU room at the time of their deaths was certainly noteworthy, but the detail that made their story particularly poignant was that Norma was holding Gordon's hand when he passed away.

No act shows love so simply—and without any lusty connotations—as holding hands.

"Hand-holding is the one aspect that's not been affected by the sexual revolution," New York University sociology department chairman Dalton Conley told *The New York Times* in 2006. "It's less about sex than about a public demonstration about coupledom."

To be sure, ask any member of the paparazzi about the value of getting a shot of a starlet and some unidentified hunk clasping paws, and the shutterbugs will tell you it's a gesture that sells. For example, when actress Scarlett Johansson was snapped holding hands with a gentleman on a morning stroll in January 2012, it was enough for E! Online to publish a whole article on what this meant for her love life. This isn't anything new: In 1935, showgirl Della Carroll claimed she spent "quality time" with famed actor Clark Gable on a cruise. But to soften their seemingly illicit tryst, she said they had fun "holding hands in the tropical starlight."

The soothing utility of hand-holding is something that is ingrained not only in humans but also in many of our primate cousins—some monkeys reconcile after a spat by holding hands. For our

Handy Music

The Beatles' first number-one single in America was **"I Want To Hold Your Hand."** While John Lennon and Paul McCartney often worked on songs separately, this 1963 hit was composed in a London basement "eyeball to eyeball," as the two music titans would describe it years later.

species, it's an act that can have meaningful medicinal purposes. A 2006 University of Virginia study discovered that holding a spouse's hand calms the brain in moments of stress. Researchers were surprised to find that even holding the hand of a complete stranger steadies nerves more than not holding any hand at all.

Some Middle Eastern cultures intuitively recognize this benefit, as hand-holding between friends is a common form of platonic affection. In 2005, for instance, President George W. Bush held hands with Crown Prince Abdullah of Saudi Arabia, during the royal's visit to Bush's home in Crawford, Texas. (Critics pointed to the hand-holding as a sign of the president's close relationship with the Saudi monarchy.)

As was the case with Bush and the Crown Prince, there are other instances when the innocence of the hand-holding depends—for better or worse—on your perspective. In 1990, two men were arrested in Cincinnati under a law that prohibited "disorderly conduct for creating a physically offensive condition" after being caught holding hands in a parked car. (The charges were later dropped.) In 2011, two lesbian students from Minneapolis were barred from holding hands while walking into their high school's annual Snow Days Pep Fest (a tradition allowed among heterosexual couples). Following protests, the school district permitted the pair to join the festivities—hand in hand.

I-L-Y Sign

Whether you're hearing impaired or not, the American Sign Language I-L-Y sign (palm facing out; pinky, forefinger, and thumb extended; other fingers turned down) is a universal sign for "I Love You."

As popular as it's become, researchers disagree on its moment of conception. One source puts it at around 1895, while another insists it was first deployed in 1905. Even academics at Gallaudet University, the world's first higher education institution for the deaf, haven't been able to pin-point its beginnings.

Still, there is one source that makes a credible claim about the sign's original use. In *Orchid of the Bayou*, Kitty Fisher's memoir of growing up deaf (and later blind), she writes that the I-L-Y sign began as a way for deaf teens to express their overheated hormones.

In the first half of the twentieth century, the only place that male and female students could mix at the Texas School for the Deaf was at the dining hall. Fisher says that the I-L-Y sign developed in the food lines as a clandestine way for budding couples to show their affection. At this point, the gesture, which according to the book dated back to around 1925, was a secret code unknown by teachers.

"Its popularity rose in the seventies [when] sign language became 'cool,'" said Gallaudet professor Benjamin Bahan. "Universities were offering sign language classes and marketers started creating T-shirts and decals with the sign *I-L-Y*."

During the 1976 presidential race, both Gerald Ford and Jimmy Carter were said to have offered up the sign to members of the deaf community. When Carter won the election, he flashed I-L-Y to some students following his inauguration. Later, Richard

Dawson, host of the game show *Family Feud*, would flash the sign, adding to its ubiquity. Variations of the gesture also developed. According to the *American Folklore* encyclopedia, rotating the forefinger in the air while doing the gesture means "I always love you."

AT THE LOUISIANA SCHOOL FOR THE DEAF, TEENS WOULD USE A SERIES OF NUMBER SIGNALS—ONE, FOUR, AND THREE—TO SAY "I LOVE YOU." ONE WAS FOR THE SINGLE-LETTER WORD *I*, FOUR STOOD FOR THE FOUR-LETTER *LOVE*, AND THREE WAS THE THREE-LETTER *YOU*.

Firmly ensconced in the public consciousness, the I-L-Y sign was commemorated on two stamps in 1993, six years after it was proposed by the National Association of the Deaf. For many in the deaf community, this might have been the sign's proverbial jumping of the shark (in other words, it was finally passé). "By the time the stamps came out, I was a little bored with it," wrote Fisher. "Whether it's a waitress in a restaurant or a tourist in the adjacent seat on a bus, that's the sign they've caught and want to make. . . . I rarely use it, except maybe to hearing people who don't know how out-of-fashion it has become."

Okay Sign

"Okay" is a worldwide phenomenon. From the Mandinka in West Africa (*o ke*) to the Finnish in the far North (*oikea*), most cultures have some form of the phrase to signify that something is correct or that all is right.

The word is "an uncomplaining workhorse," wrote Allan Metcalf in his book *OK: The Improbable Story of America's Greatest Word*. "It's the easiest way to signal agreement, whether with a written OK on a document or an 'OK' spoken aloud."

Metcalf should have added the ubiquitous okay sign (index finger touching the thumb in a circle; other three fingers apart in a fan shape). One source claims 98 percent of Americans recognize the sign, making it the most commonly understood gesture. (Take that, thumbs-up!)

While the origins linking the spoken "okay" to the hand motion are unclear, we do know that touching the index finger to the thumb has long meant something positive. The Roman scholar Quintilian mentioned the sign in his first-century opus *Institutio Oratoria*, describing it as "a graceful gesture well suited to express approval." British writer John Bulwer echoed Quintilian's sentiments in his 1644 volume on hand movements, *Chirologia*, writing that the gesture was "opportune for those who relate, distinguish, or approve."

As it connects to its modern usage, the okay sign likely followed the creation of the word. Most folks figure the circled fingers represent the O and the other digits depict the K. If so, the word's rise to prominence and the subsequent gesture can be credited to a long and sometimes contested history.

A trio of men made OK's ascension possible. The first was a successful Boston newspaper editor, Charles Gordon Greene. In 1839, his publication, the *Boston Morning Post*, was a leading voice in the city. Greene followed two journalism trends of the time: The first was mocking the competition for misspellings. The other was coming up with abbreviations. If you wanted to say "small potatoes," you'd use SP. GC would be a gin cocktail. Sometimes the two practices were combined—with the over-the-top misspellings being attributed to their opponent—yielding such questionable mash ups as KG (short for "know go" meaning "no go") and KY ("know yuse" instead of "no use").

In ridiculing the *Providence Journal*, a March 23, 1839, article by Greene offered up OK to represent "ol korrect," implying the *Journal* used the flubbed shorthand instead of the properly spelled, "all correct." Greene liked the abbreviation and began inserting it in other articles. Soon, the phrase appeared in local papers from New York to Baltimore.

Still, OK might have remained SP, if not for Martin Van Buren's 1840 presidential reelection campaign. Van Buren was in a tight race with William Henry Harrison, and the president sorely lacked something Harrison possessed: a good slogan. In a marketing coup, Harrison supporters came up with the catchy alliterative gem "Tippecanoe and

Out of This World

We can credit NASA for many things: shoe insoles, ear thermometers, and water filters to name a few. You can also add the term **A-OK** (or **a-okay**) to the list. NASA engineers used the supersized version of OK to make sure the affirmation could be heard over radio static. After astronaut Alan Shepard became the first American in space in 1961, a NASA spokesperson told journalists that Shepard had called everything on the voyage "A-OK." Shepard actually didn't use the term, but A-OK caught on with the public.

Tyler too" as part of a campaign song. (Tippecanoe was the Ohio location where military man Harrison had won a big battle against Native American forces; Tyler referred to his running mate John Tyler.) Van Buren's backers needed something equally snappy and came up with OK for "Old Kinderhook." (The fifty-seven-year-old Van Buren was from the upstate New York town of Kinderhook.) The term *OK* blossomed, thanks to the effort, but Van Buren's political career did not. He lost to Harrison.

While Van Buren's contribution was pretty well established by the twentieth century, it took the word expert Allen Read to identify Greene's role and to fend off claims that OK was not an Anglo-Saxon American invention. The Germans pointed to a few of their own potential sources, like the authoritarian sounding *Oberst Kommandant* (colonel in command). The French said it referred to a Haitian colonial town, Aux Cayes, (or, alternatively, from the statement "*aux quais*," which translates *to the docks* or *wharves* and was either what an inspector stamped on cargo cleared to ship or where Revolutionary War–era soldiers went to find women). The North American Choctaw tribe also laid a claim, saying its word *okeh*, which effectively means "it is so," came first. Still, Read, employing detailed research made a compelling argument for Greene and his Boston paper starting the trend.

Unlike the word *okay*, the okay sign hasn't always possessed the singular global meaning. During a goodwill visit to Brazil in the 1950s, then–Vice President Richard Nixon gave the okay sign with both hands at the Sao Paolo airport. The only problem, according to gestures expert Roger Axtell, was that to the Brazilian crowd, the signal represented an orifice you normally didn't flash unless you were really angry.

Salute

The salute comes from a dying breed of nice physical gestures: formal signs of respect. Others still exist, like the bow and the hat tip (see pages 61 and 97), but nowadays more casual acts like handshakes and head nods are the norm.

This wasn't the case in ancient civilizations, where bodily displays of deference were far more common (ring kissing, anyone?). The Romans were early adopters of the salute. Their version featured an outstretched arm with the palm of the hand facing down. The origins of that maneuver are hazy, but, like a number of other hand gestures, it was thought to show the person was unarmed (see Handshake, page 16).

The origin of the modern stiff hand-to-brow salute is also uncertain, but there are some fun theories. In the medieval era, knights wore their helmet visors down to shield their eyes in battle. If the armored warrior raised his visor—leaving his hand just above his eyes in a salutelike posture—it meant he came in peace. Building on that theory is the belief that the junior-ranking knight raised his visor first out of respect. Less believable is the tale that knights symbolically shielded their eyes upon seeing a beautiful woman of high rank sitting in the stands at a jousting tournament.

Centuries later, as saluting became a regular practice in the British military, historians believe it was a modification of another respectful act: removing one's hat when in the presence of a superior officer. When the soldier's basic hat gave way to more ornate and heavy headgear, a salute served as shortcut for helmet or hat removal. According to the U.S. Army Quartermaster Center and School's website, an official British form of saluting was in effect by 1745. One early book

Honorable Marksmen

The **twenty-one-gun salute** was once a moving target. In 1810, the number of bullets fired in the presidential salute were expected to correspond to the number of states (at the time there were only seventeen states, so seventeen shots were discharged). In 1842, the number was fixed on twenty-one guns. Why twenty-one? The history is uncertain. One tenuous claim is that it echoes the seven shots that were commonly fired from fourteenth-century naval cannons. The rationale, according to U.S. Army historians, is that seven is a number of biblical significance. When land artillery developed the capacity to shoot three times as much, twenty-one became the magic number.

stated: "The men are ordered not to pull off their hats when they pass an officer, or speak to them, but only to clap up their hands to their hats and bow as they pass."

An alternative for the protosalute: tugging or touching the forelock (the hair that falls over the forehead). That gesture was a popular way to defer to superiors in the nineteenth century and surely dates back well before then.

With the exception of occasionally using a salute in protest (think back to medal winners John Carlos and Tommie Smith each raising a gloved fist to the sky in the name of human rights—and black power—on the podium at the 1968 Olympics), the act is now primarily the domain of the military. But that wasn't always the case.

In the late nineteenth century, there was a tussle over how children in the U.S. should show respect for the American flag. New York City teacher and Civil War veteran George Balch devised what he called "the American Patriotic Salute" in 1889. Students were expected to touch "their foreheads and then their hearts" and say, "We give our Heads!—and our Hearts!—to God! and our Country!" The ritual ended with the kids extending their right arms with the palms down and exclaiming, "One Country! One Language! One Flag!"

The salute gained popularity in New York City, where some 6,000 children performed it daily in 1893. But not everyone was a fan. Francis Bellamy, who worked for the influential *Youth's Companion* magazine, described Balch's salute as "juvenile and lacking in dignity."

When Bellamy was appointed chairman in 1892 of a national public school event commemorating

Christopher Columbus's discovery of the New World, he used his post to challenge Balch's ritual. Bellamy introduced the Pledge of Allegiance and streamlined the salute. Instead of all the movements Balch prescribed, Bellamy's version used a simple stiff-armed, hand-facing-down tribute.

Bellamy won the battle of words, and his pledge became the morning-starting staple at schools (with some alterations along the way like "under God" being added in 1954 at the urging of President Dwight D. Eisenhower). However, his physical salute didn't have the same staying power. When the Nazis and fascists in Italy—inspired by the old Roman gesture—instituted a similar salute in the 1930s, Americans soured on it. In 1942, Congress officially banned Bellamy's salute and went with putting the right hand over the heart.

Shaka Sign
(Hang Loose)

The "hang loose" or "shaka" sign (a wave with just the thumb and pinkie sticking out) may be Hawaii's ultimate laid-back gesture. But the debate over its origins is anything but chill. In 2002, journalist June Watanabe at the *Honolulu Star-Bulletin* wrote an article on the subject, and then did a follow-up when readers offered a number of alternatives to the first story.

For starters, there's the tale of Hamana Kalili from the Laie area on the island of Oahu. Like many

Hawaiians in the early twentieth century, Kalili labored in a sugar mill, feeding sugar cane into a contraption that extracted juice from the stalks. It was a dangerous endeavor, and one day in the early 1940s, Kalili lost his three middle fingers when they were crushed by industrial-sized rollers. Left with just his pinkie and thumb, he found a new position with the company, serving as a security guard on a train that shipped sugar through the island.

"One of his jobs was to keep all the kids off the train," Kalili's grandnephew Vonn Logan told the *Star-Bulletin*. "All the kids would try to jump the train to ride from town to town." Kalili would make sure no freeloaders were milling around on the tracks and since he'd "lost his fingers, the perfect signal was what we know as the 'shaka' sign. That's how you signaled the way was clear."

Kalili was also a community leader in the local Mormon Church. As a choir director, locals watched him conduct the group with the shaka sign. In addition, the popular Kalili was the longtime king of festivities at a well-known annual event where he would be seen waving with what he had—the pinkie and the thumb. The theory goes that Kalili's involvement in so many local activities led to the spread of the gesture.

Though Kalili's story is the most complete explanation, it's not the only one. One popular alternative stars early Spanish settlers. Evidently, they'd use the sign to indicate to locals that they were friendly and wanted to share in a drink. Another option says the hand movement comes from a popular technique in marbles, "kini." One former Hawaii resident told the *Star-Bulletin* that the hand motion represented a "shark eye," which "was considered a compliment of sorts, like calling someone an 'eagle eye' here on the mainland." (Less plausible is how an extended pinkie and thumb looks like a shark's eye.)

The shaka shout-out, which accompanies the sign, also has more than one origin story. The leading claimant would be a 1960s Honolulu TV personality and used car salesman David "Lippy" Espinda. He certainly helped popularize the gesture by flashing it on TV commercials and at the end of a movie show he hosted. Some say he would also exclaim, "It's a shocker," which sounded a lot like "It's shaka" on television ads hawking cars. (He was nicknamed the "King of Pidgin" for his colorful use of English.) Then there's the assertion that it comes from Shakyamuni, a Japanese name for the original Buddha. Also in the mix:

A Flowery Welcome

A sign of both love and friendship, the orchid-festooned necklace known as a **lei** is a Hawaiian staple. A Polynesian custom that migrated to the islands from Tahiti, early versions could include stones, feathers, shells, and even bones.

a local named Bill Pacheco, who was known to say "shaka brother" (later shortened to "shaka bra").

Whatever the case, the sign really took off in 1976, when longtime Honolulu mayor Frank Fasi used it on campaign posters during a reelection bid. When asked about it in a 1999 interview, he quickly cut through the controversy over its provenance and focused instead on its positive significance. "I think it . . . meant shake it up, buddy. How's it going? Aloha. Have a good day. All those good meanings. It just meant a world of goodness," he said.

You can't get much more laid-back than that.

Thumbs-Up

As cool as the Fonz was in the old sitcom *Happy Days* (ahh, how simple were the '70s and '80s?), there was a time when his beloved practice of flashing the "thumbs-up" was decidedly uncool.

While many once believed the thumbs-up was a sign given by the Roman Emperor to spare the life of a losing gladiator who fought valiantly in the arena, researchers have concluded this wasn't the case. In fact, the signal was never used in the Colosseum, and most believe the thumbs-up was actually a harsh sign of Roman disapproval. The confusion comes from a couple of mistaken translations. When academics found the phrase *pollice compresso* in Roman texts, they thought it meant thumbs-up; they also believed *pollice verso* meant thumbs-down. As these two terms were used in connection with the great hand-to-hand battles, the myth that a straightened thumb could save the day emerged.

The misconception gained traction in 1872, when the French artist Jean-Léon Gérôme depicted spectators giving a thumbs-down to a gladiator in his popular painting *Pollice Verso*. The problem was that *pollice compresso* actually signified a compressed thumb (folded towards the palm) while *police verso* referred to a turned thumb.

Historians later recognized the error and pieced together a better understanding of the emperor's actions. If the potentate wanted the winner to slay the loser, he'd make a jabbing gesture with his thumb pointed out as if he were thrusting a sword. If the fighter deserved to live another day, he'd cover his thumb as if he were putting his weapon away.

"This made sense in an arena as vast as the Colosseum," explained the 1979 book *Gestures*,

Catching a Ride

A popular explanation for why **hitchhikers** use the thumbs-up comes from the nautically influenced verb *to hitch*. In the boating world, the term means "fastening with a hook." Later, using a similar definition, a hitch was applied to a connector between a horse and carriage or a car and trailer. Some say that a traveler's thumbs-up began as a symbolic human hitch looking for an automobile to latch onto.

"where the kill/no-kill signals would have to be strongly contrasting to be visible to all."

Although the thumbs-up signal didn't show up in the arena, it did still exist in ancient Rome. One scholarly work concluded the thumbs-up signal represented "disfavor or disgrace." And according to the first-century writer Pliny, the thumbs-down reflected approval.

There are a few explanations as to how we've come to our modern usage. At least one historian claimed that in some parts of the Roman Empire, a thumbs-up was, indeed, a positive sign. In 1644, writer John Bulwer suggested the double thumbs-up (à la the Fonz), was a Roman "expression importing a transcendency of praise."

Whether Bulwer got it right, other later traditions possibly gave the gesture its positive spin. A 1999 article in the U.K. newspaper *The Guardian* retold a story about how the thumbs-up was a vestige of early iron mines, where boys worked holding a chisel for men swinging hammers to chip away rock. When the chisel had penetrated far enough, the kids would place their thumb at the top of their tool to indicate it was time to stop. From there, the thumbs-up became a signal for a job well done. (I'm definitely not biting on this one. After getting an extended thumb mistakenly slammed once, there's no way a young miner would do it again.) An alternative option stems from a gesture that signified an old English saying, "Here's my thumb on it." Parties would seal a deal by moistening their thumbs and extending them in a sort of single-digit version of the high five. If you don't like that explanation, a final candidate comes from a venerable French practice of pushing a thumb forward to suggest something was "first class."

Wave

The wave is the Swiss Army knife of nice gestures. If you need to say hello, good-bye, sorry, or thank-you, throwing a hand in the air can do the trick (think about getting a wave from the driver who rudely cuts into your lane on the freeway; the hand motion simultaneously says sorry and thank-you and, at least for me, helps keep the blood pressure down).

In particular, waving's long-distance, no-touching aspects have made it a favorite tool for potentates, power players, and celebrities throughout history. At the end of the Revolutionary War, when George Washington resigned in Annapolis, Maryland, as commander-in chief of the American forces, he offered a weary wave to admirers, which both acknowledged his gratitude for their support and indicated just how worn out he was from the years of conflict. On the evening before the Gettysburg Address, Abraham Lincoln used a wave to calm the crowd in the Pennsylvania town. The masses wanted an impromptu speech before the memorial the next day,

THE ONION, A PUBLICATION DEVOTED TO SATIRE, ONCE DID A WEBCAST ABOUT A FAKE BOOK, DESTINED TO WAVE, WHICH CHRONICLED THE LIFE OF QUEEN ELIZABETH II. "PEOPLE SUCH AS MYSELF HAVE GROWN UP WATCHING HER WAGGLE HER HAND BACK AND FORTH," THE PSEUDO-AUTHOR SAID. "WHEN ENGLAND IS IN PERIL, SHE'S ALWAYS THERE TO WAVE."

but the president's wave, along with a few choice words, helped placate the locals and let him save the good stuff for the short, but incredibly powerful speech he gave the following day.

While it didn't mention Washington's or Lincoln's use of the gesture, a 2011 article in *New York* magazine reinforced the belief that the wave offers a nice connection between a leader and his or her people. The story noted that although Barack Obama often seemed to present the gesture grudgingly, he did it because "the president is supposed to be a friendly and folksy character, and waving as if he gives a [expletive] helps to foster such an image."

Still, not everyone has been a fan of the wave. An 1892 editorial in a Lawrence, Kansas, paper the *Daily World* compared that habit to those who indulge in end-of-the-world theories: "Why well-to-do sensible people will go wild over a doctrine that preaches their own doom is as inexplicable as why people wave their hats at a moving train." Maybe part of the answer for the wave's popularity comes from the motorcycle community. Riders are well known for giving a wave to passing strangers tooling along on motorbikes. Some suggest that similarities between the two riders' motorcycles, both in terms of brand and style (*whoo-hoo*, love those Harley's high handle bars!), goes a long way toward whether a wave will be given.

Beyond acknowledging commonality, simple kindness or even curiosity might trigger a wave.

The High Tide of Sports

Two parties have battled fiercely to earn recognition for creating the sports crowd spectacle known as **the Wave**. Professional cheerleader George Henderson (aka Krazy George) says he started the trend of fans standing and then sitting down section by section (much like a rolling ocean wave) on October 15, 1981, during a nationally televised Major League Baseball playoff game between the New York Yankees and the Oakland A's. The University of Washington counters that its marching band director Bill Bissell along with alum and former *Entertainment Tonight* host Rob Weller first initiated it at a football game against Stanford—on October 31, 1981. Over the years neither claimant has backed down.

As for whether we reply, that decision may be a genetically predetermined one. The human brain possesses mirror neurons, which trigger when a person sees a certain action—such as a wave—and gives the brain an insatiable desire to copy the maneuver.

Other Nice (Physical) Gestures

Bowing

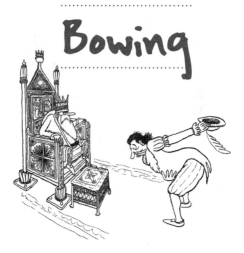

Bowing can be a seriously religious experience. Take the Zen master Hsu Yun. Over a six-year period, the man, whose name translates to "Empty Cloud," traveled to holy Buddhist sites in China and India by taking three steps and then bowing—over and over again. All told, he journeyed 3,000 miles in this fashion. The bowing must have been some sort of path to enlightenment, since he enjoyed an amazingly long mortal existence, reportedly living from 1840 to 1959.

The Ultimate Bow

The **kow-tow**, the definitive display of subservience, came from one very intense Chinese version of bowing. The word is a combination of the term *kóu*, which means "knock with reverence" and *tóu*, which stands for "head." The act includes kneeling and then bending at the waist until your head makes contact with the floor. The first known English reference to this obsequious move occurred in 1834.

Bowing and religious devotion have gone together in nearly every faith. Words for this act of submission show up in a multitude of dead languages such as Old English, Old Norse, Old Saxon, Nether-Frankish, and Sanskrit, among others.

In the tribal societies of early Western Europe where chieftains were almost godlike, bowing easily transitioned from a purely religious act into an important secular show of respect. This habit eventually took on serious meaning in European court culture. In particular, women, who were required to curtsy (coming from the word *courtesy*) rather than bow, had a lot of pressure on them to get it right.

More complicated than a straight bow, curtsies were scrutinized by royalty. A bad performance by a lady—she was judged not only on movement but also on appearance—could severely diminish her social standing.

For Colonial Americans, the bow was an accepted practice. As a seventeenth-century Puritan wrote, it was "a sign of honour and veneration . . . [and a] testimony of submission." In big cities of the early eighteenth century, it was common to see all sorts of bowing, with the person of a lesser class gesturing first.

But with the rise of democracy in the New World, the bow soon lost some of its luster. It just felt too highfalutin for an egalitarian society. While some held on to the practice even after the Revolutionary War, Andrew Jackson, who served as president from 1829 to 1837, was a particular opponent. The first populist commander-in-chief, Jackson was said to be partial to shaking hands as a more American way of greeting. High society did have difficulty letting go of the bow, but by the 1920s, even the well heeled had grown tired of motion. (Edith Wharton poked fun at the ostentatious act in her 1924 novella *New Year's Day*, calling it a gesture for old people.)

Not all cultures have discarded the bow. It remains a part of the Japanese way of life. In fact, in the 1980s, a special machine was marketed in Japan to help people practice attaining the perfect angle in their bows. And across the world, the bow is still used by actors in the theater. The origins here are unclear. It's possible that it began as an uncomplicated way to show gratitude for a crowd's adulation—or perhaps to pay respect to early aristocratic patrons in attendance.

In the religious world, it remains a central act. "Daily, across America and across the world, people begin their day by bowing," wrote Andi Young in her book *The Sacred Art of Bowing: Preparing to Practice*. "Each spiritual tradition has its own way to bow, yet despite the seeming difference between Catholic genuflection and Buddhist prostration, traditions share the common need to express their aspirations, ideals, and faith in the physical act of bowing."

Covering a Yawn

These days, most people probably give little thought to covering up their mouths when yawning. But there was a time when it was thought to be a matter of life or death.

For centuries, people, even men of science, believed that covering one's mouth when yawning prevented evil spirits from entering your body. Early doctors—grasping to understand the common tragedy of infant mortality—pinned newborn deaths, at least in part, on the yawn, according to author Charles Panati. To preserve the wee one's health, Roman physicians implored mothers to cover a baby's yawns. In truth, babies yawn as a natural reflex following birth. (Recent studies show that babies begin yawning in the womb as early as eleven weeks after conception.) The bad-spirit myth cropped up somewhere along the way, but considering that history has left no record of a hands-free yawn requiring an exorcism, we're probably safe.

As an act of modern common courtesy, the covered yawn is an enduring practice. Abigail Van Buren (aka Dear Abby) weighed in on the topic at least twice in her long career as a syndicated advice columnist. In 1963, she wrote sternly: "There is no excuse for failing to cover one's mouth while yawning." As yawns are often seen as a sign of boredom, covering up your yawn avoids giving the impression you're being put to sleep by the company. To this end, in 1974, Dear Abby added the recommendation to apologize along with hiding the wide-mouthed intake of air.

Scientists aren't completely sure why we yawn. Fatigue remains a popular claim. Others suggest that we yawn to get a burst of reviving oxygen. The physical act of yawning has also been said to

Vampire Hygiene

There is a very legitimate basis for **covering sneezes and coughs**: A single instance of either act can unleash millions of germs. While a handkerchief or hand was once an acceptable way to cover up, today the crook of the arm (a gesture called "the Dracula" by some) is preferred. The reason (as we all know but don't like to say) is that most people don't wash their hands after a sneeze or cough. Even worse, some folks don't cover up at all. A 2010 New Zealand study of 400 coughs and sneezes at a mall in the capital of Wellington found that 25 percent of people didn't even bother to use their hands or a tissue.

increase our blood pressure (though the theory has been refuted in at least one study). Other explanations exist. A personal favorite: It helps cool the brain. In 2007, researchers found that people yawned less when they pressed a cold towel to their head compared to those who put a heated towel to their brow.

Despite the disagreement, there is one ultrapolite reason to continue hiding yawns—to prevent an epidemic. Scientists agree that yawns are contagious. When a human sees another human gasp for air, he is very likely to perform "emotional contagion" and yawn as well. In fact, many animals will mimic the gesture. So, why does this happen? Reasons range from a simple reflexive reaction to a subconscious desire to empathize with the yawning individual. (See Wave, page 54, for another example of a reflexive reaction). Thankfully, avoiding demons is not under consideration.

Helping an Elderly Woman Cross the Street

For years, one of the most popular skits around the Boy Scout campfire featured a scout insisting on helping an old lady across the street, only to find out that he had escorted the woman to the wrong corner. Laughter would ensue because the ritual of aiding an elderly woman cross a road is so ingrained in the Boy Scout ethos that it's become a trope—even to them.

But it wasn't always a centerpiece of their philosophy.

The Boy Scouts were created in England by Lord Robert Baden-Powell, a lieutenant-general in the British Army who served in Africa and India. He conceived of the youth movement as a way to teach children not only manly outdoor skills but also the ways of chivalry. At the cornerstone of Boy Scout thinking was the concept of a "good turn"— small daily acts of kindness. Baden-Powell didn't want to put too much pressure on the kids, so he set the bar low. In the organization's first manual, *Scouting for Boys*, published in 1908, examples of good turns included giving water to a thirsty horse and picking up "a bit" of banana peel off a sidewalk

Snacking for a Cause

Depending on your willpower, **Girl Scout cookies** can be a nice diversion or a crushing addiction. In 1917, an Oklahoma troop was the first to try out a cookie sale. The concept was a success, and in 1936, the organization began licensing bakers to professionally produce the mouthwatering fundraising treats. The bestselling cookies are Thin Mints, which were introduced in 1951.

to avoid someone slipping. Also listed was "to help an old woman to cross the street."

Assisting an elderly person across a busy boulevard may have gone the way of the banana peel if not for a bit of American influence. In 1909, the highly successful Chicago newspaper publisher William D. Boyce was visiting London. While en route to meet with an acquaintance (some say he was trying to get to his hotel), he found himself woefully lost in London's labyrinthine streets. Adding to the lore, a thick layer of fog was allegedly making his travels especially difficult. Then, suddenly, out of the mist came a young man, who offered to navigate Boyce to his destination, no doubt assisting him across many cobblestone streets along the way. At the end of the journey, Boyce offered the boy some money in gratitude, but the fellow refused, saying he was a Boy Scout who was just doing his good turn.

Inspired, Boyce sought out Baden-Powell and established the Boy Scouts of America. This story became the stuff of legends, with the "Unknown Scout" serving as an ideal for Boy Scouts to come. While not exactly the same as assisting an elderly woman across a busy street, the scout's decision to escort an older gentleman (Boyce was 51 at the time) through London held a similar honor.

A more likely reason for the maneuver's exalted status came in 1910, when Baden-Powell's scouting manual was revised for American audiences. The same examples for good turns appeared in the U.S. edition as in the British book, but there was a notable change to the layout—an illustration of a cherub-faced scout helping an old lady traverse a street had been added. The simple sketch, which still appears in the modern handbook, perfectly encapsulated the scouts' commitment to chivalry and became an enduring symbol.

With more than 3.7 million active members in the U.S. scouting community, the good turn has persisted in popular culture. In former U.S. Secretary of State Colin Powell's 1996 memoir *My American Journey*, he makes reference to the gesture when trying to convey journalist Bob Woodward's seemingly earnest approach. "Woodward had the disarming voice and manner of a Boy Scout offering to help an old lady across the street," Powell wrote.

Even singer Taylor Swift recognized the act's power. After coming across a fan's website in 2010, Swift challenged its creator to perform a series of good deeds. Among them, you guessed it: helping an elderly woman cross the street.

Hugging

Great thinkers from the Renaissance scholar Erasmus to the children's author Shel Silverstein have written about the calming and nurturing value of hugs. (If you haven't read Silverstein's poem "Hug O' War," you're missing a masterpiece.)

The earliest known use of the verb *to hug* dates to the 1560s; hug, as a noun, emerged about ninety years later. Though the origin of the term isn't evident (some suggest it comes from the Old Norse), hugging appears to have developed as a synonym for "embrace," the word Geoffrey Chaucer was using in the fourteenth century.

Of course, arm-locking love far predates its English heritage. In fact, many believe hugging is a deeply rooted, life-sustaining imperative. "There seems to be something in the biology of the young human organism that requires physical stroking to survive, and certainly to develop healthily," University of Texas public health professor Blair Justice told *The Washington Post*. "In homes where this is missing, the central nervous system and neurochemistry does not always develop properly, and the child does not grow physically, emotionally, or mentally as well as he should."

The value of hugging is so great that, in 2011, a woman earned a patent for a contraption she called the "Infant Hugging and Comforting Device." Featuring a "cloth hugging" gadget with "adjustable arm portions," it sounds like the perfect gift for the most frigid parents in the Western world.

The world of art is chock-full of examples of comforting embraces. Along with filial depictions, there are many romantic versions of hugs. Consider the famed sixteenth-century painting by Correggio, *Jupiter and Io*, which depicts the scantily clad Io being embraced/seduced by a shadowy incarnation of the god Jupiter. (It's hotter than it sounds.) The intense painting illustrates just why some get a bit squirrelly about public embraces.

In recent years, educators around the world have prohibited hugging in schools. In 2009, an elementary school in Adelaide, Australia, deemed it "inappropriate behavior." The same year, a school principal in Hillsdale, New Jersey, explained why she banned it at her junior high school two years earlier. "Touching and physical contact is very dangerous territory," Noreen Hajinlian told *The New York Times*. "It was needless hugging—they are in the hallways before they go to class. It wasn't a greeting. It was happening all day."

This fear of the hug is not a new phenomenon. In the late nineteenth century, the *Milwaukee Sentinel* railed against hugging in public parks, arguing that benches should be removed in order to end this unwholesome practice. George Peck, who ran an opposing newspaper, strenuously objected and offered a blueprint for modern-day hugging freedom fighters. Invoking the Declaration of Independence, Peck proclaimed that "hugging is certainly a 'pursuit of happiness.' People do not hug for wages—that is except on the stage. Nobody is obliged to hug. It is a sort of spontaneous combustion, as it were, of feelings, and has to have proper conditions of atmosphere to make it a success."

He added that those who "object to hugging are old, usually, and have been satiated, and are like a lemon that has done duty in circus lemonade. If they had a job of hugging, they would want to hire a man to do it for them. . . . [Furthermore] a man who objects to a little natural, soul-inspiring hugging on a back seat in a park . . . has probably got a soul, but he hasn't got it with him." Peck concluded, "Hugging is as necessary to the youth of the land as medicine to the sick. . . . People think it is unhealthy, but nobody was ever known to catch cold while hugging."

If anyone questions the wisdom of Peck's words, it's worth noting that the writer would go on to be elected mayor of Milwaukee in 1890 and then serve two terms as governor of the state of Wisconsin.

Perhaps hugging's biggest champion is the Hindu religious leader Mata Amritanandamayi. Known as the "hugging saint," Amritanandamayi has traveled widely since the 1980s, preaching love and compassion across the world. Along the way, she claims to have given some 30 million hugs.

Kissing

Some may balk at including a section on kissing in a book about "nice." After all, if you do it well with the right person, calling kissing nice is a vast understatement.

But kissing is many things to many people. A kiss can be given as (but not limited to) a greeting, a show of reverence, a plea for good fortune (come on, lucky dice!), a sign of reconciliation, an act of friendship or betrayal, and everyone's favorite, a moment of deep love. (Fun fact: A one-minute kiss of the love category supposedly burns 26 calories.)

The Romans had three primary words for a kiss, depending on whether it was friendly, loving, or passionate. The Germans, showing their longstanding penchant for precision, allegedly have thirty different words for types of kisses. (My favorite: *Nachküssen*, which is a smooch to make up for kisses you should have given but didn't.) Even if we focus on just romance, there are variations. The *Kama Sutra* features multiple types from the nominal to what we call the French kiss (described in the book as "fighting of the tongue"). One seventeenth-century author identified twenty different kinds of kisses in a thousand-page encyclopedia devoted to the topic.

The biggest debate over kissing, beyond figuring out an appropriate time to lay one on, is over its origins. There are scientists who believe the act is innate. Chimpanzees, for example, are known to kiss as part of apologizing after a fight. Some anthropologists describe it as a "relic gesture" from primates, who would chew food for their young and feed it to them, mouth-to-mouth. For humans, the theory goes, it evolved from a baby's need to pucker up when breast-feeding.

Holiday Kisses

Why does hanging **mistletoe** make us kiss during the Christmas season? Druids in the second century B.C. initially placed the plant in doorways to ward off evil and encourage good tidings. (It was also used to increase female fertility and as a poison antidote.) But it was the Scandinavians who associated mistletoe with the Norse goddess of love, Frigg, which likely led to the kissing connection.

Then there are those who argue the kiss is a human-made creation. Texas A&M University professor Vaughn Bryant told *The New York Times* in 2006 that the first kiss occurred in India circa 1500 B.C. It was described in ancient Vedic scriptures as "sniffing" with one's mouth and later as "setting mouth to mouth."

From there, the kiss moved west when Alexander the Great conquered parts of India in 326 B.C. In one of the least shocking moments in history, his soldiers liked kissing so much they brought the practice back to Europe. The Greeks adopted kissing as more than just a lip-lock. They also kissed hands, feet, and even knees as a salutation. To honor the warrior Diocles, who died defending his lover, there were annual festivals that included kissing contests. Unfortunately, details on the judge's criteria do not appear to have survived.

The Romans regarded kissing as an essential sign of respect. "Under the emperors," wrote the scholar Isaac Disraeli, "kissing hands became an essential duty even for the great themselves." Writer Joshua Foer joked, "The Romans were inveterate kissers, and along with Latin, the kiss became one of their chief exports."

The medieval period bolstered the reputation of the kiss as a romantic gesture. Troubadours traveling throughout Europe spinning tales often spoke of a kiss as an essential part of amorous adventure—albeit with results that were not always for the best. After all, the legendary affair between Lancelot and Guinevere that brought down King Arthur's Camelot was sealed with a kiss. Also during this era, another type of powerful smooch—kissing a Bible to seal one's oath—emerged (see XOXO, page 284). While Renaissance writers and artists ratcheted up a kiss's hot quotient in poems and paintings, it was reined in by the Puritans (a Boston man, who had been at sea for three years, was once charged with "lewd and unseemly behavior" for kissing his wife on the Sabbath) and later, by the Victorians (there were strict rules about when kisses were allowed).

It's a shame they didn't have the advanced science of our time. In the 1980s, researchers found that men who kissed their spouses before going off to work lived longer, avoided more car accidents, and had higher incomes than their married counterparts who didn't pucker up. If nothing else, the study proved that under the right circumstances, kissing can be connected to a nice life.

Kissing Hits

Number one songs on the **Billboard Hot 100** charts featuring "kiss" in the title:

1952–53: "I Saw Mommy Kissing Santa Claus" (Jimmy Boyd)

1969: "Na Na Hey Hey Kiss Him Good-Bye" (Steam)

1976: "Kiss and Say Good-Bye" (Manhattans)

1978: "Kiss You All Over" (Exile)

1981: "Kiss on My List" (Daryl Hall and John Oates)

1986: "Kiss" (Prince)

1991: "I Like the Way (The Kissing Game)" (Hi-Five)

1995: "Kiss from a Rose" (Seal)

2007: "Kiss Kiss" (Chris Brown, featuring T-Pain)

2008: "I Kissed a Girl" (Katy Perry)

Nice Thoughts About Kissing

"*A kiss is a lovely trick designed by nature to stop speech when words become superfluous.*"

—Ingrid Bergman, actress

"Any man who can drive safely while kissing a pretty girl is simply not giving the kiss the attention it deserves."

—Albert Einstein, scientist

"*Everybody winds up kissing the wrong person good night.*"

—Andy Warhol, artist

"People who throw kisses are hopelessly lazy."

—Bob Hope, actor

"A word invented by the poets as a rhyme for 'bliss.'"

—Ambrose Bierce, humorist

"The sound of a kiss is not so loud as that of a cannon, but its echo lasts a great deal longer."
—*Oliver Wendell Holmes, Sr., physician*

"Kisses are a better fate than wisdom."
—e.e. cummings, poet

"Political baby-kissing must come to an end—unless the size and the age of the babies be materially increased."
—*W. C. Fields, actor*

NICE FACTS ABOUT KISSING

// An old English superstition says that bubbles on tea mean kisses are coming.

// Hershey's teardrop-shaped chocolates, dubbed "kisses," went on sale in 1907.

// Kissing is hard work: Researchers concluded each person uses 34 facial muscles and 112 postural muscles to successfully smooch.

// The most important muscle in kissing is probably the obicularis oris. Often called the kissing muscle, it allows people to pucker their lips.

// The first filmed kiss was between actors May Irwin and John C. Rice in 1896. That thirty-second movie was called *The Kiss*. The most kisses in a movie: 191 in the 1926 Warner Brothers production *Don Juan*.

Nodding

Charles Darwin.

As simple as the nod seems—a vertical head movement signifying yes or a quick flip upward as shorthand for hello—it is a gesture complex enough to have fascinated none other than Charles Darwin.

In 1872, the father of evolution devoted six whole pages to the head movement in his book *The Expression of the Emotions in Man and Animals.* Along with the negative side-to-side head shake, Darwin observed that, "These signs are indeed to a certain extent expressive of our feelings, as we give a vertical nod of approval with a smile to our children, when we approve of their conduct; and shake our heads laterally with a frown, when we disapprove."

"[Among] Anglo-Saxons," Darwin concluded, "these signs are innate or instinctive." He pointed to an example of a blind and deaf woman who, without being taught, reflexively responded in the affirmative with the up-down nod. Darwin also reflected on the fact that babies make a sort of nodding motion when latching on for mother's milk, suggesting the move may very well be intrinsic.

So in his typical fact-finding style, Darwin began questioning his sources around the globe (including one guy with the intriguing name "Captain Speedy") to figure out whether the nod was indeed a universal action. Much to his surprise, it wasn't. Among those who embraced the nod were Malaysians, the Chinese, and some aboriginal people of Australia and South Africa. Still, there were many cultures that didn't follow the custom. Even today, the vertical nod in countries like Bulgaria and Turkey can have a negative meaning.

Interestingly, Darwin discovered that the affirmative nod was far less common than shaking the head side to side for no. Unfortunately, beyond collecting the data, Darwin gave little explanation, not even a hypothesis, for why the affirmative nod wasn't universal.

Although there is debate as to why we nod, the word itself has a firmer history. It's believed that the term comes from the Hebrew term *nad*, meaning, among other things, "to waver or wander." In English, *nad* was translated into *nod*. It comes from the biblical story of Cain and Abel in which Cain wanders to the Land of Nod after killing his brother. The theologian John Wesley believed Cain's restless spirit shook as he faced this land as an outcast. Some scholars suggest that this existential wavering inspired the head-shaking meaning of the word *nod* today.

In modern times, a nod has taken on additional linguistic meaning. To "give the nod," as in to provide support to a person or cause, made its first appearance in a 1924 *New York Times* article, according to the *Oxford English Dictionary*. When a powerful politician gives the nod to a piece of legislation, it means it has his backing.

As for why we issue the head nod as a hello, like the use of the affirmative up-down maneuver, the answer may very well be unknowable. Much to my disappointment, I don't have Darwin's Captain Speedy around to offer some insight.

Opening a Door for a Lady

The genteel male custom of opening a door for a lady is an example of the shifting landscape of nice. What was once considered a kind gesture is now a questionable act.

Although many believe the tradition dates to the Middle Ages and the time of gallant knights, this is unlikely. The chivalric code laid out acts of courtesy toward women, but door duty doesn't appear in a vast body of literature studied by chivalry expert Richard Kaeuper.

Though no one has pinpointed its beginnings, opening doors for ladies probably made its way into polite European culture by the 1700s. During that century, the French term *place aux dames* ("make way for the ladies" or "ladies first") was used both in England and on the continent. The opening of doors seems to fit well with this show of deference.

Another theory suggests that the practice started in royal courts where women wore cumbersome clothing. Recognizing the difficulty females faced in navigating portals while dressed in tight corsets and bulging gowns, men would open doors to ease the process. If this theory is accurate, the custom could date back even earlier than the eighteenth century.

Whichever is the case, men were expected to provide this courtesy well into the twentieth century. Still, the contemporary world hasn't been as certain about the value of the gesture. In 2011, a study by a group of psychologists concluded that men who, among other actions, opened doors for women were guilty of "benevolent sexism," which was defined in 1996 as "a paternalistic attitude toward women that idealizes them affectionately."

This can lead to some bad consequences "if gallantry begets the notion that women are less than or need special favors in order to succeed," argued *Forbes* writer Jenna Gourdreau following the study's release. "Men *and* women might subconsciously receive that message and carry it with them to their schoolyards, workplaces, and marriages."

Not everyone responded with such measure. The British newspaper the *Daily Mail* ran a story on the subject with the snarky headline: "Men who hold open doors for women are SEXIST, not chivalrous, feminists claim."

So where do etiquette gurus stand on this controversy? *Emily Post's Etiquette* (18th edition, 2011), takes the middle ground: "Whether a man should open doors and hold chairs for a woman depends largely on whether the woman will appreciate these gestures," the book explains. "On a date, the man's best bet is to ask. Like so many matters of modern etiquette, a little communication between the people involved removes awkwardness."

Smiling

What makes the perfect smile? Just reading the question probably brings a particular image to mind. Alas, history has not had such an easy time coming up with a consensus on the matter.

Consider what's generally judged the world's most famous smile: Leonardo da Vinci's *Mona Lisa*. There are many art experts who believe her expression is "a miraculous achievement in the history of art," according to Angus Trumble, author

Camera Etiquette

Why do we immediately light up when a photographer tells us to *say cheese*? Various sources make a claim for the term's invention, but it likely started with kids at fancy English prep schools like Oundle and Rugby School in the 1920s. While uttering cheese does seem to make your mouth go wide for a smile, at least one source claims photographers were playing off a popular phrase of the time, "quite the cheese," which meant fashionable.

of *A Brief History of the Smile*. But Trumble points out that even Mona Lisa's "widely celebrated" expression has its detractors. John Ruskin, a well-known nineteenth-century critic, wasn't a fan. He called Da Vinci "the slave of an archaic smile." Even Sigmund Freud had issues. The revered psychoanalyst believed Mona Lisa's smile represented Da Vinci's longing for his mother Caterina, whom the artist hadn't seen since he was an infant.

As a natural physical reaction, the smile is as old as our species. Babies quickly master the ability to smile, and they generally use this skill to great effect, as most parents know. However, some behavioral scientists believe early smiles were more akin to dogs showing their teeth in a combat-ready posture than a child's sweet gesture.

In civilized society, art has often served as a snapshot for an era's perfect smile or, equally as often, worst smile. Homer mentioned smiling a number of times in the *Odyssey* but seemed to suggest the act, when sincere, should not be an outward grin but, instead, a figurative internal gesture. At times, a controlled, closed-mouth smile has represented wisdom in both Eastern culture (example: ancient Buddha sculptures) and Western religious works.

For a long stretch of history, the longstanding rule on public smiles was: Don't show teeth. For centuries, only the worst of the worst went toothy. Trumble's investigations of smiles in eighteenth- and nineteenth-century European paintings discovered depictions of teeth-bearing grins or open mouths generally "belonged to dirty old men, misers, drunks, whores, gypsies, people undergoing experiences of religious ecstasy, dwarves, lunatics, monsters, ghosts, the possessed, the damned, and . . . tax collectors."

Indeed, flashing teeth was such a big-time no-no that a Catholic saint weighed in on the topic. The seventeenth-century educational reformer and patron saint of teachers St. Jean-Baptiste de la Salle wrote that showing teeth in public was "entirely contrary to decorum, which forbids you to allow your teeth to be uncovered, since nature gave us lips to conceal them."

Another perceived offshoot of smiling—laughter—was also ruled bad form in good company. In 1748, Britain's Lord Chesterfield wrote to his son: "I could heartily wish that you may often be seen to smile, but never heard to laugh, while you live." Despite Lord Chesterfield's concerns, many scientists believe smiling and laughing are not inherently connected. Rather, they evolved separately, both physically and psychologically.

So how did we get to our modern smile? Trumble argues that toothy grins are welcomed today because of better dentistry and advances in photography.

There was a good reason to keep your teeth hidden in the days of St. Jean-Baptiste: Bad oral hygiene meant discolored and decayed teeth. In the second half of the nineteenth century, improved dentistry made people feel more comfortable showing off their increasingly pearly whites.

At the same time, photography was also developing. In the 1840s and 1850s slow shutter speeds meant it could take up to 45 minutes to shoot a

Ugly Grins

In modern language, the word **grin** is synonymous with smile. But up until the nineteenth century, a grin was regularly defined as making a grotesque face. In fact, grinning matches, in which contestants would contort their mug in the most sickening way possible to earn a prize, were regular features in eighteenth-century England.

picture. When the technology improved to allow for candid shots, it became easier to catch people in the act of smiling. Such pictures helped break down the taboo of the toothy smile.

Nowadays most any smile is good, as long as you mean it. While you might reflexively look at the shape of a beaming person's mouth to gauge sincerity, think again. It's the eyes that determine the honesty of a smile. An 1862 study by French doctor Guillaume Duchenne revealed that while we can control our mouth—and, if necessary, flash a disingenuous smile—wrinkling at the corner of the eyes is involuntary, making it a true sign of whether your grin is sincere. So, if genuineness counts, the Duchenne smile may be the closest we have to perfect.

Nice Supporters

CHEERLEADING:
An American invention, cheerleading started with students at Princeton University. Around the 1880s, an all-male "pep club" was charged with leading fans in chants and yells during the Ivy League school's football games. When Princeton grad Thomas Peebles moved to Minneapolis, he introduced the practice to the students of the University of Minnesota. In 1898, during the last football game of the season, Minnesota student Jack "Johnny" Campbell took a megaphone onto the field to rouse the crowd, giving birth to the modern cheerleading tradition. (The Princeton fellas had stuck to the stands.) Girls weren't initially cheerleaders, but by the 1940s, they were in the majority. Today, 90 percent of cheerleaders are female.

FAN CLUBS: Though it wouldn't have been called a "fan club" (at the time, the term *fan* described a baseball enthusiast), admirers of British actor Lewis Waller were the first to organize a club in tribute to a celebrity around 1902. Members of the Keen Order of Wallerites wore a badge with Waller's likeness and the actor's favorite flower, a pansy. According to the group's rules, only the club's secretary was allowed to approach Waller. Around the same time, actor Sir Herbert Beerbohm Tree, star of the first Shakespearean film (*King John* in 1899), was also honored with a club of admirers. It was called the True-to-Trees. The first known American fan club, the Peggy Snow Club, was founded in 1914 in Northboro, Massachusetts, to laud the popular actress.

Tip of
the Hat

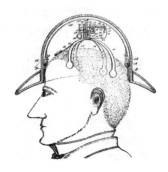

While you can find claims on the Internet that hat tipping is a relic of knights raising their helmet visor as a sign of reverence (also see Salute, page 41), author Charles Panati provides a more revealing explanation. According to his book *Extraordinary Origins of Everyday Things*, the seeds of the concept date back to ancient Assyria. Enemies captured in battle were required to take off all their clothes as a sign of deference to the victors. As far-fetched as it seems, similar stripping practices were picked up, although modified, by other cultures. For example, the Greeks insisted servants starting in a new household undress from the waist up. The Romans also saw removing attire as a sign of respect. They required that sandals be removed before entering a holy shrine. As for head coverings, Romans considered them a sign of social or political significance. Thus, in some circumstances, a bare head would indicate inferiority.

This potpourri of gestures was eventually tailored into the hat tip. It was particularly fashionable in Victorian England, where modesty was paramount and, no doubt, undressing in any other way would have shown the opposite of respect.

How popular was this practice? So much so that, in 1896, an enterprising inventor patented a self-tipping hat. The "novel device for automatically effecting polite salutations" was powered by clockwork hidden under the headgear (see illustration on page 97). When a man bent forward, the hat would automatically lurch forward "without the use of the hands in any manner."

Needless to say, the robo-chapeau did not sell well enough to capture the zeitgeist. Still, the hat tip remained an essential part of culture in most parts of the world, including the United States, well into the twentieth century. Manners maven Emily Post dedicated a whole section to the dos and don'ts on the topic in her 1922 etiquette book.

BY THE 1890s, BASEBALL PLAYERS WERE TIPPING THEIR BRIMMED CAPS TO ACKNOWLEDGE FANS' APPLAUSE.

"Lifting the hat is a conventional gesture of politeness shown to strangers only," Post wrote. Apparently, bowing was the appropriate custom when running into friends and acquaintances. As for the mechanics of the hat tip, Post was equally exacting: "In lifting his hat, a gentleman merely lifts it slightly off his forehead and replaces it; he does not smile nor bow, nor even look at the object of his courtesy," she explained. (In terms of fully taking off a hat, Post also had many rules, including the requirement to hold it with one's left hand if stopping to talk to a lady on the street, and removing it entirely in hotel, club, and apartment elevators, but not in business elevators.)

Maybe it was all the rules or just the increasingly less formal nature of social interaction—or the fact that men stopped wearing hats—but by the twenty-first century this nicety has faded considerably. In fact, in the seventeenth edition of Post's book, which was edited by her granddaughter and published in 2004, there were just a few passing mentions on when to take off a hat, and the discussion centers more on baseball caps than other forms of headdress.

Even so, the tradition lives on in a couple of very different pockets. Since at least the late 1930s, publications have used the phrase "tip of the hat" when they wanted to offer plaudits. For Comedy Central fans, talk show host Stephen Colbert keeps this tradition alive on his program *The Colbert Report*. (His satiric hat tips have been bestowed on everything from scented razors to Casio, makers of musical keyboards and old-school digital watches.)

If you're looking for the physical act of the hat tip, it can best be found in the sports world. Baseball players have a long tradition of acknowledging the crowd's applause with a doff of the cap, and golfers have taken to removing their hats when shaking hands with their playing partner at the end of eighteen holes of golf.

Winking

I f ever there was a potentially nice gesture that needed to be deployed carefully, it's the wink.

The 1980 classic movie *Coal Miner's Daughter* did it right. When country music's Patsy Cline (played by Beverly D'Angelo) is singing at the Grand Ole Opry, she looks over to the wings and locks eyes with fellow star Loretta Lynn (Sissy Spacek). With a smile, Cline winks, which modestly, yet fully, encapsulates the solidarity and understanding shared between the two women.

A wink can also be a sign of endearment from a rakish type if it's not taken too seriously. Prominent early twentieth-century journalist H. L. Mencken once wrote: "If, after I depart this vale, you ever remember me and thought to please my ghost, forgive some sinner and wink your eye at some homely girl." Sure, he wasn't PC (Mencken rarely was), but suggesting a little flirtation with a person who might not normally get attention is nice on some level.

When used correctly, the wink can even propel a wildly successful brand. In 1904, the Brown Shoe Co. licensed the rights to a comic strip featuring a dapper but mischievous little boy, Buster Brown. The logo of the winsome lad sporting a sly wink was beloved and helped build the company into a $1.8 billion behemoth. In fact, collectors still pay big bucks for memorabilia of the winking kid.

And, still, the world has its winking doubters. As a *Chicago Tribune* reporter was told in 2004, after winking at a friend, "winking is for seedy old men." The comment drove the journalist to the streets to investigate whether her pal represented conventional wisdom on the subject. Opinions ranged from calling it a "nice gesture" to deeming it "too overt." Her conclusion: "The Wink is all about context."

So while a cheeky little boy can wink when selling shoes, Jesus is another story. In 2011, a U.K. cell phone company, Phones 4 U, featured a depiction of a winking Christ giving a thumbs-up in an advertisement. The image was borrowed from filmmaker Kevin Smith's 1999 movie *Dogma*, but that didn't matter. Explaining their banning of the ad, the country's Advertising Standards Authority said, "Although the ads were intended to be light hearted and humorous . . . [they] gave the impression that they were mocking and belittling core Christian beliefs."

Part of the problem may be the wink's longstanding difficulty to define itself. In the seventeenth century, the word was more commonly used in reference to sleeping rather than picking up ladies or signifying that one was in the know. William Shakespeare employed it in this fashion many times, popularizing the phrase, "I have not slept a wink." (*Hoodwinked* also comes from this meaning; it refers to thieves putting sacks over the heads of victims, which effectively closed their eyes.)

By the nineteenth century, the question became what word should be used to describe the gesture: blink or wink. Scientific journals used wink in the way we'd use blink on more than one occasion.

An 1830 dictionary went with "to shut the eyes; to close the eyelids" as wink's primary definition.

Some writers of the time did campaign for the wink's more playful usage. In 1889, author Charles John Smith backed the notion that the gesture had a naughty side (or as he put it, an "active connivance"), but added that it was an undertaking of some energy. Winking is "not only a blinding of the eye, but much more significantly a purposed twinkling of it, as of a mind at once awake to what is going on, and, as it were, purposely asleep," he wrote wryly. To some extent, this wink to the wink opened the door for the maneuver's more benign modern applications.

Nice Words to Say

Amen

AMEN

If you want to unite three of the world's most popular faiths, just say "amen." Whether you're Christian, Jewish, or Muslim, *amen* comes up in your religious ceremonies. The word, which has a variety of English translations including "so be it," "verily," and "truly," is a linguistic oddity. Most religious words are tweaked from language to language, but when it comes to *amen*, speakers across the world have adopted it, using essentially the same pronunciation and definition. Maybe

MUSLIMS USE THE WORD ĀMIN WHICH FIRST APPEARED IN EARLY TEXTS AS A TERM OF AFFIRMATION, WHEN READING CERTAIN HOLY SCRIPTURES.

it's that sonorous combination of *ahh* and *men*, but whatever the case, it is *the* all-purpose affirmation during religious services.

In the beginning, so to speak, *amen* was used as an adjective or noun, and came from the Hebrew verb *aman*, which meant "to strengthen" or "to confirm." The word showed up thirteen times in early texts of the Jewish Bible, and by the beginning of the first century, it was uttered during Jewish religious ceremonies.

Early Christians adopted the word, making no attempt to translate it out of the Hebrew, as was their practice with other religious terms. The reason: the word's popularity with Jesus Christ. "So frequent was this Hebrew in the mouth of Our Savior," decreed the Catechism of the Council of Trent, "that it pleased the Holy Ghost to have it perpetuated in the Church of God." Jesus says the word twenty-eight times in the Bible, according to the *Catholic Encyclopedia*.

The term eventually crossed over to secular speech and writing. One riff—"amen to that"—

shows up in Shakespeare's *Othello*, and again over 200 years later in Dickens's *Pickwick Papers*, and then almost 200 years after that on a Justin Bieber Facebook fan page. (How's that for universal?)

Despite unanimity about its usage, there is disagreement over its origins. Some claim the Hebrew people borrowed *amen* from Egypt, where the word (or a variation, *amun*) was used for its greatest god, Amen-Ra. By this thinking, the Egyptians would exclaim, "By Amun!" to reinforce a point, and the Hebrews, who were familiar with Egyptian theology, adopted it. Others believe that there is a connection between the Eastern world's use of the meditative term *om* (or *aum*) and *amen*. But although the words predate the Hebrew term, most are skeptical of any direct ties.

Bless You

Pope Gregory I sure liked speaking out in the name of God. Gregory the Great, as he was also known, ascended to the papacy in 590, and among his many contributions during his fourteen-year reign was the Gregorian Chant, a form of divine praise in song still practiced today. But perhaps more important to our daily lives, he was the first to bring the word of *god* (as in "God bless you," later shortened to "Bless you") into the world as a post-sneeeze exclamation.

Unlike his solemn yet celebratory liturgical chants, Gregory's "Bless you" decree was deadly serious. You see, he'd become pope after the untimely death of his predecessor Pelagius II. Like many of his fellow Romans, Pelagius had succumbed to a version of the bubonic plague; this particular strain was alarmingly dubbed by at least one contemporary as the "plague of the groin." The devastating affliction quickly spread through Rome and people were known to perish suddenly, even in the middle of a sneeze.

Folklore had long warned about the danger of sneezes. The most popular tale revolved around evil spirits trying to capture the soul, which could escape the body through the reflexive reaction. Others claimed a sneeze "puts a healthy person as close to death as a healthy person is likely to get." The Romans believed the reflexive act might forecast terrible things. They would exclaim, *"Absit Omen!"* ("May the omen come to nothing!") following a

SCIENTISTS NOWADAYS SAY WE SNEEZE PRIMARILY AS A "PHYSIOLOGIC RESPONSE TO THE IRRITATION OF THE RESPIRATORY EPITHELIUM LINING OF THE NOSE." OR MORE PLAINLY, BECAUSE THE INSIDE OF OUR NOSE ITCHES.

sneeze. Not everyone was so gloomy. Greek philosophers like Aristotle and Thucydides held that sneezes could have heavenly meaning, reflecting divine favor. And the Maori in New Zealand and the Zulus in southern Africa share the belief that a sneeze is a sign from a kindly spirit.

But when Gregory was in charge, the sneeze had a solidly bad reputation, especially after the whole dying-during-sneezing bit. To combat it, the pope put out a memo, as it were, to his subjects, telling them to exclaim, *"Deus te adjuvet!"* ("God help you!") whenever someone had a nose-exploding moment.

The pope's influence was such that the custom spread faster and farther than the plague that inspired it. If anyone doubted Gregory's greatness, it should be noted that the plague of the groin ran its course relatively quickly, suggesting that the pontiff may have been on to something.

Many other cultures have gone with more secular wishes post sneeze. The popular *Gesundheit* means "health" or "healthiness." The German term comes from the proverb *"Gesundheit ist besser als krankeith,"* or "Healthiness is better than illness." (That's a saying worth supporting.) It came to the U.S. largely through the Pennsylvania Dutch and

Sexy Sneezes?

Despite the fact it feels pretty satisfying, a sneeze—or multiple sneezes depending on the story—does not produce an **orgasm** (the popular myth-busting website Snopes.com debunks that one). But one weird fact that *is* true: about one in four Americans sneeze when they look into bright light.

Eastern European Jews, who used the Yiddish variants "*tsi gesundt*" or "*zay gezunt*." Elsewhere in the world, the Chinese say "*bai sui*" ("May you live one hundred years"), Russians go with "*bud zdorov*" or the more formal "*butye zdorovy*" ("Be healthy"), and the Spanish-speaking world opts for "*salud*" ("Health"). Although we're reasonably certain that souls are safe when someone sneezes, the emphasis on health remains a good one. However, we should probably be wishing health to everyone *around* the sneezer instead. After all, each "ah-choo" produces tens of thousands of germ-laden droplets.

Compliments

Receiving a compliment is literally an emotional payday. As a 2008 study found, hearing words of praise activates the same happy area of the brain that's stimulated when you receive money.

When considering compliments, the story has largely centered less on the actual words of praise, and more on the spirit with which they're delivered. The reason: insincerity. If someone gives a genuinely nice comment, then great—it's a compliment.

But if warm-and-cuddly praise is given with ulterior motives, it's flattery and a tool philosophers have long feared for its potentially nefarious means.

Not all early cultures worried about this issue. The Egyptians assumed that any positive rhetorical flourish was given in earnest. Their language doesn't even appear to have a word for "lying." "What seems like fulsome praise of the pharaoh was just someone trying to use language to capture something beyond language," wrote Richard Stengel, in his book *You're Too Kind: A Brief History of Flattery*. "Saying something that was not yet the case might have the effect of causing it to happen. It was not false speech but perhaps wishful-thinking speech."

But the Greeks pondered whether certain compliments were something more akin to manipulation. Philosophers weren't particularly worried about this on a micro level—if a beau could con a lady into an amorous tryst with a false compliment, so be it. But if an ambitious citizen could use flattery to sway the masses, you had a problem. Aristotle was among the many who derided flatterers for using verbal niceties for personal gain or self interest. The Greek word *demagogue*, which simply means "leader of the people," earned its negative connotation from the populist leaders who might say all the right things with little regard for the truth. (Sound familiar?)

In contrast to their Greek predecessors, the Romans were troubled with the difference between true compliments and flattery on a more individual level. With ultrapowerful rulers ("All hail Caesar!") replacing the purer Greek democracies, the challenge was protecting the powerful from unscrupulous, fawning advisers. Plutarch, a popular writer of the era, pulled no punches on this one. The flatterer, he wrote, who has a place "in great houses and great affairs . . . often times overturns kingdoms and principalities." The writer even put together a commonsense cheat sheet on how to spot a dubious flatterer. For instance, if you change opinions and an adviser abruptly alters his view to yours, it's a bad sign. Another red flag: lots of third-party praise ("Claudius says your toga parties are the best!").

Either future leaders didn't read Plutarch or didn't really care, because flattery persisted long after the fall of the Roman Empire (no doubt some self-serving flattery helped spur the empire's demise). Most notably, courtiers were royal suckups for centuries. Even Dante's fourteenth-century critique of flatterers in his epic work *Inferno* hasn't helped stem the tide of false praise. He placed them in the eighth circle of hell: a worse place than thieves and hypocrites and only one ring better than murderers and tyrants.

Still, when you get the real thing—a sincere compliment—it can be sublime. As Mark Twain once said, "I can live for two months on a good compliment." And apparently it doesn't take much. Linguists Nessa Wolfson and Joan Manes found that two thirds of all compliments in the U.S. use just one of five adjectives: nice, good, beautiful, pretty, or great. And 85 percent of compliments come in one of three simple syntactic structures: *Your book is totally interesting* (noun/pronoun + is/ looks + (intensifying word) + adjective); *I really love your book* (I + (intensifier) + like/love + (possessive word) + noun/pronoun); or *That's a very good book* (pronoun + is + (intensifier) + a + adjective + noun/pronoun).

But what we lack in originality, we make up for in quantity. According to Wolfson, Americans offer up compliments quite frequently compared to other cultures, meaning another touchy-feely payday is always just around the corner.

Congratulations

Congratulations entered the English language through the Latin verb *gratulari*, which means "to thank." By adding the *con* prefix, the Romans created *congratulari*, which meant "to express one's joy." English speakers picked up the term by the sixteenth century, although they used the singular *congratulation*. The plural version, *congratulations*, didn't emerge until the following century. It's unclear why the "s" was added, but presumably it gave extra heft to the sentiment.

After all, why congratulate once when you can do it multiple times with a single word!

In the late 1800s, the humorist Ambrose Bierce wrote that *congratulations* should be defined as "the civility of envy." While that cynicism never caught on, people have tried to put their own spin on the encouraging word, with varying levels of success.

Some heavyweights were using the shortened *congrats* by the first decade of the nineteenth century. In a 1805 letter, Rufus King, a signer of the U.S. Constitution and a presidential candidate in 1816, offered his "sincere and cordl. congrats" in a letter to Supreme Court justice Samuel Chase, who had just evaded a politically motivated impeachment effort in the U.S. Senate.

The move to inject the variation "congratters" into common speak was less successful. The British

How to Congratulate

Some tips from the experts on how to write a proper congratulatory note: Use the word **congratulations** early on; explain how you learned about the happy news; be sure to wish future success; keep it short and somewhat formal.

Congrats: His and Hers

"**B**ravo" first rang out at Italian operas in the 1700s. The English-speaking world co-opted it a century later. If you want to be linguistically correct, you're supposed to say **"bravo"** in celebration of a male performer's work and **"brava"** if she is female.

poet Rupert Chawner Brooke used it in a 1905 letter, and it was still kicking around in the 1960s. I'm pleased to say the awkward word has all but died out now.

Despite that epic fail, efforts continue in search of new abbreviations of the expression. *Gratz* has emerged as a truncated Twitter-friendly option (with only 140 characters, you have to cut somewhere). But those displeased with the five letters required in that shorthand have taken it to the next level—a simple *gz* is a choice among some über-text-happy folks.

Eulogy

Chilon of Sparta is probably one of the smartest men you've never heard of (and if you have heard of him, I bow to your deep classical knowledge). Chilon (pronounced KYE-lon) lived circa 556 B.C. and was a great judge and philosopher who wisely steered the bellicose Spartans into a more collaborative foreign policy with the creation of the Peloponnesian League.

He may be largely forgotten, but his words are not. He is credited with the Greek versions of such golden nuggets of wisdom as "Judge not, lest ye be judged" and "Know thyself." He also gave the world a very clear directive on eulogies: "Never speak ill of the dead."

His line, along with the orators of Greece's other great city-state, Athens, have shaped how Western society has handled speeches following a death ever since.

While Chilon had the pithy quote, Athenians are considered to be the eulogy's first great innovators with the *epitaphios logos* ("funeral oration"). These weren't the personable, anecdote-laden walks down memory lane we know today. Instead, they were grand speeches lauding those who fought and died for Athens, focusing less on the greatness of the person and more on how the person's life reflected on the greatness of the city-state. Even so, Greek orator Demosthenes claimed that Athens was the only locale in the world at the time that delivered funeral orations for its citizens.

This may not be entirely true: There's evidence that other early cultures, such as some in Mesopotamia, praised their dead. Still, the Greeks' affinity for funeral speeches certainly spurred the Romans to take the ritual seriously. Our word *eulogy* comes from the Latin *eulogium*, which is defined as a formal expression of praise and was derived from a Greek term meaning "praise" or "blessing." At Roman funerals, the eulogy was called the *laudatio funebris* and, as Chilon counseled, it was a glowing speech about the recently departed.

For important figures, the address was given in front of the masses and the best of them would be recorded for posterity, which could give a boost to the speaker's popularity. (Julius Caesar enjoyed a big bump in public regard after his eulogy for his aunt Julia in 69 B.C.)

In the Judeo-Christian faiths, an early endorsement for eulogies came in the second century B.C. book of Ecclesiasticus. The tract called on people to "Praise famous men and our fathers in their generation." As for what few examples we have of

Poetic Remembrances

Another form of remembrance is the **elegy**, a poem that laments the loss of a person. Though not as common as today's eulogies, elegies emerged in the Greek and Roman eras and enjoyed particular popularity among Americans and Brits in the seventeenth and eighteenth centuries.

funeral oration in Christianity's formative years, we do know that they tended to be formulaic, following the style of the Greeks and the Romans. Even in the centuries that followed, most Christian eulogies were formal, emphasizing religion as much as the person.

Contemporary eulogies, which at their best mix humor and wit with a deep understanding of the departed, are a relatively new phenomenon. A great example of this comes from playwright Neil Simon's 1987 eulogy for famed choreographer Bob Fosse: "He was one of those people who you had to gear yourself up to be with because you always wanted to be at your best. If you were going to have lunch with him, you had to go out and have lunch someplace else first, just to break in your conversation."

Memorable Passages from Eulogies

SUSAN B. ANTHONY, SUFFRAGIST

"She was in the truest sense a reformer, unhindered in her service by the narrowness and negative destructiveness that often so sadly hampers the work of true reform. Possessed by an unfaltering conviction of the primary importance of her own cause, she nevertheless recognized that every effort by either one or many earnest souls toward what they believe to be a better or saner life should be met in a spirit of encouragement and helpfulness."

—*Rev. Anna Howard Shaw (1906)*

MARK TWAIN, WRITER

"Nothing is more false than to think that the presence of humor means the absence of seriousness. It was the showing up of the unreal sham, the untruth that made Mark Twain's humor. He was serious in his humor. But we know Mark Twain never laughed at the frail, the weak, the poor, and the humble. He used his humor, but for things good and wholesome. He made fun without hatred."

—*Rev. Henry Van Dyke (1910)*

ALBERT EINSTEIN, PHYSICIST

"He liked to stand alone on his own two feet and never lean on anyone or anything, nor did he have much sympathy for the feelings of those who needed something to lean on. [He said:] 'Nothing is so hateful to me as to belong in any group, be it a nation or a party, an academy or an institute. One always has the responsibility for actions on which one has no influence. My only refuge is not to take it too seriously.' "

—*Ernst Straus, assistant (1955)*

JOHN D. ROCKEFELLER JR., INDUSTRIALIST

"Mr. Rockefeller would be the last person to wish a eulogy pronounced upon him. Some men are forever courting observation, are never so happy as when basking in the sunshine of popular approval. He was not one of them. With all the weight and influence at his command, he was the most unassuming of men, innately modest and humble."

—*Dr. Robert J. McCracker (1960)*

ELEANOR ROOSEVELT, ACTIVIST AND FORMER FIRST LADY

"Her life was crowded, restless, fearless. Perhaps she pitied most not those whom she aided in the struggle, but the more fortunate who were preoccupied with themselves and cursed with the self-deceptions of private success."

—*Adlai Stevenson, politician (1962)*

HELEN KELLER, ACTIVIST

"Although she was denied the light of day, Helen Keller cast more of the radiance of heaven than any person on this earth. Within this radiance and the light and example of her life, may we carry on in our troubled world, worthy of her deeds, her hope, and her faith."

—Senator Lister Hill (1968)

JACK BENNY, COMEDIAN

"For a man who was the undisputed master of comedy timing, you'd have to say that this was the only time when Jack Benny's timing was all wrong. He was stingy to the end. He gave us only eighty years, and it wasn't enough. . . . Jack was one of the richest men I know. He was happy with who he was. He was happy with what he was. He was happy with where he was. Few are as rich as that." *—Bob Hope, comedian (1974)*

LUCILLE BALL, ACTRESS

"Lucille Ball told a friend of hers once that the essence of her comedy was to take the unbelievable and make it believable and true. And what she came up with was so true that people in eighty-three countries felt that she was giving them a revelation about their lives. Laughter of that kind, it seems to me, is not just unifying, it is humanity's holiday."

—Diane Sawyer, journalist (1989)

GIANNI VERSACE, DESIGNER

"I slept in Gianni Versace's bed. Of course, he wasn't in it at the time, but I couldn't help feeling that I was soaking up some of his aura. . . . There was a lot of nervous energy around Gianni's bed, and I must say I never slept very well in it."

—Madonna, musician/actress (1997)

PRESIDENT RONALD REAGAN

"In his lifetime, Ronald Reagan was such a cheerful and invigorating presence that it was easy to forget what daunting historic tasks he set himself. He sought to mend America's wounded spirit, to restore the strength of the free world, and to free the slaves of communism. . . . Yet [these tasks] were pursued with almost a lightness of spirit, for Ronald Reagan also embodied another great cause, what Arnold Bennett once called 'the great cause of cheering us all up.' "

—Margaret Thatcher,
former British Prime Minister (2004)

ExCuse Me
(Pardon Me)

Emily Post took the world of manners seriously. But after her book *Etiquette in Society, in Business, in Politics and at Home* became a bestseller in 1922, she made it her life, writing a syndicated column that appeared for decades in some 200 newspapers across the country.

No point of propriety was too small. Case in point: the distinction between "Excuse me" and "Pardon me." She wrote in a 1937 column, "The expressions 'I'm sorry' and 'Excuse me' can be said almost interchangeably for an offense that is unavoidable and yet one which might be unpleasant to others." And she added, "'I beg your pardon'" was also okay for "an offense that is caused by one's own awkwardness." But when it came to "Pardon me," she proclaimed, it was "a social tabu if separated from the complete sentence, 'I beg your pardon.'" For Post, this was a long-standing no-no. In her 1922 book, "Pardon me" made her "NEVER SAY" list; in at least two other locations in the volume, she reinforced the point. When a man bumps up against another person in a crowded streetcar, he "should *not*" say "Pardon me," but "Excuse me." An equally damning faux pas would be saying the phrase when moving past seated patrons at the theater.

Nice gestures should have some internal logic, and Americans weren't buying this one. The banning of "Pardon me" vexed enough readers that Post was compelled to justify her seemingly immovable rule. Her explanation was less than satisfactory. "I can only answer that this choice is purely an arbitrary one of social tradition," she said in a 1941 column. "'I beg your pardon' (four words) and 'excuse me' have long been established. 'I'm sorry' or 'sorry' come from England and have been made welcome, but 'pardon me' and 'pardon' have always been labeled bad taste."

In her defense, there may be an explanation from the world of etymology. *Pardon* comes from Old French and, by the twelfth century, referred to an act of forgiving a fault or offense. "Excuse me" emerged around the same time in Middle English, and is simply an offer of apology. Considering those definitions, "Pardon me" is almost a crass command lacking any politeness (in other words, it's insisting the wronged party forgive you). In contrast, "Excuse me" is a straightforward alternative for "Sorry," requiring no action from the aggrieved.

Other manners mavens haven't been so caught up in the minutiae of the two phrases. In 1961, Ann Landers called them "virtually interchangeable." Two decades later, Abigail Van Buren (Dear Abby) actually stumped for "Pardon" as the preferable form of a light apology. It "sounds a tad more elegant than 'Excuse' because of the French '*pardonnez-moi*,'" she wrote in 1982.

"Today, the terms are interchangeable," she said, "unless, of course you are referring to what Gerald Ford did for Richard Nixon."

Good-bye

GOD BE WITH YOU

ood-bye comes from a simple heavenly wish.
Scholars believe that the term developed as a contraction for the common farewell "God be with you." (The *Oxford English Dictionary* also suggests that "God be with you" was sometimes interchangeable with "God buy you," meaning "God redeem you.")

Dating back to at least the start of the fifteenth century, "God be with you" was a basic blessing used in all sorts of situations. ("You're going to take

a bite of that moldy mutton? God be with you!")
It was also common practice for most Sabbath
services in Judeo-Christian faiths to close with a
prayer asking God to be with and protect all present
in the coming week. Offering the same when parting under secular circumstances seemed natural.

As for how we got to *good-bye*, we can probably thank William Shakespeare for popularizing
the truncated phrase. The bard, who loved to coin
terms—from "faint-hearted" to "one fell swoop"—
used both "God be with you" and "good-bye" in a
number of his plays.

While Shakespeare wasn't likely the first good-
bye guy (sources suggest the term might have been
inspired by the already established expressions
"Good day" and "Good night"), the popularity of
the bard's writing helped put it into the vernacular.
According to one study, *good-bye* was the definitive
closing by the middle of the 1700s. By the 1800s,
most people had even forgotten its tie to the more
pious "God be with you." As it was sometimes
abbreviated in literature, "God-b'w'y" made a brief
comeback in the second half of the nineteenth century as a general statement of encouragement—like
Obi-Wan Kenobi saying "May the force be with
you" to Luke Skywalker.

Over time, *good-bye* has suffered the same fate as "God be with you." Starting as early as the seventeenth century, the word has been shortened to *bye* or *bye-bye* (on the plus side, it's an easy phrase for babies to learn). But how nice is "bye-bye"? In 1969, a sociologist named Sandor Feldman wrote that if a woman signed off a conversation with a man by saying "Bye-bye" rather than "Good-bye," it was a suggestive maneuver. Women, he asserted, used "Bye-bye" with men they aspired to get cozy with. "They think," he wrote, "by using the phrase, that men may accept the familiarity graciously."

While that doesn't seem to jibe with my understanding of the words—I remain confident that my wife saying "Bye-bye" to our dentist has no subtext—the term, whichever way you use it, owns a unique place in nice salutations.

After all, often one good-bye won't do. Invariably there are times when we end up saying good-bye over and over again. For example, during that awkward moment when we part ways but then head off in the same direction. Why do we feel a need to repeat the phrase? God only knows.

Hello

Inventors Alexander Graham Bell and Thomas Alva Edison were rivals on a grand scale. Most notably, the pair, among others, sparred over who would receive the first U.S. patent for the telephone (winner: Bell, in February 1876, three months before Edison). But it was their disagreement over what simple salutation would open telephone conversations that carried them out of the technical realm and into a linguistic street fight.

ACCORDING TO HELLO-OLOGIST ALLEN KOENIGSBERG (YEP, THERE IS A HELLO-OLOGIST), THE FIRST KNOWN "HELLO" NAME TAG POPPED UP IN 1880 AT A TELEPHONE OPERATORS CONVENTION IN NIAGARA FALLS, NEW YORK. THE MINUTES FROM THE EVENT GLEEFULLY REPORT THAT THE GROUP HAD "A NEW WORD TO GO ON OUR NAME TAGS."

Edison was a big fan of *hello*. While the term's etymology is a little hazy, some suggest it stems from *hail* and *ho*, morphing into *hallo* or *halla*, and was a crude way of getting another's attention. Although various forms had been kicking around since the fourteenth century, it was an obscure word in the 1870s when Edison was toiling over his version of the telephone. It's unclear how the Wizard of Menlo Park, New Jersey, came to love the term, but he would champion it as the perfect phone greeting.

However, some saw *hello* as a vulgarity. (In fact, as late at the 1940s, there was at least one manners book that cautioned the polite set to use *hello* only in rare circumstances.) Edison's adversary, Bell, had his own favorite: *Ahoy*. Originally a Viking war cry, *ahoy* was a greeting well known among nautical types. It doesn't seem like Bell was much of a sailor, but he was enamored with the term, so much so that when he performed the first long-distance call (between Boston and Cambridge, Massachusetts), he opened the conversation with "Ahoy." Apparently, he even enjoyed it enough to insist that the word be used twice— "Ahoy, ahoy"— to signal it was time to talk.

As odd as *Ahoy* might sound today, this wasn't a matter easily settled since both men had influence in all things telephone. Bell had considerable power, but Edison had a contract with Western Union, which gave him the advantage.

For the original public telephone exchange, which opened January 28, 1878, in New Haven, Connecticut, Western Union's official manual offered its operators two optional greetings: "Hello" or "What is wanted?" But within two years, the awkward "What-is-wanted" phrase was overshadowed by the elegant "Hello."

Interestingly, in many languages, the telephone greeting never crossed over into everyday conversation. For example, the Italians say "*Pronto*" ("Ready") when they take a call, but they don't use that word when they see a friend on the street. And in Spain, the telephone greeting "*Diga*" ("Speak") isn't typically used face-to-face.

When There Wasn't "Hello"

Before "Hello" took over as the catch-all introductory statement, "How do you do?" was deemed most appropriate at a first meeting. "Pleased to meet you" was also common, but it was considered impolite to presume you were happy to meet someone you didn't really know. If you had done some serious reconnaissance on a person, "Pleased to meet you" was okay.

So why did Americans embrace "Hello" as an all-purpose, go-to greeting? Frederick Perry Fish, who served as president of AT&T from 1901 to 1907, argued that the word developed greater meaning because it was a pure expression of the American attitude.

"When the first telephones came into use, people were accustomed to ringing a bell on the box and then say ponderously, 'Are you there?' 'Are you ready to talk?'" Fish said. "Mr. Edison did away with that awkward, un-American way of doing things. He caught up the receiver one day and yelled into the transmitter one word—a most satisfactory, capable, soul-satisfying word—Hello!"

Mr./Mrs./Ms.

Call it a rite of passage into middle age. At some point, young people cease referring to you by your first name and you become *Mr.*, *Mrs.*, or *Ms.* This distinction ties into the time-honored axiom of respecting your elders. It is also an age-old tradition that has some noteworthy historical twists.

The abbreviations Mr. and Mrs. come from the terms *mister* and *missus*, which are derived from *master* and *mistress*. Emerging in the thirteenth century, *master* was used as a title of respect for men below the level of knighthood, morphing into *mister* by the seventeenth century. The term was so revered that physicians in the United Kingdom, Australia, and South Africa appropriated it as a way to distinguish themselves from barbers.

Say what?

Yes, there was a time when barbers and doctors were considered kindred professionals. Barbers would, of course, give you a trim and a shave. But they were also trained to do a broad array of surgical procedures including amputation, tonsil removal, and blood letting. Beginning in 1540, the United Barber-Surgeons Company was a professional guild in England for some 200 years. As both barbers and full-fledged medical professionals could be called "doctor," proper physicians wanted a distinction befitting their additional education, so they adopted *mister*.

Much like *mister*, *mistress* was initially a term of respect bestowed on women of social importance like teachers and housekeepers. In the seventeenth century, the word took a turn for the unseemly, and was used in association with concubines and prostitutes. "Respectable" women were happy to use *missus* as an alternative.

Initially, *Mrs.* didn't have anything to do with marital status, but by the nineteenth century it was the honorific for married ladies, with *Miss* going to the unmarried. This led to a glaring linguistic inequality: Men didn't have to tele-graph the status of their love life when introduced, but for women, it was front and center. This fact was not lost on the American feminist movement in the second half of the twentieth century. *Ms.* had been kicking around since at least the 1760s and was used interchangeably with *Mrs.* as an abbre-viation for missus. It was little used until it began popping up in secretarial manuals in the 1950s as a substitute title for women whose marital status was uncertain.

Feminist organizations seized the term in the late 1960s, and in 1970 called for *Ms.* to be used as the universal female honorific. The introduction of *Ms.* magazine in December 1971 gave the fight a national stage. "The use of Ms. isn't meant to pro-tect either the married or the unmarried woman from social pressure—only to signify a female

THE *NEW YORK TIMES* WAS SLUGGISH IN EMBRACING *MS.* THE NEWSPAPER OF RECORD WOULD CONTINUE TO REQUIRE THE MRS./MISS DISTINCTION UNTIL 1986.

Names and Marriage

Should women have to relinquish their maiden names? Lucy Stone, a feminist who fought eloquently for women's rights, addressed this very question in the nineteenth century. When she married in 1855, she opted not to take her husband's surname—an unheard of decision in that day. In the first half of the twentieth century, women who followed Stone's example and kept their birth name were dubbed **Lucy Stoners**.

human being," the editors wrote in an explanation of the publications title. "It's symbolic, and important. There's a lot in a name."

As for those folks who would prefer not to be reminded of their age, there is hope. "We still teach children to address adults using dignified titles," according to Bethanne Patrick, author of *An Uncommon History of Common Courtesy*, "but experts in manners advise teaching children flexibility by instructing them to call adults by the titles the adults prefer. In this way children learn that showing respect for adults' wishes is more important than adhering to rigid rules."

Please

"Please" is the sugar sprinkled on the top of any request. As the Rotarians (those paragons of civility) wrote in their monthly magazine in 1937: "The stiffness and curtness of many an order is cancelled by that word of six letters." Indeed, *please* is the embodiment of courtesy, a word that reflects respect no matter the circumstances. (Heck, even the down-and-out Oliver Twist mustered a "Please, sir, I want some more" when asking for a second helping of gruel.)

But the central role of *please* in the manners of the English-speaking world is one that could easily have gone another way. In Elizabethan England, there were a number of options when making a courteous request. While *please* was in the mix, terms like *beseech*, *prithee*, and *to pray* (example: I pray thee give me back my tunic) were very popular. At this point, *please* was used as a verb, as in "if you please" or an adverb, as in "I'd be pleased to."

But by the nineteenth century, the word *please*, as we use it today—in such well-worn requests as, "Can you please take out the garbage"—began dominating everyday conversation. Grammatically, this form of *please* is a bit difficult to characterize. Dictionaries have classified it as an adverb, an interjection, or an exclamation, though other linguists place it in a special category, referring to it as a *courtesy marker*.

It's unclear why words like *beseech* and *prithee* didn't make the long-term cross over into the courtesy-marker world. After all, it would be fun to say, "Prithee, clean up your room!" Perhaps the soothing rhythm of the word *please* helped its cause. As one late nineteenth-century writer explained: "We like the word 'please'; there is something about it that sounds like a friendly word from a gentleman."

Even as a staple, *please* has weathered numerous debates over its necessity. In 1907, for example, controversy swirled regarding a decision by the Philadelphia-based Keystone Telephone Company to ban its 450 operators from saying "please" when connecting calls (as in, "please hold for a moment"). One bean counter calculated the term was uttered 900,000 times every day, and cutting it out would reclaim 125 hours of lost productivity every twenty-four hours. *The American Telephone Journal* lauded the maneuver: "There are some people who say that courtesy pays. It does, but one has to exercise discretion." Another publication, *Telephony*, disagreed. "No doubt, the word 'please,' sweetly uttered in cooing tones by the girl at the switchboard, has often assuaged the wrath of him (or her) who was becoming impatient at some delay in getting the right number." Nice won in the battle as Keystone's efforts did not catch on. In fact, a year later, the post office issued a notice advising operators to use the word *please* "wherever it can be conveniently introduced."

In 1920 a similar discussion swirled when some newsmen questioned the worth of using the term in telegrams. It was so common that estimates placed the annual cost of *please* to telegram writers—who paid by the word—at between $8 million and $10 million. But, again, the practice had strong defenders. "Its cost to the sender is amply compensated for by the good feeling, the cordiality, and the sense of self-respect that it promotes in the mind and the heart of the man who receives it," editorialized *The American Stationer and Office Outfitter*.

More recently, in 1999 the New York City Transit Authority attempted to keep conductors from using *please* in announcements like "please stand clear of the closing doors." Following public outcry, a Transit Authority spokesman backtracked. "You'll not only hear 'please,' we expect you'll hear 'thank-yous.'"

But, as Oliver Twist learned, saying please doesn't always mean getting what you want. In 1859, a defense lawyer in a California court argued that his client didn't have to pay a debt because the creditor used *please* in a letter requesting reimbursement. The creative attorney claimed adding *please* in the document proved that the creditor was simply asking payment as a "favor" rather than requiring it.

Lest you think that the case was a slam dunk, *Wheatley v. Strobe* made it all the way to the Supreme Court of California before a judge finally

Please Respond

Using **R.S.V.P.** (*Répondez s'il vous plaît,*
meaning "respond if you please") on invitations
became a popular tradition in America during the
late nineteenth century's Gilded Age. While some
stuck with the formal English saying, "The favor of
a reply is requested," large numbers of the country's
well-heeled believed the French option added an air
of sophistication.

ruled that being civil didn't mean the borrower
could sidestep paying up. The decision has since
been cited by lawyers across the United States as
proof that even *please* has its nice limitations—at
least in a legal sense.

PLEASE and THANK YOU
From Around the World

Language	# of Native Speakers*
1. Mandarin	845 million
2. Spanish	329 million
3. English	328 million
4. Arabic	221 million
5. Hindi	182 million
6. Bengali	181 million
7. Portuguese	178 million
8. Russia	144 million
9. Japanese	122 million
10. German	90.3 million

Top 10 most spoken languages and how they say please *and* thank you

Please	Thank You
qǐng	xiéxié
por favor	gracias
please	thank you
min fadlak/lau samaht	shukran
krpaya	dhan-ya-vaad
daya kare	d'oh-noh-baad
por favor	obrigado
pazhalsta	spaseeba
kudasai	arigato
bitte	danke

*AS OF 2009

Saying Grace

When early hunters and gatherers said a few words to higher beings before digging into a meal, it was more of a request than a thank-you. With spotty knowledge about which foods could have poisonous effects, and even less know-how about keeping edibles fresh, some clans, according to anthropologists, explicitly asked the heavens for protection. This prayer would often be accompanied by a sacrifice. (If you're going to ask your god for a favor, you ought to provide more than pleasant words.)

Even as food safety improved, the prayer habit continued—more out of gratitude for the feast than a save-me-from-this-potentially-rancid-wild-boar-meat plea. Cultures throughout the world, regardless of their chosen religion, share the tradition of offering thanks for their daily bread.

The ancient Greeks and Romans placed wine in a flat bowl and sang before pouring some of the drink onto the floor to honor the gods. The Igbo people from Nigeria take a pinch of food and throw it outside while uttering words of thanks. In Japan, the Ainu aborigines sprinkle drops of soup or sake on the floor and say a prayer before dinner.

THE WORD GRACE EFFECTIVELY MEANS "THANKSGIVING" AND WAS PRIMARILY USED IN THE PLURAL— SAYING GRACES— UNTIL THE SIXTEENTH CENTURY.

The major modern monotheistic religions also have customs for grace. The Jewish faith has a variety of formal pre-meal blessings depending on the food and drink. In an early Christian custom, the leader would mark a round loaf of bread with a cross while providing an introductory prayer. Islamic Arabs will roll up their right sleeve and say,

"*Bismil'lah ir-rahman ir-raheem*" ("In the name of God, the merciful and compassionate") before starting a meal.

Why is this custom so prevalent? One early twentieth-century author posited that "a natural piety and 'the law of reason' account in part for the prevalence of this tribute paid to the Supreme being."

Grace is an act primarily used at dinnertime— typically a more formal event than a rushed lunch or breakfast. However, for many, the formality (and

Table Manners

Although ideas about table manners go back to ancient Egyptian and Greek cultures (the poet Hesiod counseled not to cut your fingernails at the table), many of our modern practices—like keeping elbows off the table—developed in the Middle Ages. Still, not every rule fits with our current notions. The Dutch humanist Erasmus said it was okay to throw a piece of tough meat you couldn't swallow somewhere in the room. And, when the fork landed on tables in eleventh century Tuscany, it was disparaged by the Roman Catholic Church, which insisted that human hands were nature's proper eating implements.

religiosity) have diminished. While not as spiritual as traditional graces, which can be found in book form under titles like *Table Prayer* and *Hear Our Grace*, the trend has moved toward a kind of secular grace. These are neither a thank-you to a divine presence nor a request that the eaters be spared from dangerous foods, but more a show of cheer or gratitude, on a human level.

AS DEFINED BY THE OXFORD ENGLISH DICTIONARY, GRACE IS "A SHORT, PRAYER EITHER ASKING A BLESSING BEFORE, OR RENDERING THANKS AFTER, A MEAL."

Famed cookbook writer and TV chef Julia Child popularized the French phrase "*Bon appétit!*" (or "Good appetite") in America when serving up dishes. The Germans similarly say "*Guten Appetit,*" and in Slovakia it's "*Dobrú chut´,*" meaning "Enjoy your meal." The Japanese often offer "*itadakimasu*" or "I graciously accept this" to a host, and in many Spanish-language countries, it's "*buen provecho*" ("to a good meal").

Of course in the U.S., even those who still want to give thanks to a higher being can make allowances for a little light humor. There's always, "Rub-a-dub-dub, thanks for the grub" or "Good food, good meat, good God, let's eat."

Sorry

There was a time when offering an apology meant never having to say you're sorry. Rather than showing remorse or repentance, an *apologia*—from the Greek *apologos*, meaning "story"—was originally a formal defense of an opinion. Socrates famously offered one against accusations of corrupting the youth of Athens. (Sadly, his effort failed to win the day and he was sentenced to death.) Many early Christian scholars, like the writer Tertullian, delivered apologias

NICE WORDS TO SAY

to defend their religion to Roman Emperors. The concept still survives in the word *apologist*—a person who argues in defense of something.

Scholars aren't exactly sure how the apology moved from a form of verbal argument to an act of contrition, but some say that Judeo-Christian theology helped shift the tide. Certainly those religions focused heavily on the concept of forgiveness. The twelfth-century Jewish philosopher Maimonides argued that apologizing entailed far more than words. The offender had to acknowledge his actions, assume responsibility, and solemnly promise not to do it again. The sincerity of a sorry couldn't be known until the wrongdoer, when faced with an opportunity to repeat the transgression, chose not to commit the act again.

The word *sorry* began popping up in English in the fourteenth century, according to the *Oxford English Dictionary*. At the time, it typically meant to wound, hurt, or injure, but could also reflect grieving or sorrow. (It was a popular word; cognates for *sorry* existed in Middle Dutch, Middle Low German, and Old English.)

Over time, *sorry* became shorthand for apologizing. "The commonplace phrase, 'I am sorry,' conveys a simple description of one's own condition—a condition that, if accepted as *authentic*, would then warrant forgiveness by the other," explained Nicholas Tavuchis, author of *Mea Cupla: A Sociology of Apology and Reconciliation.*

Simple though it may be, the humbling required to make an apology has not always sat well with people. "This imperious never-apologize-never-explain code of conduct probably began in 1970, when Eric Segal gave [the film] *Love Story* its one unforgettable line: 'Love is never having to say you're sorry,'" wrote journalist Marilyn Gardner in the *Christian Science Monitor* in 1990. "That same year California became the first state to pass a no-fault divorce law, marking the beginning of a nationwide no-fault mentality that seemed to absolve everyone, including politicians, of any wrongdoing—and thus of any need to apologize. From Watergate to the Iran-Contra affair to the Savings and Loan scandal, stonewalling was In. Confession and contrition were Out. An apology became the ultimate form of wimpishness."

And yet, less than a decade after Gardner's lament, the British newspaper *The Independent* declared 1997 as "the year of the apology." Among those who said "sorry" in 1997: Boxer Mike Tyson for biting off part of opponent Evander Holyfield's ear; British Prime Minister Tony Blair for the nineteenth-century Irish potato famine; the German government for invading the Czech Republic before World War II; and various Christian sects in England for such actions as slavery, racism, and the Crusades.

THE HOLY ROMAN EMPEROR HENRY IV CROSSED THE ALPS IN 1077 IN ORDER TO APOLOGIZE TO POPE GREGORY VII AFTER A RELIGIOUS POWER PLAY WENT AWRY. THE POPE MADE THE KING SPEND THREE DAYS KNEELING—IN THE SNOW—BEFORE ALL WAS FORGIVEN.

With so many apologies out there, we have become far more discerning in how we react to *sorry*. As author Tavuchis put it, the key comes down to authenticity. When Bill Clinton apologized in 1998 for having an affair with intern Monica Lewinsky, he offered this limp statement: "Indeed I did have a relationship with Miss Lewinsky that was not appropriate. In fact, it was wrong. . . . I misled people, including even my wife. I deeply regret that."

American didn't buy it and, according to *TIME* magazine, Clinton has since said "sorry" publicly more than a half dozen times.

In the twenty-first century, many apologies have migrated to Twitter. They've ranged from the famous—Kanye West's apologizing to Taylor Swift nearly a year after he snubbed her at the 2009 MTV Video Music Awards—to the mundane—the British supermarket Sainsbury's saying sorry to a customer after he complained about a chicken sandwich. They can also be prolific: A Malaysian social activist tweeted an apology to a magazine publisher one hundred times in 2011 as part of a defamation settlement (a number that puts Clinton's apologies to shame).

Thank You

THANK YOU!

T hank you is a rock star in the world of nice.
No other word conveys gratitude better, or
more concisely, than *thank you* or its pithy
cousin *thanks*.

"Thanking is so widely used partly because
'thank you' is easy to say and can offend no one,"
wrote Margaret Visser in her book *The Gift of
Thanks*. A 2011 survey in Great Britain found that
the average Brit says "thank you" nearly 5,000
times a year.

The singular *thank* was first used as a noun in the eighth century. Linguists believe the term stems from the Old English words *thonc* or *thanc* meaning "thinking" or "thought." (The German word for thanks, *danke*, also has a similar lineage.) How we got from thinking to gratitude is uncertain, but philosopher Martin Heidegger took an interesting crack at it. "In giving thanks, the heart gives thought to what it has and what it is," he said. "Pure thanks is not giving back. It is simply thinking. . . . This thinking . . . does not need to repay, nor be deserved, in order to give thanks."

We don't know whether Ye Olde English speakers had such equivalent deep thoughts, but we do know it took a while before the phrase *thank you* developed from the noun *thank*. *Thanks* as the "courteous acknowledgement of a favor or service" (so defined by the *Oxford English Dictionary*) emerged in the fifteenth century. William Shakespeare likely deserves some credit for popularizing the truncated *thanks* some two centuries later, using it in his comedy *Love's Labour's Lost*.

The phrase is also a cornerstone of a branch of linguistic studies known as pragmatics. These academics see *thanks* "as neither a noun nor a verb, but a stem, susceptible of expansion, compounding, and ironic subversion," according to Visser. (In other words, if you want to add a little snark to your conversation, a tongue-in-cheek *thanks* will do quite nicely.)

More important for us regular folks, the phrase is a "behabitive," which means, like the word *sorry*, it can communicate a person's disposition: Whether your friend thanks you multiple times for washing his car or just takes the keys and says nothing, tells you a lot.

Researchers have also honed in on the role *thank you* plays when faced with a compliment. Almost reflexively, we teach our kids to say "thank you" when someone pays them a compliment. But adults often don't feel comfortable taking their own advice because it seems akin to praising oneself.

One study came up with twelve (yes, twelve) wonderful techniques to sidestep a basic thank-you. They include the *reassignment*, in which we transfer credit to a third person or an object (for example, "the scarf really knitted itself"); or the *scale down*, where we point out flaws ("thanks, but look at that poor needlework near the scarf's fringe"); or, my personal favorite, the *return*: "thank you, but the scarf *you* knitted is doubly fantastic."

No matter how we use it (or don't, as the case may be), like most aging rock gods, thank-you's star may be starting to fade. The same British survey that counted daily *thank-you*'s found signs that other words are encroaching on the term's supremacy. One in three people used "cheers" or "ta" instead, and one in twenty used "nice one" as a *thank you* substitute. (Other alternatives included "fab" and "much appreciated.") While most of these phrases haven't crossed the Atlantic, one day we may be saying something other than "thanks" for a job well done.

Toasting

The original toast was a way to welcome otherworldy guests. The Greeks raised their glasses to give thanks to the gods—and spilled some wine as sort of an offering to the deities (see Saying Grace, page 150). Rather than toasting, it was called "drinking a health" or "drinking healths."

Some sources also suggest there may have been a more self-serving reason for raising one's glass: fear of poisoning. Spiking the drink of your enemy

WHILE MANY CREDIT THE GREEKS FOR TOASTING, ONE 1912 COMPENDIUM, *TWENTIETH CENTURY ENCYCLOPAEDIA: A LIBRARY OF UNIVERSAL KNOWLEDGE*, MAINTAINS THAT RAISING GLASSES AS DEFENSE AGAINST POISONING PRACTICES DEVELOPED IN TENTH–CENTURY EUROPE.

was a common strategy for getting ahead in Greek politics (so much for good old-fashioned democracy). As a result, to assuage any fear, the host would make a speech and take a swig to prove the alcohol wasn't spiked. After that, everyone could relax and enjoy the evening.

Poison also figures in the origin of the tradition of clinking glasses. Smacking tankards allowed the alcohol in both cups to slosh out and mix, serving as a deterrent for poisoning. In another variation, the host offered his glass to a guest to prove there was no tampering. If a visitor felt it unnecessary, he'd clink his glass with the host's and keep what he had. Different explanations range from clinking to ward off evil spirits to simply liking the sound.

In any case, the toasting tradition was embraced by most Western cultures. During Roman times, revelers began substituting powerful leaders for gods as the target of toasting affection. The ritual would migrate throughout Europe with some taking it a little too seriously. "The gallants of the sixteenth and seventeenth centuries frequently bled themselves, and let the blood drop into their cups before toasting,"

LEGEND HAS IT THAT QUEEN ELIZABETH I ONCE SAID ON THE TOPIC OF TOASTS, "I NEVER FARE WORSE THAN WHEN MY HEALTH IS DRUNK."

a journalist claimed in 1903. The writer also quotes St. Augustine as denouncing the practice, calling it the "filthy and unhappy custom of drinking healths."

Most believe the term *toast* originated in seventeenth- or eighteenth-century Britain. The story goes that in an effort to make their wine more flavorful, drinkers literally dropped pieces of toast into glasses of alcoholic beverages. What the bread did for the wine is up for debate. Some say that the toast, sweetened with nutmeg and sugar, added a nice flavor to the brew. Others suggest that the burnt toast was employed to soak up some of the liquid's acidity. (There's a popular but hard-to-believe tale that the term came from a specific instance in the English town of Bath. When two friends passed a beautiful woman, one said he'd drink to her, while the other, a teetotaler, pledged to eat the toast placed in the drink instead.

History of "Cheers"

Nearly every language has their standard toast. For most, it's a version of "to health" or "good luck." In America, it's **"cheers."** The word comes from the Middle English for "face" or "countenance." Later it referred to a person's outlook or mood. In 1720, it was first used as a shout of encouragement, like giving a cheer for the home team. By the 1920s, people were raising their martini glasses to the word, perhaps in the same sort of rah-rah spirit as the eighteenth-century definition. Other popular toasting terms range from SKÅL (pronounced SKOAL) in Swedish to SALUD in Spanish. The popular German choice is *prost* which comes from the Latin PROSIT, essentially meaning "may it benefit (you)."

The British have long loved the concept, turning it into an art. Upper-class English partiers would raise glasses not only to those around the table but also to people not present—most often beautiful ladies adored either locally or throughout the British Empire (much like the buddies in Bath). This led to the popular phrase "the toast of the town," to represent someone—usually a woman—whose fair virtues deserved special celebration.

As the British migrated to the American colonies, so did the toast. Volumes filled with ready-to-use toasts were commonly available at most local booksellers. Prohibition in the 1920s posed an obvious threat (toasting with apple juice just lacks the gravitas of lifting a snifter of brandy).

Thankfully, the tradition persisted. No one proved this more than Douglas McElvy. When the New Yorker died in 1973, he bequeathed $12,000 to his friends so they could toast him each year on the anniversary of his death. The toasts must have been really special: The five-figure sum only lasted his pals three years.

You're Welcome

Although the word *welcome*—or *wilcuman*—dates back to Old English (it appears in *Beowulf*, circa 399), using the phrase in response to "thank you" is relatively new.

The Oxford English Dictionary pinpoints 1907 as the first year the idiom showed up in print in conjunction with "thank you." It's so new that welcome mats in front of houses, which became popular at the end of the nineteenth century, seem to predate the phrase.

At first, definitions for *welcome* just referred to receiving visitors or loved ones to a home (hence, the welcome mats). *Welcome* did have another lesser used meaning—"acceptable, agreeable, or pleasing"—which popped up in the thirteenth century and was spoken somewhat regularly by the 1500s. Perhaps "you're welcome" was devised to indicate pleasure taken from a thank-you.

Once "you're welcome" entered the mainstream, most people gave little thought to its meaning, making it a commonplace coda to all sorts of conversations that conveyed thanks. Yet, some critics argue that the phrase can seem almost arrogant. For example, Henry Kissinger was once approached by a supporter who thanked the Secretary of State for preventing nuclear war during the height of the Cold War. Instead of deflecting such a grandiose compliment, Kissinger supposedly responded, "You're welcome." The statement came off as a cocky way to take credit for something that was far more complicated.

"You're supposed to say something that minimizes the pleasure when you do something for someone," Georgetown University professor Deborah Tannen said in a 2009 interview. Employing "you're welcome" doesn't properly reassure the grateful party that whatever you did wasn't such a big deal. Instead, Tannen said, "no problem" is a better, low-key response.

But Geoffrey Sampson, a linguistics professor at the University of Sussex, has suggested that even "no problem" is unnecessary. The simple "please" and then "thank you" combination is enough. With those pleasantries, "the transaction was complete and no further words were required," he claimed.

"You're welcome" does have its defenders. The *New York Times* language columnist William Safire was one. "As if decreed by a dictatorial Academie Americaine," he wrote in 2007, "the only answer now socially permitted to even the most perfunctory 'Thank you' is 'Thank you!'" Such verbal deflection is "an obsequious 'I deserve no thanks at all; you are the one to be thanked for graciously accepting such a meager and unworthy offer of my time, talent, and money.'"

Alas, Safire's wish to continue the use of a bold response to "thanks" may be a long shot. University of Toronto linguist Jack Chambers believes "you're welcome" (or, no doubt, alternatives such as "my pleasure") just feels too formal nowadays. "You're welcome," he said, "will eventually be quaint and then it will be obsolete."

Extra Credit

A-1: The term refers to something (or someone) that's top class, and was created by the famous insurance company Lloyd's of London, which has insured just about everything from rock star Bruce Springsteen's vocal cords to football player Troy Polamalu's distinctively long hair. In 1775, Lloyd's ranked ships with a letter grade based on the quality of each ship's hull and used a number system to evaluate the condition of the boat's other vital parts like the anchor and cables. The absolute best seafaring vessels would receive an A-1 rating. Charles Dickens supposedly popularized the term outside of its maritime context in the late 1830s.

HALCYON DAYS: Oddly, this phrase used to recall happy days of the past comes from a less-than-joyful mythological tragedy. The Greek tale centers on Aklyone, the daughter of the god of the winds. When Aklyone's husband died at sea, she threw herself into the waves in despair. Her deity dad saved his bereft daughter by transforming her into a kingfisher. Now a bird, Aklyone nested on the sea, and during the winter solstice, her presence would calm the winds and the waves. The word *Aklyone* eventually evolved to *halcyon* and its definition developed from "calm and peaceful" to our more sentimental notion of the past.

HUNKY DORY: Meaning "all is right or good," the phrase may be derived from the Dutch *honk*, meaning "base" or "home," which morphed into *hunk* (as in "he's a hunk") on the streets of New York. Others suggest that it came from a Japanese term for a main street, *honcho-dori*. U.S. sailors who had enjoyed a fun time on a *honcho-dori* in Japan allegedly brought it back America. We do know that it was used by a popular singing group, Christy's Minstrels, by 1862 when they crooned, "With your smiling faces round, 'tis then I'm hunkey dorey."

TICKER—TAPE PARADE:

On October 20, 1886, a parade was held in New York City in honor of the dedication of the Statue of Liberty. The sight of some 20,000 people marching through the city led to an impromptu addition to the celebration on Wall Street. "All the display was an inspiration to so many imps of office boys, who, from a hundred windows began to unreel the spools of tape that record fateful messages of the 'ticker,'" wrote *The New York Times*.

TLC:

Chalk this one up—at least initially— to William Shakespeare. He first used the phrase "tender loving care" in *Henry IV, Part II*, but it took another 350 years for it to turn into a go-to acronym. *TLC*, used to describe sweetly helping a patient, began popping up in dictionaries for medical secretaries in the 1950s. Ultimately, it was James Bond who made the term cool. In Ian Fleming's famed 1959 book *Goldfinger*, Bond refers to it while getting intimate with a lady, calling it "TLC treatment." Fleming does credit the acronym's medical roots, saying it was "what they write on most papers when a waif gets brought in to a children's clinic." From there the phrase took off. According to one study, around a dozen songs were penned between 1960 and 1983 with *TLC* in the title.

Nice Offerings

Anniversary Gifts

Lists of symbolic wedding anniversary gifts (and their meaning) are more than just cheat sheets for gift-giving. Their ever-changing contents reflect the customs and values of their time.

The routine of commemorating years of marriage with keepsakes started during the medieval period in the Germanic region of Europe. Presents were reserved only for very special anniversaries: For twenty-five years of marriage, a couple would receive a silver garland from family and members of the community. For fifty years of nuptial fidelity, a gold reward was handed out, though, considering how few people lived past their fifties, most could breathe easy knowing that they wouldn't have to dole out such an expensive gift.

As one nineteenth-century author lightly put it, these tokens were bestowed "partly in congratulation of the good fortune that had prolonged the lives of the couple for so many years, and partly in recognition of the fact that they must have known a fairly harmonious existence, otherwise one or the other would long ago have been worried into the grave."

In Victorian England, the upper classes, who loved to conjure up social rules and make lists, formalized anniversary gift etiquette. Around 1875, giving wood on the fifth year joined silver and gold. Soon, the list grew to about fifteen anniversaries that required gift giving.

There wasn't universal agreement on what tokens should be given when. Numerous nineteenth-century guides advised paper for the first anniversary, while others went with cotton. Many publications list fine linens for the twelfth anniversary, while at least one puts it at the thirty-fifth. (At the time, the value of linen was high—these days it's typically given at the four-year mark.)

Birthday Gifts

I f you need good inspiration when it comes to gifts, look to history. **Birthday presents** likely date back to the beginning of birthday celebrations—around 3000 B.C. In 238, the scholar Censorinus wrote a book for the nobleman Quintus Caerellius's birthday (not bad, although it was chock full of philosophy so it wasn't the wildest of gifts). For something a little more romantic, the German composer Richard Wagner penned the symphony *Siegfried Idyll* as a present for his second wife's thirty-third birthday. He even brought in an orchestra on the big day to perform it. Now that's hard to beat.

To further confuse matters, in 1897, Queen Victoria celebrated sixty years on the British throne. It was dubbed her Diamond Jubilee, and although the seventy-fifth wedding anniversary had typically been the year for diamonds, they were added to the sixtieth year as well. (After all, we must respect the Queen!) No doubt, very few wives complained about the duplication.

Leave it to good old American capitalism to expand and clarify this gift-giving tradition.

In 1937, the American National Retail Jewelers Association published an authoritative year-by-year directory of anniversary gifts. In the interest of increasing their industry's bottom line, the group added a number of fine stones like jade, agate, and aquamarine to the must-buy list.

While the Association's litany remains America's traditional cheat sheet (England has a slightly different list), an alternative option is out there with a more modern take. The Jewelry Industry Council unveiled it in 1948 to reflect a unique moment in history. World War II had ended two years earlier and people were getting hitched at a monumental rate. In fact, 2.29 million couples married in 1946, the most to wed in a single year at that point in U.S. history. With the economy booming, the council saw an opportunity not only to make sales but also to reflect the period's optimism and wealth. Newlyweds were focused on feathering their nests and the new list's first nine gifts—which included electrical appliances and silverware—were devoted to basic home improvement.

"After the ninth wedding anniversary, personal gifts are suggested for a span of five years," wrote one newspaper, "because by then children are usually out of babyhood and parents have more freedom to leave the house." Later, gifts aimed at updating the house, like changing out furniture, were added because "as growing children show an increased pride in their home as a place to entertain friends," decor upgrades were necessary.

The options may be overwhelming, but married couples should take solace in the words of the ever-reliable etiquette expert Emily Post. In 1922 (and then in later editions of her books), Post counseled her readers that these lists were just recommendations, and civilized folks weren't required to follow them to the letter. Still, dedication to a certain year—the twenty-fifth silver anniversary—*was* essential. "Silver is always serious," she warned.

THE BOOK OF NICE

Nice Love Tokens

*T*he "right" anniversary gift is a moving target. Below are the traditional and modern recommendations (though keep in mind many of the modern choices are decades old). Some choices are timeless, like silver on a twenty-fifth anniversary and gold on the fiftieth.

KEY: **T**- *traditional* | **M**- *modern*

First
T · Paper | **M** · Clocks

Second
T · Cotton | **M** · China

Third
T · Leather | **M** · Crystal, glass

Fourth
T · Fruits and flowers, books
M · Appliances

Fifth
T · Wood | **M** · Silverware

Sixth
T · Iron or candy
(or other sugary treat)
M · Wood

Seventh
T · Wool /copper
M · Desk sets

Eighth
T · Bronze | **M** · Linens, lace

Ninth
T · Pottery, willow | **M** · Leather

Tenth
T · Tin, aluminum
M · Diamond jewelry

Eleventh
T · Steel | **M** · Fashion jewelry

Twelfth
T · Silk or linens | **M** · Pearls

Thirteenth
T · Lace | **M** · Textiles, furs

Fourteenth
T · Ivory or agate
M · Gold jewelry

Fifteenth
T · Crystal | **M** · Watches

Sixteenth
M · Silver hollow ware

Seventeenth
M · Furniture

Eighteenth
M · Porcelain

Nineteenth
M · Bronze

Twentieth
T · China | **M** · Platinum

Twenty-first
M · Brass or nickel

Twenty-second
M · Copper

Twenty-third
M · Silver plate

Twenty-fourth
M · Musical instruments

Twenty-fifth
M · Silver

Twenty-sixth
M · Original art/pictures

Twenty-seventh
M · Sculpture

Twenty-eighth
M · Orchids

Twenty-ninth
M · Furniture

Thirtieth
T · Pearls | **M** · Diamonds

Thirty-first
M · Timepieces

Thirty-second
M · Conveyances

Thirty-third
M · Amethyst

Thirty-fourth
M · Opal

Thirty-fifth
T · Coral | **M** · Jade

Thirty-sixth
M · Bone China

Thirty-seventh
M · Alabaster

Thirty-eighth
M · Tourmaline/beryl

Thirty-ninth
M · Lace

Fortieth
M · Ruby

Forty-fifth
M · Sapphire

Fiftieth
M · Gold

Fifty-fifth
M · Emerald

Sixtieth
M · Diamond

Sixty-fifth
T · Blue sapphire
M · Star sapphire

Seventieth
M · Platinum

Seventy-fifth
M · Diamond

Eightieth
T · Oak

Birthday Cake

When it comes to birthday cakes, the ancient Greeks had the right idea. Rather than offering yearly birthday praise to Artemis, the god of the moon and the hunt, devotees would offer up a cake surrounded with torches, (those are some big candles!) once a month. While not quite the same as today's Baskin-Robbins ice-cream cake, according to a 1914 encyclopedia, it was "a striking prototype of [the modern] birthday cake" and is considered by most to be the first time baked goods and fire came together to honor a birth.

Cakes have been around since humans mastered baking. The Persians were said to have particular talent in this area, and the Nordic people must have had some skills since the word *cake* derives from an Old Norse term *kaka*. As for the birthday treat, many early civilizations did this informally. The Romans certainly did. In *Tristia*, a collection of letters written by Ovid after his exile from Rome in the year 8, the poet talks about receiving a cake on his birthday. Regrettably, he was too bummed about his banishment to enjoy the confection.

The birthday cake began to take shape as a regular tradition in Germany during the medieval age. On birthdays, the Germans celebrated their children in an event called *Kinderfest*. Loved ones would gather at dawn to present the child with a cake adorned with candles. The candles would burn until that evening and, much to the birthday child's frustration, no doubt, he or she had to wait until then to dig into the cake. Some suggest this fete was more about fear than affection, since the celebration—cake, candles, and all—was designed to help protect the child from evil spirits.

A Wedding Treat

The **wedding cake** tradition appears to have been in place before its birthday counterpart. Brides in ancient Rome were traditionally showered with wheat, which represented fertility and prospective wealth. Opting for a more practical use of the wheat, bakers began making cakes as an alternative. In a weird twist, wedding partygoers who missed throwing wheat were known to toss pieces of the cake at the bride. Over time, smart guests realized the dessert was better eaten than thrown.

The British added their own wrinkle to the proceedings. In some instances, small symbolic objects were baked into cakes for birthdays and other special occasions. The person who received the slice with the little bauble would be given a fortune—a coin (you'd be rich), a thimble (you'd never marry), a horseshoe (you'd have luck).

While wealthy Europeans baked birthday fruitcakes and other rich bready treats, birthday cakes as we know them weren't common until the nineteenth century when more middle-class families had the means to make them.

Americans deserve a lot of credit for the modern design. Access to relatively inexpensive staples like sugar, butter, and flour, and the availability of quick-heating ovens allowed American bakers to innovate. The result was "[a] cake constructed in layers, filled, and frosted, [which] became the image of the standard birthday cake," explained *The Oxford Companion to American Food and Drink*.

Immortalizing the start of this American tradition is an 1887 painting, *The Birthday Party*, by John Singer Sargent, depicting a boy with a tasty-looking cake complete with candles. The only question nowadays is which is better birthday cake: homemade or store-bought?

Box of
Chocolates

The migration of chocolates into lavish boxes was initiated by a man in dire straits. To paraphrase the well-worn quote from the movie *Forrest Gump*, Richard Cadbury's life at the start of the 1860s was like a dreadful box of chocolates. Most notably, his family's chocolate business was floundering in the English city of Birmingham. As purveyors of "drinking" chocolate ("eating" chocolate—the precursor to candy bars and boxed chocolate—wasn't common in Britain at the time),

Cadbury's was struggling as the British turned to tea as their go-to hot beverage. To make matters worse, a competitor, Fry and Sons, became the first British company to figure out how to produce pieces of edible chocolate. (Geek note: While it took a while for chocolate bars to reach England, a French pharmacist, Jean-Antoine Brutus Menier, is widely credited with creating solid chocolate in 1836.)

Although they lacked a popular product, Richard and his brother George made a hard choice and spent the last of their inheritance to keep the company from failing. They then moved quickly to begin selling their own eating chocolate. In 1861, the family produced a variety of tantalizing options—chocolates filled with orange, raspberry, and almond nougat, as well as spice-flavored pieces.

In 1868, Fry, which continued to be Cadbury's main competition, began a battle of the boxes when they issued an ornately illustrated candy container portraying kids in a goat-drawn carriage. But Richard Cadbury had a better feel for this type of marketing. Manufacturing what was described as the "first specially produced commercial design" for boxed chocolate, Cadbury wowed the masses with his more elegant presentation. The lids on his four-ounce oval boxes, depicting his six-year-old daughter, were considered quite artistic by the masses. (Anything was probably better than goats, but still it was impressive.)

Boxed candy quickly became a perfect present for courting. Long before we began doling out heart-shaped containers full of the confection (another Cadbury creation), chocolate was an iconic symbol of love and lust. Ancient peoples in Latin America exchanged cocoa beans during nuptial vows and, following the ceremony, drank the stuff to toast the marriage. These indigenous folks certainly believed the sweet had sexual power. Supposedly, at least one potentate would drink up to fifty goblets of liquid chocolate to prepare for private time with his harem.

European explorers like Christopher Columbus and Hernán Cortés came upon chocolate in the early sixteenth century in the New World and brought it back to Europe, where it was embraced as a bracing drink and, for some, an aphrodisiac.

Scientists have since concluded that chocolate's combinations of stimulants (both caffeine and theobromine) as well as phenylethylamine, which is believed to be a mood upper, does trigger a bit of amorous euphoria. Lovers around the world must

You Never Know What You're Going to Get

The iconic line from the movie *Forrest Gump*, **"Life is like a box of chocolates,"** was screenwriter Eric Roth's improvement on the opening line from Winston Groom's novel on which the film is based: "Let me say this: bein' an idiot is no box of chocolates."

believe it—or at least like the symbolism of giving sweets to their sweetie—because some 35 million boxes of chocolate are sold annually for Valentine's Day alone.

As for the Cadburys' success, their victory was a win for nice. At a time when horrible labor conditions were the norm, the brothers, who were Quakers, treated their employees with incredible grace. They used their boxed-chocolate proceeds to raise wages, give workers Saturdays off, and provide pensions, among other benefits.

Bread, Salt, and Wine

When Habitat for Humanity finishes building or renovating a home, the occupants are sometimes given bread, salt, and wine along with the keys to their new abode. And countless others welcome newcomers to the neighborhood in a similar fashion. The custom, which the *Austin* (Texas) *American-Statesman* once described as "traditional" for housewarming, is actually a relatively recent trend and actually can be largely attributed to the magic of movies.

The triumvirate of goods made its debut as an American ritual in the indelible 1946 Oscar-nominated film *It's a Wonderful Life*. George and Mary Bailey (Jimmy Stewart and Donna Reed) present bread, salt, and wine to Giuseppe Martini (William Edmunds) and his family before they move into a new home financed by Bailey's Savings and Loan.

"Bread! That this house may never know hunger," Mary begins as she hands out the gifts. "Salt! That life may always have flavor," she continues. Then, George interrupts to present the last offering: "And wine! That joy and prosperity may reign forever."

With a handful of writers receiving credit for penning the film, it's hard to know who actually wrote the speech. But the inspiration for the kind offering came from traditions in Eastern and Central Europe.

The fictional Martinis might have hailed from Italy, but it is Russia where at least two-thirds of this custom is known to exist. There, bread and salt are time-honored house-warming items—and it's not hard to imagine a few fun-loving neighbors throwing in a bottle of wine (or more regionally appropriate, vodka).

The bread, salt, *and* wine custom is most often tied to Poland, where those gifts are typically presented to newlyweds. According to the book *Planet Wedding: A Nuptialpedia*, the custom is deployed for similar, albeit slightly different, reasons: "The bread represents the hope that the bride and groom never go hungry. The salt is a reminder that life may be difficult at times, but that they will learn to cope. The wine symbolizes the desire that the couple will never go thirsty and that their lives will be filled with health and happiness."

Bread, salt, and wine have also served as a catch-all gift in countries as far-flung as Romania, Great Britain, and Israel. For example, in 1982 when French president François Mitterrand visited Israel to show his support for the embattled nation, he was greeted at one town with the bounty. The Reverend Philip Watson explained the three objects' significance in 1999 when dedicating a newly renovated building in the English city of Leicester: "Wine is a symbol of joy, while bread and salt are symbols of prosperity and wealth," he said.

The good rector most likely delivered his words well, but odds are he didn't move the audience quite like Hollywood's Baileys.

Charity

Most agree on what the word *charity* means: help for the needy, generally in the form of money, tangible gifts, or physical assistance.

What isn't so easy is explaining what the concept of charity entails. Who deserves charity? Who should give it? When should it be given? Why should it be given? These questions were debated long before the word itself became a fixture in the English language in the thirteenth century.

The Roman scholar and statesman Cicero was an early proponent of charity. In his 44 B.C. writings *On Moral Obligation*, he laid down some rules: A donation should not reflect badly on the person giving or the person receiving; the benefactor should not give beyond his or her means; and the gift should be in line with what the recipient deserves based on the relationship between the two parties and the character of the beneficiary. Cicero believed such regulations were necessary because "no action," he wrote, "can be at the same time generous and unjust."

It didn't take long for others to tweak Cicero's parameters. Seneca the Younger, who lived from 4 B.C. to A.D. 65, added a caveat, insisting that the social station of both parties be taken into consideration. "Some gifts are too small to come fittingly from the hands of a great man, and some are too large for the other to take," he wrote.

Jewish thinkers also weighed in, coming out strongly in support of charity. The book of Deuteronomy in the Old Testament of the Bible commanded the pious to give to the poor in whatever way was most appropriate, and in return God would smile favorably on them. In the twelfth century, the Jewish writer Maimonides built on that

Big Givers

The twenty-first century boasts its fair share of generous folks. Famous financial wizard Warren Buffett made headlines in 2006 when he pledged vast sums, estimated to be worth around $36 billion, to charitable causes. (He's earmarked barrel loads of cash for charity on other occasions as well.) Other famous names who gave big over the last few decades include Bill and Melinda Gates, Helen R. Walton (of Walmart fame), William Hewlett (Hewlett-Packard), and Joan B. Kroc (McDonald's). Not to be forgotten: Hotel magnate Leona Helmsley, who died in 2007 and was dubbed by some as the "Queen of Mean," also left billions of dollars to her charitable trust.

basic sentiment, setting up eight degrees of charity. At the bottom of the charity ladder is giving out of obligation. At the top is helping a needy person become self-sufficient.

The New Testament also strongly espoused a commitment to giving. Jesus was said to have told his disciples they should always give to those who asked. Moreover, the piety in the gift giving wasn't determined by the amount that was offered but by the personal cost of the charity. In other words, those who dug deep to help others got far more points than the rich who gave a lot but with little impact to their bottom line.

While these early mandates seem pretty clear (Islam also incorporates charity as one of its five foundational pillars), the last thousand years has seen a variety of interpretations.

The philosophers Francis Bacon and Thomas Hobbes were at odds on this matter. Bacon (1561–1626) believed that goodness was ingrained in our nature and that giving charity with a specific purpose flowed from this human characteristic. Hobbes (1588–1679) wasn't so generous. The writer argued that humans are reflexively selfish and protective of their own interests. When charity did occur, it had nothing to do with the recipient and everything to do with the giver's ego.

Americans brought charity into the modern era with what we now call philanthropy. In the early 1800s, the word *philanthropy* broadly meant "love of mankind," and was reflected in the support of any humanitarian cause like women's suffrage or the abolition of slavery.

This all changed with the boom in American wealth at the start of the twentieth century. In

1892, there were 4,047 millionaires, but by 1916, that number had jumped to more than 40,000, with the likes of John D. Rockefeller and Henry Ford boasting fortunes in the billions. Now the rich were looking for ways to spend their money. Around this time, the term *philanthropy* came to reflect large-scale institutional giving.

Rockefeller and Andrew Carnegie emerged as two of the biggest philanthropists. But, like Cicero, these fat cats had rules about how their money should be spent. "The best philanthropy . . . is not what is usually called charity," Rockefeller said. Instead, the industrialists aspired to the top rung of Maimonides's ladder of generosity, offering the kind of charity that helped people help themselves, often in the form of supporting educational institutions. As Carnegie would say, the biggest mistake a wealthy man could make was giving funds to the "unreclaimably poor."

Despite the industry barons' power, there are still those who focus their charitable efforts on the "unreclaimably poor," guaranteeing that arguments over the true meaning of charity will continue.

Chicken Soup

Follow this train of thought: sick . . . in bed . . . hungry . . . Grandma. I'll wager that for most people, it leads to one thing: chicken soup, or possibly some specific hot, constitution-rejuvenating variation like chicken noodle soup or matzo ball soup.

To be sure, chicken soup is the reassuring home remedy for a loved one with the sniffles. But the elixir is more than just something to sip. It's become a metaphorical salve for many of life's ills. Just ask the accountants for the publishers of the *Chicken Soup for the Soul* series of inspirational books, who have the pleasure of counting the money earned from spin-off titles like *Chicken Soup for the Soul: NASCAR* and *Chicken Soup for the American Idol Soul.*

While I'm not certain chicken soup can fix a blown gasket in Dale Earnhardt Jr.'s stock car, a small but vocal chorus in the medical community has championed its medicinal value. In the second century, the Greek doctor Galen claimed chicken soup was useful for battling a broad array of ailments, including migraines, ongoing fevers, and constipation. He went so far as to prescribe it to combat leprosy. Twelfth-century Jewish philosopher Maimonides added asthma to the list of problems that could be remedied by a "soup of fat hens," and the great Greek physician Hippocrates (of the Hippocratic Oath fame) was also a fan.

Modern medicine is more skeptical of the chicken soup hype (the likes of Galen overselling it with that leprosy claim probably didn't help its overall profile). Many relegate chicken soup to the old wives' tale section of medical books.

However, in recent decades, it has made somewhat of a comeback in scientific circles. One 1978 study argued that the soup could lessen cold symptoms like mucus buildup more than sipping hot water (and far better than drinking cold fluids). Based primarily on that study (along with words from the likes of Maimonides), two academics argued in a 1999 article that "chicken soup be classified as an essential drug" by the World Health Organization.

While you probably won't be able to pick up a prescription for a quart of soup anytime soon, other studies have further bolstered the contention that Grandma should be on speed dial for a little bit of the hot stuff when you're sick.

In 2000, University of Nebraska Medical Center researcher Stephen Rennard found that diluted versions of the soup lessened lung congestion. Although he couldn't identify the ingredients causing this useful reaction, he did establish that chicken soup slows the movement of certain white blood cells, which in turn makes you feel better. Interestingly, just chicken broth without all the fixings didn't lead to the same healing result. It should also be noted that Dr. Rennard used his grandmother-in-law's recipe, so be warned: Results may vary from grandma to grandma. Side effects can include cheek pinching and excessive hugging. As for leprosy, please consult your doctor.

Flowers

If you think a bouquet of flowers says a lot, you probably don't realize just how right you are. With an enticing combination of beauty and sweet aroma, flowers have, through the ages, been an offering imbued with significance. Cultivated for thousands of years, flowers appear in writings and images from ancient cultures on every continent.

From the start, red roses were an amorous symbol steeped in legend. Favorite origin tales include the first rose turning red after a kiss from Eve in the

Garden of Eden; or Cupid bleeding on a white rose and turning it red. The Romans loved the flower's romantic symbolism. Dionysus the Younger, who lived in the fourth century B.C., was known to throw big parties and fill his house with heaps of roses for big parties to impress fetching ladies.

Other flowers have also enjoyed long-held importance. Garlands of flowers (often orange blossoms) were placed on the heads of brides, and in some instances grooms, for millennia—from the Egyptians and Moors to the early Gauls and Anglo-Saxons.

That said, flowers weren't used in wedding bouquets until a few centuries ago. Instead handfuls of wheat sheaths were typically carried down the aisle to represent a hope for a bountiful marriage. Alternatively, the wedding party held herbs to counter any evil spirits or, in the case of dill, to instill lust.

In Japan, cherry blossoms hold an ancient reputation as flowers for springtime celebration. While in Mexico, the Aztec tradition of cultivating orange marigolds to honor the dead continues today for *Dia de los Muertos* (Day of the Dead) celebrations.

But credit goes to the Europeans for giving every flower its own meaning. The Turkish practice of *sélam*—a rhyming language using a flower's name as a code for the sender's intention—was introduced in Europe in the early eighteenth century. Inspired by that practice, writers developed the language of flowers, which spelled out what a broad catalog of stunning plants symbolized. It proved to be a good piece of commerce. So much so that by the start of the Victorian Era, dictionaries focusing on flower meanings became a cottage industry.

MANY CULTURES HAVE USED FLOWERS FOR FUNERAL CEREMONIES; EARLY CIVILIZATIONS SAW THEM AS A GRAVE GOOD—AN ITEM INCLUDED IN A TOMB THAT THE DEPARTED COULD USE AS A SHOW OF STATUS IN THE AFTERWORLD.

At a time when public displays of affection were considered crass, floral shorthand was incredibly useful. It's unlikely that lovebirds conducted long conversations through the constant exchange of bouquets, but, when necessary, the gift of flowers could provide a relatively reserved emotional message. For example, if a woman received jonquils, a vibrant yellow flower, it meant the sender was showing his desire and looking for a return of affection. For married couples, ivy represented the promise of fidelity. Fighting

Catching the Bouquet

The traditional battle for a bride's tossed **bouquet** was an offshoot of a similar tradition with garters, which started in the fourteenth century. A bride's wedding attire has long been considered good luck, so much so that men would sometimes try to pilfer garters or ribbons right off the leg of the bride if she didn't fling them out to the crowd in a timely fashion (women often wore many on their wedding day). Throwing a bouquet was a way to share some of that wedding day good fortune with the single women at the event.

couples could send hazel for reconciliation. And while red roses reflected love, white roses meant chastity (surely the worst flower for any pining guy to receive from a lady).

The Victorian's slavish attention to detail faded with the start of the twentieth century, but the practice of giving flowers to loved ones has never diminished. After all, with more than $30 billion in annual floral sales in the United States alone, most people continue to believe, as one author put it, that flowers "say that which cannot be said, and . . . say it with beauty and with grace."

The Language of Flowers

Although there is no definitive source on the meaning of each and every flower, here are some popular ones.

- *Amaranth:* Immortality
- *Basil:* Hate
- *Carnation:*
    Pink - I will always remember you
    White - Sweetness
    Red - Heart breaking
    Yellow - Disdain
- *Chamomile:* Energy in adversity
- *Chrysanthemum:*
    White - Truth
    Yellow - Love that's been slighted
- *Columbine:* Desertion
- *Cowslip:* Pensiveness
- *Crocus:* Do not abuse
    Spring - Youthful happiness
    Saffron- Merriment

- *Cypress:* Mourning or death
- *Daisy:* Innocence
- *Forget Me Not:* True love
- *Geranium:* I made a mistake
- *Goldenrod:* Precaution
- *Hazel:* Reconciliation
- *Hemp:* Fate
- *Hibiscus:* Fragile beauty
- *Honeysuckle:* Generosity or affection

- *Hydrangea:* Boastful
- *Iris:* Message of good tidings
- *Ivy:* Fidelity
- *Jasmine:* Friendliness
- *Jonquil:* Desire for affection
- *Juniper:* Need for assistance or protection
- *Laurel:* Glory
- *Lavender:* Distrust
- *Lilac:*

  Purple - Emotions of first love

  White - young innocence

- *Lily:*
    White - Purity
    Yellow - Falsehood
- *Lotus:* Eloquence, articulate
- *Magnolia*: Affinity for nature
- *Mandrake:* Horror
- *Marigold:* Deep sorrow
- *Orchid:* Elegant and graceful beauty
- *Pansy:* A request to be in one's thoughts
- *Periwinkle:*
    White - Warm memories
    Blue - New friendship
- *Poppy:*
    Scarlet - Opulence
    White - Sleep
    Red - Consolation
- *Rose:*
    White - Chastity
    Pink - Grace
    Red - Love
    Purple - Under one's spell
    Orange - Irresistibly drawn
    Yellow - Infidelity or jealousy

- *Rosemary*: Remembering another
- *Sage:* Domestic ability
- *Sunflower:* False riches
- *Tulip:* Fame
    Red - Declaring one's love
    Yellow - hopeless love
- *Violet:*
    Blue - Faithfulness
    White - Purity
- *Wallflower:* Fidelity in adversity
- *Weeping willow:* Deep and enduring sadness

Greeting Card

Thinking of you.

If you're looking for a sign that we might be reaching greeting card Armageddon, consider that in England you can buy a card wishing congratulations for passing a driving test. Granted, the British driving test is hard, but a formal congratulations? Civilization may be on the brink.

Although the industry may be awash in blatant capitalism today, it all started so innocently.

The first commercial greeting card is believed to have been produced in London in 1829. The simple but elegant design featured a medallion and scroll work and made it pretty easy on the buyer: "To [fill in the blank] on the ANNIVERSAIRIE of [fill in the blank] Day. From [fill in the blank]."

At the time, delivering such a note to anyone outside your local village was prohibitively expensive. That all changed with a little progressive government reform in 1840. That year, Great Britain enacted the universal penny postage, which made it affordable to send all sorts of mail, including greeting cards, across the country.

The first holiday-oriented card was to celebrate an occasion we don't typically consider a Hallmark moment. Created by a printer and publisher from Leith, Scotland, in 1841, the card wished a friend or loved one a very happy New Year's Day. But it was Valentine's Day that really put the greeting card business on the map.

Writing letters to loved ones on Valentine's Day was a long-held tradition. But mustering up the proper sentiment—particularly for the stiff-upper-lipped English—wasn't an easy task. Before the greeting card, many relied on books that offered heart-warming poems and comments for inspiration. Combining these ready-made thoughts with a finely produced card complete with fancy

Good Business

The greeting card industry was assisted by a bit of good press in its formative days. In 1864, none other than Charles Dickens lauded the conditions in a greeting card factory. "The rooms are well lighted and airy, and the girls exhibit none of the languor and weariness which are painfully apparent in the workrooms of the milliner and dressmaker," he wrote. Not bad, considering squalid work conditions can be described as "Dickensian."

embossing and beautiful lacing—something that would have seemed very artistic at the time—was a no-brainer.

Early adopters were "men and women caught up in a commercial society, a world already transformed by the 'market revolution,' . . . whose most private feelings were at least partially determined by their public material circumstances," wrote Barry Shank in his book *A Token of My Affection: Greeting Cards and American Business Culture.* Shank insists that even if sentiments were conjured up by others and printed on paper, those "emotions were no less powerful, no less sincere, no less authentic for having been produced in that context."

With business going well, the industry quickly added Christmas cards. In the United States, one critic worried that the move set a dangerous precedent. "Surely a new Pandora had been sent forth by the gods!" wrote Janet Huntington McKelvey in an 1886 essay about the new Christmas tradition. She was right; the holiday cards became socially essential in the twentieth century. The Forbes family (famous for their magazine and enormous wealth) sent out nearly 200 Christmas cards in 1949, up from 107 in 1938. In 1957, more than 4 billion cards were sold and the industry was bringing in $500 billion annually in the United States alone. (Geek note: Women accounted for 80 percent of all card purchases in the twentieth century.)

From their humble Valentine's Day beginnings, greeting cards are now looked on as an art form, meriting exhibitions by major institutions like New York's Metropolitan Museum of Art. For the average consumer, they've also become incredibly convenient: You can go online and purchase cards with personalized greetings printed directly on the paper, making it that much easier to offer your congratulations after your kid passes his driving test.

May Basket

For many big-city folks, the May basket is probably a complete unknown. For those in smaller locales—from Newton, Kansas, to Dover, Delaware—it's a tradition that persists, even in these more cynical times.

A brief explanation for the uninitiated: On or just before May 1, bags are filled with flowers and candy (a modern addition) and hung on the front door knobs of friends or family. Teenagers take the meaning up a notch and leave a present for a beau or a crush. The gift-giver must then ring the doorbell and run away before being seen by the recipient. (Consider it a benign version of ding-dong ditch.) If caught, the giver is duty bound to give the basket receiver a kiss, which is probably what the teens hoped for all along.

This custom stems from a long history of May Day celebrations. As spring begins to give way to summer, many cultures mark May 1 as a time to party. The Romans held a *Floralia* festival in honor of Flora, the goddess of flowers. In the British Isles, ancient Druids would erect bonfires and give thanks for the coming summer's softer climate and longer days.

Along the way, as these summer festivals developed, young men thought it would be a good idea to head into the forest and chop down trees to fashion into "maypoles." These decorated logs became a hive of activity as young girls danced around them, interlacing colorful ribbons over the large wooden posts. While the church often frowned on these events (there were seen as a bit heathen), the Victorian English transformed the pagan tradition into a child-centric opportunity to frolic.

The 1895 book *The Young Folk's Cyclopaedia of Games and Sports* offers up a plausible claim for how the May basket became part of the festivities. *May-buskets* was an Old English term for bouquets of fresh flowers given in early spring. The transition to May baskets, which appears to primarily be an American tradition, was simply a lost-in-translation "corruption" of May-buskets.

In the United States, May baskets were common by the middle of the nineteenth century and particularly popular in New England. Louisa May Alcott, author of the classic novel *Little Women*, devoted a whole chapter to the custom in her 1880 book *Jack and Jill: A Village Story*. Set in a New England town following the Civil War, the story focuses on two young friends. Alcott goes into great detail discussing the logistics of basket making: "The job now in hand was May baskets, for it was the custom of the children to hang them on the doors of their friends the night before May-day; and the girls had agreed to supply baskets if the boys would hunt for flowers." The drama of the chapter revolved around who would get baskets and whether the boys would come through with flowers (spoiler alert: they do).

More than a century later, some Americans still enjoy the tradition. "You can't send May baskets by text, u kno, or by Gmail, Facebook, or

Tweets (a gift in 140 characters, the length of this paragraph really)," a journalist at Nebraska's *Lincoln Journal Star* wrote in 2011. "To do it right, you have to make something real. Something with your hands from something that takes shape in your heart. Something with color and sugar and softness and, if you're doing it right, a little fear. And then— and this should be the hardest part—you have to do something. You have to let go of your big sister's hand and take your first step across the lawn, toward the closed door that suddenly seems so far away."

The article ends with this piece of advice: "Then you knock and then you run, but not too fast."

Mint on Your Hotel Pillow

For decades, the sight of a chocolate mint on a perfectly white puffy pillow at bedtime was a sure sign that a hotel was certified fancy. Considering the pillow mint's original high-class connotations, it makes sense that the tradition is credited to one of the most suave and debonair actors of Hollywood's Golden Age.

Enter Cary Grant. On a trip through St. Louis in the 1950s, he wanted to add a sugary dash of romance to a liaison at the local Mayfair Hotel.

Although he was married to actress Betsy Drake at the time, Grant had another, *ahem*, friend lined up. He allegedly fashioned a trail of chocolates, leading from his penthouse suite's sitting room into the bedroom before ending up on his pillow. Along with the chocolate was a letter. Unfortunately the contents of his note were lost to time (though somehow I doubt it said, "Compliments of C. Grant: Have a restful sleep").

The manager on duty caught wind of Grant's ploy and, though discreet about its provenance, started the regular practice of leaving a nighttime chocolate on guests' pillows. You may not think of St. Louis as the arbiter of up-scale offerings, but at the time the Mayfair did have an air of sophistication. Famous guests in this era included presidents Harry Truman and Lyndon Johnson and composer Irving Berlin. The Mayfair also prided itself on trend setting, being the first hotel west of the Mississippi to boast a rooftop swimming pool.

Whether the Mayfair's high-end patrons spread the word about the hotel's chocolate touch or other hotels simply caught wind of it, the practice spread. One business to capitalize on the trend was the Andes Candies company. In 1950, the confectioner stepped in with just the right chocolate mint—small, rectangular, and wrapped in distinctive bright green foil—at just the right moment.

Sadly, trends change and the chocolate mint is no longer a compulsory offering at posh hotels. With many diet-conscious guests (one estimate claimed that a hotel mint a week could add 1½ pounds to the waistline in a year), some in the industry figured a less weighty option might keep the chocolate tradition alive. In 2004, Sheraton Hotels launched a low-carb mint for its pillows. But not long after, most chic spots decided to just ditch the chocolate treat.

"The chocolate has become commodified," Ross Klein, president of W Hotels Worldwide, told *The New York Times* in 2005. "You can buy it in bulk. And the low-carb trend has made it not such a treat."

Even the Mayfair no longer provides mints. Still, the hotel's eighteenth floor does have a Cary Grant suite in honor of the actor and, presumably, his tasty affair.

Party Favors

Getting invited to the right party means more than just having a good time. It's an opportunity to walk away with some sweet swag.

When Cleopatra threw a lavish fete for her lover Mark Antony, the big winners were the invitees. The event was "celebrated with such magnificence that many of the guests who came poor, returned wealthy," wrote the Roman historian Plutarch.

The desire to ensure guests go home happy likely grew out of an early effort to please the gods with sacrifices. Party favors were "inspired by the ancient practice of proffering symbolic gifts to ensure a positive outcome such as love, fertility, long life, or prosperity," according to *Entertaining from Ancient Rome to the Super Bowl: An Encyclopedia.*

Beyond the riches doled out at Mark Antony's celebration, the Romans were sometimes known to provide partygoers with a pair of napkins—one to use around the neck, the other to wrap up leftovers as a sort of edible party favor. Gatherings in the Middle Ages often featured actors and musicians performing between courses of food. Along with the entertaining, they would throw little keepsakes (like the colored beads similar to those thrown around during Mardi Gras in New Orleans) to the partygoers. Larger gifts, like intricately carved pieces of wood or handmade banners, would be bestowed on the more important guests.

Celebrations have long been ripe for party favors. At weddings in England, it was customary in the sixteenth and seventeenth centuries to hand out "love knots" of lace or ribbon to those in attendance. And while it might seem odd today, party favors were common at funerals among New England Puritans in the eighteenth century. The tradition of funerary gifts was brought to the U.S.

from England, and the Puritans could get pretty over-the-top in their choice of presents. At one funeral, a thousand pairs of gloves were given away to mourners. Other gifts included mourning rings, needlework, scarves, and books.

This extravagant spirit lives on today. In 2006, for instance, planners at the Academy Awards gave the ultimate prizes to the Oscar nominees just for attending, lavishing them with gift bags worth approximately $55,000 each. Presents included vouchers for a stay at the Mirage Hotel in Las Vegas, a mug with a special mechanism to cool your drink, and diamond-encrusted flip-flops. That year, gifts at TV's Emmy Awards were worth a slightly less impressive $30,000 but nevertheless featured such nice freebees as a New Zealand vacation package and fancy skin-care products.

But not everybody embraces the gift-giving. Most notably, the Internal Revenue Service began cracking down on these presents in 2006, requiring recipients at high-profile events to pay taxes on their bags.

The Academy of Motion Picture Arts and Sciences immediately announced it would no longer distribute gift bags, ending a practice more than thirty years old.

Tipping

Nowadays, tips are seen as a must-give form of monetary thanks for a job well done, but it wasn't always this way.

Most credit the English with this nice maneuver, though the verb *to tip* and the noun *tip* weren't initially used. Starting in the Middle Ages, wealthy landowners would pay their servants an extra fee, known as a *vail*, for their hard work.

The modern term *to tip* comes from a darker place. It dates back to the early seventeenth-century

England when thieves communicated in their own underworld language known as the Rogues' Cant. In this world, *to tip* meant "to give to" or "to share with," and probably had more to do with divvying up ill-gotten gains than a pecuniary hat tip to someone for their service. The word took hold among polite society—and in the context we know today—in the eighteenth century.

MOST SCHOLARS DISMISS THE CLAIM THAT THE WORD *TIP* IS AN ACRONYM FOR "TO INSURE PROMPTNESS" OR "TO INSURE PROMPT SERVICE."

While a majority of Europeans embraced the tipping concept, Americans were conflicted. Many naysayers believed that a wage alone should suffice for a solid job performance. For example, the nineteenth-century poet and philosopher Ralph Waldo Emerson expressed embarrassment about tipping. "Though I confess with shame that I sometimes succumb and give the dollar [as a tip], yet it is a wicked dollar which by and by I shall have the manhood to withhold," said Emerson, who seemed to be taking his belief in self-reliance a bit too far.

The attitude grew particularly strong at the start of the twentieth century. The widely read *Gunton's Magazine* typified the antigratuity stance when it declared tipping to be "offensively un-American and positively uneconomic." The publication asserted that workers should get their agreed-upon payment, and angling for any more was simply "fawning for favors."

Many big names of the day jumped on this bandwagon. It probably comes as no surprise that leading industrialists John Rockefeller and Andrew Carnegie weren't big tippers. They weren't alone. During the 1908 presidential campaign, William Howard Taft declared he was the "patron saint of the anti-tip crusade."

So why did things change? Well, for one thing, workers—particularly those at restaurants—began expressing their dismay at wealthy clientele holding out on them. An extreme case: In Chicago during the early 1900s, waiters who felt wronged by cheapskate patrons would slip them a Mickey Finn. The concoction was a combo of antimony and potassium tartrate and could cause everything from headaches to vomiting (there were even three cases of customers dying from the concoction).

Beyond that harsh retribution, a more likely explanation for our changing attitudes on tipping was simply, "Americans are a generous people," claimed author and self-proclaimed guru of gratuity

Steve Dublanica in his book *Tipping: An American Social History of Gratuities*. "Many people tip out of sympathy for the workingman . . . [and] customers—whether they liked tipping or not—wanted to avoid appearing mean-spirited and cheap, so they ponied up."

In fact, today, Americans are among the world's best tippers. While those in the U.S. typically throw in a 15 to 20 percent tip, most Europeans cap their gratuity at 10 percent. In many parts of East Asia, tipping isn't even expected.

But some habits die hard, even for Americans. In 2011, the *Boston Herald* listed Tiger Woods, Madonna, and Barbra Streisand as the three worse celebrity tippers. Perhaps they all quoted Emerson as they snuck away from the table.

Wedding and Engagement Rings

J.R.R. Tolkien fans may disagree, but if ever there was a ring of power, it's the wedding ring. The token not only represents something intimate to a married couple, but it's also a signal to the larger world that a person is committed.

Some date the first symbolic rings of marriage to ancient cultures, which would use lengths of grass to fashion something for a wife's finger. These items were a one-way street—women wore them to show they were the property of their spouse.

The Horrific Honeymoon

The original **honeymoon** was far from romantic. The practice comes from the early custom of abducting women from other tribes. The new "couple" would head off to a safe location until the bride's tribe gave up on the search. The term *honeymoon* comes from keeping the woman sedated by forcing her to drink honeyed wine once a day during the first month of marriage. Some credit Attila the Hun with coming up with both the abducting and drinking. Early Norse tribes in Scandinavia were also practitioners.

While it's difficult to ascertain the prevalence of these ring forerunners, we do know that both the Egyptians and Romans ascribed a lot of meaning to finger bands—rings were worn in Egypt as early as 2800 B.C., according to one source. For the Egyptians, and many other cultures that followed, the never-ending circle represented the eternal bond of marriage. Roman authors also spoke of the power of the ring. Plautus, a playwright who lived sometime during the final two centuries B.C., is said to have been among the first to write about its meaning as a gift of love.

Not all these bands were of great monetary value. The Roman poet Ovid, who lived from 43 B.C. to A.D. 17, described a ring he planned to give to a lover as "having no worth except the love of the giver." It's possible that the ring was made of iron, which was the metal of choice for most bands at the time. Even those who could afford gold would fashion two rings—one of iron for around-the-house use and another of gold for going out.

Contemporaries of Ovid placed added significance on the ring. Piggybacking off physicians from earlier cultures, who believed the third finger possessed a vein that ran directly to the heart—dubbed the vein of love—the Romans placed bands on what we now call the ring finger. In Christian traditions, placing a ring on the third finger became part of the marriage ceremony. The official first placed the ring on the index finger, then on the middle finger, and finally on the ring finger. While moving it, he'd say "in the name of the Father" on the first finger, then "and of the Son" for the second, "and of the Holy Ghost" on its final destination.

Still, not all cultures put their wedding bands on their ring finger. Early Hebrews opted for the index finger while Indians preferred the thumb. Even in England in the early eighteenth century,

DURING THE REIGN OF ENGLAND'S KING GEORGE I, THE THUMB PROVED A FASHIONABLE LOCATION FOR WEDDING BANDS AMONG THE WEALTHY BECAUSE IT ALLOWED FOR LARGER RINGS.

some women, following the wedding, would move their ring to a different finger.

Engagement rings also have a long history. In early Anglo-Saxon Teutonic law, after a marriage was agreed to, the father of the bride received a valuable item (call it a down payment) from the groom's family. By the thirteenth century, these protoengagement rings, which also popped up in Roman times, were commonplace.

As for adding a diamond to this betrothal keepsake, the first high-profile example occurred in 1477, when Archduke Maximilian of Austria offered up a sparkler to Mary of Burgundy. While there's no word on whether he was on bended knee, others followed. For centuries, it was equally (if not more) popular to present a ring encrusted with the bride-to-be's birthstone.

That changed in the 1930s when the diamond company De Beers advertised heavily on behalf of the diamond ring's symbolism. Its 1947 slogan A "Diamond Is Forever" (like a good marriage a diamond was resilient and long-lasting) put the bedazzling stone over the top.

Ladies, one word of advice: If you want to keep your ring, you better go through with the marriage. Legally, in the U.S. a gift is a gift and the recipient is under no obligation to return it. But in most states an engagement ring is considered a conditional gift, and if the couple never makes it to the altar, the bride can be forced to give the ring back.

NICE BABY
Items and Traditions

Baby Powder: Brothers Robert, James, and Edward Johnson founded Johnson & Johnson in 1886 in New Brunswick, New Jersey. Their first success came two years later, with one of the original commercial first-aid kits. But it was their decision to go into the baby business that was the real moneymaker. In 1894, the brothers launched a line of maternity supplies that included such fun products as umbilical tape and an abdominal binder . . . and their wonderful white baby powder.

Baby Shower: Parties, presents, and a pregnant woman didn't come together until the 1950s. Before that, people still got excited about the birth of a child, but high mortality rates made them more circumspect. Early civilizations like the Egyptians and the Greeks threw parties celebrating a baby's birth a week or more after the child was born. But even then, those were less about celebrating the mom and more about the baby. The baby shower, as we know it, developed in Victorian England. As in the past, parties didn't take place until after the baby was born, but once the child came, women would throw tea parties for the mother, which included games and a shower, so to speak, of gifts. Thanks to medical advances, in post–World War II America, it became safe to throw the party in the months before the birth.

Blue for Boys/Pink for Girls: Consensus on which gender should wear which color is relatively new. In the nineteenth century, all babies wore white. This was a practical choice, because it was a lot easier to bleach white clothing after baby made all those wonderful stains. Until around the age of seven, even the style and cut of clothes were gender neutral. Suiting up infants in colorful attire began around the early twentieth century. At first, there were no gender-specific hues (colors were often chosen based on the season and the fashion of the day). Both pink and blue were popular shades for baby attire—in fact, boys often wore pink, while many believed the pastel blue was a dainty shade better suited for girls. Our notions of pink for girls and blue for boys didn't become widely accepted until the 1950s. Most credit the fickle hand of fashion for the ultimate designation, but one neuroscience study did find that genders do have different tastes in colors. Females tend to like shades closer to pink, while males show an affinity for colors in the region of blue.

Disposable Diapers: With a creation as ingenious as diapers you don't have to wash, it's not surprising that many claim paternity (or maternity, as the case may be). The company that most likely first cracked the wear-then-soil-then-throwaway process was the Swedish business Pauliström in the early 1940s. (They were said to have made the diaper out of creped cellulose paper.) Other models would follow. In England, a tired mother, Valerie Hunter Gordon, made a pad out of cellulose tissue and soft cotton wool to insert in an underwearlike garment made of used nylon parachutes and later PVC plastic. The product, which she devised in 1947, was called the Paddi. Around the same time, a Connecticut housewife, Marion Donovan, came up with a similar concept, building a prototype out of a shower curtain (and eventually, like Gordon, surplus nylon parachutes). Called a Boater, it made a big splash, going on sale at New York City's Saks Fifth Avenue in 1949. It was such a success that by the time she received her patents in 1951, she'd already sold the product rights for $1 million. The famed Pampers brand didn't come onto the market until 1961.

Passing Out Cigars: This tradition likely comes from the Native American custom of distributing gifts when good fortune smiles on a person. Some tribes, such as those of the Pacific Northwest, have a gathering called a "potlatch" in which wealth is redistributed to all guests during a celebratory event. Tobacco has been used ceremonially among some Native American tribes and is often handed out—or smoked—as part of celebrations. Cigars would come later; they weren't widely used in the United States until the mid-1800s. Others say that this explanation is overthinking it, and that passing out cigars was simply a way for proud fathers to make an opulent manly nod to their involvement in the birth.

Rattle: While high priests and shamans used rattles (often gourds stuffed with pebbles) in ceremonies to scare away bad spirits, the item was likely introduced into the nursery in Egypt around 1360 B.C. Rattles from this era have been discovered in children's tombs. Rather than our iconic round ball and handle, these early clay shakers were in the shape of animals such as pigs, birds, or bears. They were often covered in silk and painted bright colors.

Stroller (Baby Carriage): Tired parents have been devising ways to lug around their wee ones for thousands of years, but William Kent is generally credited with developing the first modern solution around 1733. Kent was a man of many skills; along with being a painter, landscape designer, and architect, he was an adroit tinkerer. When the Duke of Devonshire asked him to come up with a method to carry a baby, Kent snapped to attention. He designed a stroller in the shape of a scallop shell. It featured a folding hood, 21-inch wheels in the back, and 16-inch wheels in the front. Across the English Channel, a similar contraption was supposedly built for one of King Louis XV's children, but there is debate over which one came first.

Teddy Bear: Teddy Roosevelt was a tough guy—after all, he was the man behind the famed U.S. cavalry unit known as the Rough Riders. But these cute little stuffed bears prove that he was not without a soft spot. One day in November 1902, Roosevelt, who was president at the time, went game hunting in Mississippi and came across a wounded bear. Party members encouraged the chief executive to off the animal, but Roosevelt refused (another ended up doing the deed). A journalist heard the story and dubbed the creature a "Teddy bear." The name stuck, and stuffed animal manufacturers soon jumped onboard.

Wrapping
Paper

Gift wrap, those colorful rolls of decorative paper, can be attributed to the luck—both good and bad—of Joyce Clyde Hall.

A full-blooded entrepreneur at age sixteen, Hall joined his two brothers, Rollie and William, in starting a business importing postcards during the first decade of the twentieth century. When the business didn't take off in his hometown of Norfolk, Virginia, J. C. jumped on a train to Kansas City in an attempt to sell postcards there.

For five years, he built up the business with Rollie, who'd followed him to the Midwest. Then, in 1915, a fire destroyed the company's inventory of postcards, putting the brothers in severe debt. Undeterred, they borrowed cash, purchased engraving equipment, and embarked in a new trade—creating and selling greeting cards.

The hard luck proved fortuitous and their business boomed—so much so that they opened a specialty store under the name Hall Brothers, Inc. The company still focused on their cards, but the new space allowed them to branch out into other paper goods.

The Halls were aware that wrapping gifts was a long-held trend dating back to the invention of paper in China during the second century. (The first paper mills were established in Europe around 1085.) The English took to wrapping gifts and tried all sorts of papers, including wallpaper, which came to the country in 1509. But the stiff stuff proved too brittle to put around presents.

By the Victorian Era, the British were using dainty tissue paper or sturdy plain-brown paper to conceal their presents. The first known reference to wrapping paper, also known as gift dressing, in the U.S. appeared in the December 1860 issue of

Godey's Magazine in a story mentioning Christmas "packages, wrapped in paper." As the nineteenth century came to a close, the combination of colored ribbon and white tissue was popular in America.

Keeping with history, the Halls stocked their store with tissue paper in white, green, and red (as well as a holly pattern) for the 1917 Christmas season. As the story goes, the wispy paper sold out, leaving J. C. to ponder an alternative. Looking through the inventory, the brothers stumbled onto a lucky find. They had some pretty yet hard-wearing French paper used for lining envelopes that could serve as an alternative. This being one of those almost mythical moments of discovery, there's a slightly different version of the story that says this paper was already being used as part of a display for the wrapping paper. Either way, the brothers marveled as customers readily purchased the thicker paper at 10 cents a sheet. The following year, three sheets at 25 cents quickly sold out again.

J. C. and Rollie knew they'd hit on a money-maker. The company, which was renamed Hallmark in 1954, started a second line, manufacturing wrapping paper. In many ways, Joyce Clyde Hall was the ideal steward to develop this new style of giftwrap. He cared deeply about getting his products just right. "Good taste is good business," he was known to say. As chief executive for fifty-six years, J. C. would go on to build the company and the wrapping paper venture expertly, turning Hallmark into an industry

BEFORE THE ADVENT OF CLEAR TAPE, GIFT WRAPPERS WOULD SOMETIMES USE STRAIGHT PINS TO KEEP THEIR FOLDS TOGETHER.

behemoth. When he died in 1982 at the age of 91, his business boasted total annual sales of more than $750 million.

Nice Images and Writing

Doves

What's in a name? Just ask the poor pigeon.

Nobody likes pigeons. To wit: In 2011, the city of Albuquerque, New Mexico, enacted a "pigeon nuisance" law to rid the beasts from congregating in public areas. The good people of Albuquerque were certainly not the first and won't be the last to fight the little scavengers.

But when we speak of doves, there is much rejoicing. The dove has a happy history as a symbol

Heavenly Messengers

The earliest artistic representations of **winged angels** as we depict them today date back to the fourth century. (Before that time, angels were typically portrayed as humans, sometimes sporting beards.) As uplifting as those heavenly creatures may appear, at least one biologist from University College London isn't buying it. In 2009, he compared artistic renderings of winged angels with the physiology of earthly flying species and concluded that the divine messengers wouldn't be able to get off the ground. Regardless, angels definitely have their defenders. In 2008, a survey conducted by the Baylor University Institute for Studies of Religion found that 55 percent of Americans believe they've been protected by a guardian angel at some point in their lives.

of both love and peace. The funny thing is that the dove has a deep, dark secret: it's just a small, white . . . pigeon. "When we malign [the bird], we call it a pigeon, not a dove," explained the authors of the book *Winged Wonders: A Celebration of Birds in Human History*. "It is pigeons that defecate everywhere and have to be discouraged from gathering in public places. Pigeons are attacked in proverbs: 'Pigeons and priests make foul houses.' "

So how did the dove earn an elevated spot in our hearts? Looks matter. Like a ladybug compared to a creepy crawly insect, snow-white doves are simply more attractive than pavement-gray pigeons. It also helps that doves tend to be found in the wild—rather than gathering and begging for food at your local park.

While this might explain why doves are more palatable than their urban cousins, it doesn't explain how they've become a lasting emblem for some of our most important virtues. Doves were part of the iconography of love in ancient Egypt, Crete, and Greece. The Hindu faith reveres the animal so much that the birds are allowed to nest in temples. Even William Shakespeare described the dove, along with the phoenix, as "co-supremes and stars of love" in "The Phoenix and the Turtle," a poem published in 1601.

The dove's connection to *amore* probably has something to do with the bird's impressive fertility—it lays two eggs nine or ten times a year. Its beautiful cooing also adds a romantic effect. The turtledove's soothing sound is so beloved in Southeast Asia that well-trained ones can fetch sums of more than $50,000, and a single egg goes for up to $1,500. Finally, doves mate for life, which is a reassuring proof of love (or, if you're a little more cynical, just proof of fidelity).

While the dove's symbolic significance predates Christianity, the New Testament reaffirms the sentiment in a spiritual way. In the book of Mark, the Holy Spirit is likened to a dove. Great artists, such as El Greco and Giambattista Tiepolo, found inspiration in the association, and included the white winged creature in paintings and church adornments.

In addition to its loving reputation, the dove has a connection to peace that can also be attributed to religious references. In the famous story of Noah and his ark, the dove is sent out from the boat to scout for land. It returns clenching an olive branch (some early translations say an olive leaf or sprig) in its beak—proof that land had reemerged from the flood. Some Christian interpretations suggest that the bird's arrival with the olive branch—long a symbol of amity—also represents the harmony between God and man.

By the fifteenth century, the dove was showing up in secular statements of peace. Early Americans were also fans of the symbol. Along with some eighteenth-century New World currency depicting the dove, George Washington had a weather vane erected in 1787 at his home Mount Vernon featuring the bird with an olive branch in its beak.

In 1949, Pablo Picasso cemented the dove-as-peace connection with his painting *La Colombe*. The simple illustration of a dovelike bird and an olive branch was embraced a year later by the World Peace Congress in Paris as the perfect image for its cause. And, for those who believe the pigeon has gotten a bad rap while the dove has soared, you can take solace in this fact: Picasso is said to have used a plain everyday pigeon as his inspiration.

Awareness Ribbons

Ribbons have an extensive history of symbolism. In the age of chivalry, knights wore them to reflect their social standing. During the late nineteenth century, wearing a yellow ribbon was a sign that you were thinking someone who was far away—most often, serving in the military. The symbol was cemented for baby boomers with the 1973 number one hit song "Tie a Yellow Ribbon Round the Old Oak Tree." (Geek note: Though the song was associated with families of Vietnam War soldiers yearning for their loved ones, the lyrics suggest another use for the yellow ribbon: showing a willingness to accept someone who was just released from jail.)

The red ribbon took on meaning in 1991, when Jeremy Irons wore one on his lapel at the Tony Awards to bring attention to AIDS. The symbol spread quickly. Just a year later, *The New York Times* dubbed 1992 The Year of the Ribbon. "Crosses took almost two millenniums to change from handmade icons of fervent belief into abstract decorations worn anywhere but church," the newspaper wrote. "In less than one year, the AIDS ribbon has come nearly as far."

Other causes would quickly find their own ribbons. So if you want to tie a periwinkle or teal ribbon around your oak tree, you'll be making some kind of statement. Though which meaning you intend may not always be clear since many colors have multiple connotations.

BLACK: mourning, melanoma, gang prevention, or for those military personnel missing in action (MIA)

BLUE: (pale) prostate cancer, thyroid disease, or Grave's disease; (dark) arthritis, child abuse prevention, colon cancer, victim's rights, or water safety

BROWN: antitobacco

BURGUNDY: brain aneurysm, hospice care, or multiple myeloma

GOLD: childhood cancer

GREEN: environmental issues, bipolar, celiac disease or organ transplants; (lime) lymphoma, Lyme disease, or Sandhoff disease

GRAY: diabetes or brain cancer

INDIGO: bullying (among other colors), harassment and stalking awareness

JADE: hepatitis B and liver cancer

LAVENDER: cancer awareness, epilepsy, or Rett Syndrome

MULTICOLORED: (puzzle shapes) autism awareness

ORANGE: leukemia, multiple sclerosis, hunger, or motorcycle safety

PEACH: uterine cancer, or endometrial cancer

PERIWINKLE: eating disorders, esophageal cancer, or pulmonary hypertension

PINK: breast cancer, or cleft palate syndrome; (pink and blue) antiabortion, or infant/baby loss

PURPLE: pancreatic cancer, Alzheimer's disease, cystic fibrosis, multiple system atrophy, or victims of 9/11

RED: HIV/AIDs, heart disease, stroke, or substance abuse; (red and black) atheism

SILVER: Parkinson's disease

TEAL: ovarian and cervical cancers, tsunami victims, or sexual abuse/assault

TURQUOISE: Native American reparations

VIOLET: Hodgkin's lymphoma

WHITE: lung cancer (also clear ribbon), safe motherhood during childbirth, or multiple hereditary exostoses

YELLOW: support for the military and/or prisoners of war and those missing in action, or suicide prevention

Fairy Tales

Drama. Conflict. Love. Sure, fairy tales have all of that. But did you know that the tales behind the fairy tales are also juicy?

First, there is what I'll call the Tale of the Fighting Scholars. The oral tradition of edge-of-your-seat children's sagas dates back thousands of years with many of the themes, including such nasty ones as kidnapping and murder, spanning cultures. But the impact of these early tales on the stories we know today is an area of hot debate.

Take *Little Red Riding Hood*. Most agree the Frenchman Charles Perrault was responsible for the Western world's first written account of the story in the seventeenth century (see also page 381). But a 2009 study found thirty-five variations on the wolf, Grandma, and the red-hooded girl, with some dating back more than 2,600 years. There are differences—for example, Little Red is a boy in Iran—but the essential theme has remained the same.

The study's author, Jamie Tehrani, argued, "Over time these folktales have been subtly changed and have evolved just like a biological organism. Because many of them were not written down until much later, they have been misremembered or reinvented through hundreds of generations."

But other scholars wouldn't let Tehrani ride off in the sunset with his findings. They argue that the written fairy tale is a singular work—one that stands outside any oral folk tradition. And to conflate the two is to undermine the artistry of the literature. As one professor, Ruth Bottigheimer, fumed: "Tehrani has bought into the newest wave of biology-based understanding of literature, taking evolutionary genetics as his model. But his views are based on slippery assumptions that can't be verified and that have no legs in the real world."

Jack Zipes, a renowned expert on fairy tales, came to Tehrani's defense: "Anyone who says [fairy tales] arrive only with print is just stupid. People have similar experiences around the world and always have had." Spoken just like a prince charming (well, sort of).

And then there is the Tale of the World Weary Authors. The Brothers Grimm and Hans Christian Andersen were among the first and most successful to publish printed collections of these stories. One can only wonder how much the Grimm Brothers or Andersen drew on their own stirring lives for their stories.

Born one year apart, Jacob and Wilhelm Grimm looked like they would live happily ever after from day one. Their father, Philipp, was a successful lawyer who had the means to give his wife and six children a very comfortable life. Alas, their dad died of pneumonia at age forty-four in 1796, before Jacob and Wilhelm were teenagers. Eleven-year-old Jacob, the eldest boy, was forced to become the man of the house.

Without their father's income, the family's circumstances worsened dramatically. Still, through industrious hard work, the brothers were able to save money and attend school. In scenes out of

Cinderella, the boys were bullied by other students because of their financial standing. Their situation eventually improved, sometimes with the help of kindly benefactors (sounds pretty storybook-ish to me), and they established themselves as professors. The brothers began collaborating on collections of fairy tales, beginning in 1812.

While life seemed stable for a number of years, there was a late-in-life plot twist, when the brothers, who were ardent German nationalists, lost their jobs over political protest. Ultimately, they would find new positions, and while their story was not wrapped up as neatly as the Disney version of their far darker rendition of *Snow White and the Seven Dwarves*, the two were able to live out their years in a somewhat comfortable fashion.

As for Andersen, his life also had intrigue from the beginning: We do know that the Dane came from poor means and was forced to venture out early in life, moving to Copenhagen in his early teens. But despite his humble beginnings, stories swirled that he was related to royalty (though they've never been confirmed). After a failed singing career, he became a successful writer, receiving tremendous praise for such works as *The Ugly Duckling* and *The Little Mermaid*.

Still, Andersen had his share of problems. He was a lovelorn man, who made efforts to woo several women (and men as well, according to some scholars) but failed on all accounts. Andersen died in 1875, having never married and wearing a leather pouch around his neck containing a love letter from his childhood sweetheart. The deathbed moment proved that while a modern fairy-tale character may have thoroughly happy endings, the same may not be the case for all fairy-tale writers.

Heart Symbol

We all know what a pretty red heart represents. Try going one hour without coming across a heart serving as contemporary shorthand for love, romance, affection, or pretty much any warm, snuggly emotion you can name. But how we got to its unique shape isn't quite as certain. After all, it looks nothing like a human heart.

The story of the symbol's shape stretches back to the formative days of humans. Cro-Magnon pictograms depicting the design have been discovered in Europe, though what those cave paintings mean is unclear. The first credible candidate for the loving (or at least lusting) use of the heart symbol comes from the ancient North African city-state Cyrene.

In the seventh century B.C., Cyrene was doing a cracking trade in silphium plants. The leaf of the now-extinct herb looked exactly like the modern heart shape and, for the amorously inclined, it was marketed as a type of birth control. The plant's efficacy in the bedroom is unknown today, but we do know that it was so beloved that the people of Cyrene put its shape on coins, which traveled far beyond North Africa.

There are other plausible explanations. One hypothesis argues that it comes from an early European physician's erroneous diagram of the human heart. If that doesn't work for you, there's the claim that it was inspired by the shape two swans make during mating rituals. Another says it was taken from ivy designs used on ancient Asian and Greek pottery. Even the famed feminist Gloria Steinem has a theory on this one. "The shape we call a heart—whose symmetry resembles the vulva far more than the asymmetry of the organ that shares its name—is probably a residual female genital symbol," she once wrote. "It was reduced from power to romance by centuries of male dominance."

All or some of these theories may have factored into the heart shape's beginnings, but it's the Christian church that really ratcheted up the tie between the symbol and its touchy feely connotations. The heart has long served as a metaphorical vessel for kind and caring emotions in Judeo-Christian texts. The Old Testament refers to the heart in that context 850 times, according to one study. So it should come as no surprise that early Christian art depicted the heart in its iconography—often in the shape we recognize today.

FIFTEENTH–CENTURY MERCHANTS MADE THE HEART SYMBOL A SUIT ON THOROUGHLY NONRELIGIOUS PLAYING CARDS.

In the seventeenth century, when St. Margaret Mary Alocoque had a vision of a heart surrounded by thorns, dubbed the Sacred Heart of Jesus, the icon took on a deeper meaning of love.

More recently, the symbol is used to represent feelings of affection for just about anything. Take, for example, Milton Glaser's iconic I ♥ NY logo, which he created for the New York State Department of

Commerce in 1977 as a way to attract tourists to New York City. Glaser, a successful graphic artist, was dismayed that his hometown, which had fallen on hard times, was getting such a bad rap. His heart-themed work not only helped New York tourism—shirts sporting his design becoming best sellers on the city's street corners for decades—but it also spawned copycats around the world. Astonishingly, Glaser created the logo for free and never complained that his inspiring work led to lots of money in the pockets of others. He was just happy to have helped the town he loved.

And if that attitude doesn't truly represent the heart symbol, nothing does.

Nursery Rhymes

There once was a man from Nantucket . . .
Okay, that's the start to everyone's favorite
dirty limerick, not a nursery rhyme, but what
is astonishing is that nursery rhymes can be every
bit as inappropriate for kids. In fact, the meanings
of many of our favorite children's verses are quite
R-rated, or worse.

As one 1952 study concluded, in a typical book
of 200 nursery rhymes, approximately half include
"'unsavoury' material for children, including,

murder, racial discrimination, cruelty to animals, lost children, and body snatching."

Others believe that number is higher. Steeped in the oral tradition, many kids' ditties started far from the nursery. Instead, they sprang from the "adult code of joviality," according to *The Oxford Dictionary of Nursery Rhymes*. In other words, they were typically composed in drinking halls by people downing more than one tankard of grog.

Some nursery rhymes date back to before the twelfth century, but the golden age was between Henry VIII's reign in the 1500s and the Stuart monarchs in the following century. This era was one of deep social unrest and conflict in England. Catholics and members of the newly formed Church of England clashed and there were great divisions between the rich and the poor. Though seemingly frivolous and bawdy, these songs often held deep social or economic commentary. (For example, "Baa, Baa, Black Sheep" was actually protesting an unfair tax on wool.)

It was also a period when children grew up very quickly. Many parents, particularly during the seventeenth century, regarded their children as "grown-ups in miniature." (Adults would commonly use swear words in front of little ones.)

Unsurprisingly, their light tunes and heavier words quickly trickled down to youngsters.

At the start of the nineteenth century, writers began collecting the rhymes in books with such Harry Potter–sounding names as *Grammer Gurton's Garland or the Nursery Parnassus* and *Infant Institutes*. By then, many of the original meanings had been forgotten.

Maybe that was for the best. After all, one theory suggests "Pop Goes the Weasel" was a sly bit of social commentary on the sweatshop conditions in London's textile factories. The story of "Humpty Dumpty" is widely believed to be about a clash during the English Civil War of 1642 to 1651. Humpty Dumpty was a large cannon used against rebels by those loyal to King Charles I. When the huge gun fell from its perch on a tower, the royalist forces fell hard, too.

One interpretation of "London Bridge is Falling Down" is particularly grim. While some believe it's a reference to a Viking attack that destroyed an early version of the bridge or simply a description of its deterioration, human sacrifice is also a popular explanation. Apparently, there was a long-held belief that a person should be buried in the foundation of a bridge to serve as a "guardian spirit."

Hush, Little Baby . . .

Lullabies are thought to be positively ancient. Even certain animals coo their young to sleep. The first known English-language tradition of setting words to calming tunes (or cradle songs) dates to at least the 1300s, but the practice likely stretches back much earlier. The Romans used the phrase *Lalla, lalla, lalla, aut dormi, aut lacte*, when rocking their kids to sleep. The translation isn't exactly clear, but there is reference to two baby favorites, sleep and milk, with *lalla* being just a relaxing sound, which probably serves as our inspiration for the "lulla" in lullaby.

The ghost would make sure the bridge remained sturdy. (Skeletons have been uncovered during the renovation of some European bridges, like one in the German town of Bremen during the nineteenth century.) It's believed the poem's popular words are about this delightful practice with "my fair lady" being the unlucky sacrifice. Try explaining that to your wee one right before bed.

Obituaries

A good obituary has the feel of an epic story. Sure, the person's peccadilloes and mistakes may be noted in these final odes, but from the beginning of this art form, writers have told stories that for the most part have you rooting for the recently departed.

This was evident in the first English-language obituary ever published. Following the death of Maurice of Nassau, Prince of Orange, in 1625, the periodical *Continuation of our Weekly Newes* was

Laugh After Death

When Colorado resident Michael Blanchard died in 2011, he'd prewritten most of his death notice. "Weary of reading obituaries noting someone's courageous battle with death, Mike wanted it known that he died as a result of being stubborn, refusing to follow doctors' orders, and raising hell for more than six decades," his notice said in the *Denver Post*. "He enjoyed booze, guns, cars, and younger women until the day he died."

thoroughly upbeat. The paper lauded the man as "having left behind him the fame of a wise and valiant [sic] Prince, that had commanded in a popular state with great care and d[i]scretion for many years together."

From that first effort, obituaries, which initially focused only on the elite, have become history's first drafts. They not only reflect people's lives but also give future readers insight into the values and concerns of bygone eras.

For example, in the early 1700s, the English were focused on stretching their dominion over the world. So when the Duke of Marlborough died in

1722, his obituary centered on the role he played nurturing that growth with military victories against the French and Germans. A little more than a century later, piety was of utmost importance, so when John Maguire, the long-time mayor of Cork, died, the focal point wasn't on his worldly accomplishments but on how he was an "eloquent and earnest . . . defender" of Christianity.

By the Victorian Era, obituaries were must-reads. (Taking a page from their cousins across the sea, American newspapers were invested deeply in obituary writing during this period.) But World War I, with its heart-wrenching casualties, led to obit fatigue on both sides of the Atlantic. World War II also blunted this tradition. As the owners of Britain's *Daily Telegraph* once said about that period: "Readers were only interested in live people."

While there were both death notices (brief articles often written and paid for by family members) and news stories (reporting the basics when an important figured passed), in-depth meditations on the departed didn't make a comprehensive comeback until the second half of the twentieth century.

In the U.S., this return was driven by journalists who could combine sympathy with just enough

I'm Not Dead Yet

Many notables have been the victims of the **premature obituary**, including Apple cofounder Steve Jobs, sci-fi writer Arthur C. Clarke, and Black Nationalist Marcus Garvey. But the famous Mark Twain quote: "The report of my death was an exaggeration" (often paraphrased as "reports of my death are greatly exaggerated") wasn't one of those instances. In 1897, a journalist acting on a tip Twain had perished visited the author. The still-breathing humorist greeted the newspaperman with his quip, preventing the obit from going to print.

detachment. For instance, *The New York Times*'s chief obituary writer from 1964 to 1976, Alden Whitman, helped reinvigorate the practice. He was not your average reporter. The Harvard grad wore a bow tie and a cape (yep, a cape), and while his coworkers would run around the newsroom rushing to meet deadlines, he would sip tea in the corner, as one colleague put it, "dwelling in this strange little world of the half living, the half dead."

But he knew how to effectively sum up a life, so much so that before Harry Truman's death, the former president allowed Whitman to interview the man planning his funeral. Along with Truman's obit, Whitman had the last word on the likes of Helen Keller, Pablo Picasso, and Charlie Chaplin.

While Whitman continued the tradition of obituaries for the famous, a journalist in Philadelphia brought the practice to the common people. Jim Nicholson had worked as a cement finisher, a dock laborer, an oil field hand, and a private investigator, among other gigs, before becoming a reporter at the Philadelphia *Daily News*. His blue-collar background prepared him in 1982 to become a pioneer of in-depth obituaries about otherwise obscure folks.

"He would listen very hard to family and friends and find something in the person's life that was singular," a fellow journalist once said. Proving that mining for nice can have rewards, Nicholson, who was the first in his generation to win industry awards for obit writing, would say of his experience: "It turned me from a very cynical investigator into more of a Pollyannish kind of person."

NICE EPITAPHS

Broadly, epitaphs are statements or phrases penned in memory of a dead person, but we best know them as tombstone inscriptions. Some of the best are either poignant or funny.

"That's All Folks"
MEL BLANC
LOONEY TUNES
VOICE ARTIST

"Quoth the Raven, 'Nevermore'"
EDGAR ALLAN POE
POET

"I had a lover's quarrel with the world"
ROBERT FROST
POET

"There goes the neighborhood"
RODNEY DANGERFIELD
COMEDIAN

"Called Back"
EMILY DICKINSON
POET

"I'm a writer but then nobody's perfect"
BILLY WILDER
WRITER/DIRECTOR

"She did it the hard way"
BETTE DAVIS
ACTRESS

"I will not be right back after this message"
MERV GRIFFIN
–TV HOST/PRODUCER

"The best is yet to come"
FRANK SINATRA
SINGER /ACTOR

Peace Symbol

The peace symbol's original meaning was not the broad call for peace we know today, though that would have been a nice by-product. The symbol's creator, Gerald Holtom, was a British textile designer. Born in 1914, he received conscientious-objector status during World War II and cared very much about world peace. But his symbol was aimed at what he believed was the greatest threat to the planet—nuclear weapons.

In early 1958, an English anti-nukes group, the Direct Action Committee Against Nuclear War (DAC), began planning a major traveling demonstration from London to the town of Aldermaston, where the British military was developing nuclear weapons. Holtom showed up one day at the offices of a publication called *Peace News*, which was also involved with the protest, and proposed the insignia as a rallying sign for the march.

A number of explanations for the design have been given over the years. The most popular is that it's a play on semaphore, a code primarily employed in the navy using flags to convey information. The two diagonal lines represented an N, while the straight middle line was a D with the two letters standing for "nuclear disarmament."

In reality, Holtom's inspiration appears to have come from a darker place. Initially, he'd hoped to integrate the Christian cross into his symbol. He met with about a dozen religious figures from various denominations, but received a unanimously chilly response. "The face of one [clergyman] turned into a gargoyle's expression as he crossed himself," Hotlom later said.

The final product's resemblance to a drooping cross was probably no accident, but he would say that his ultimate touchstone was his own sadness about the state of the world. "I was in despair," he wrote. "I drew myself: the representative of an individual in despair, with hands palm outstretched outwards and downwards in the manner of Goya's peasant before the firing squad. I formalized the drawing into a line and put a circle round it."

Needless to say, the march organizers were uncertain about the seemingly random symbol's impact. After some debate, they decided to go with it, and Holtom manufactured some 500 circular pieces of fabric mounted on wooden sticks. Holtom hoped that these lollipops, as they were dubbed, would be "stuck into the ground on their wood laths at stopping places so that they would appear like a Field of Remembrance." But, instead, marchers carried them. The event received a lot of media attention and the odd new symbol went global.

Before long, the peace sign was co-opted by other causes from civil rights to Vietnam War protests. Holtom never copyrighted the symbol, so it was also available to those trying to make a buck. San Francisco concert promoter Bill Graham famously used the emblem in posters announcing concerts for musical acts such as the Doors, Chuck Berry, the Grateful Dead, and Jefferson Airplane.

But not everyone was pleased with the sign. Hawkish types believed the symbol represented weakness and joked that its likeness to a bird's foot made it a "footprint of the American chicken." The ultraconservative John Birch Society was more scathing. In a 1970 editorial in its publication *American Opinion*, a writer claimed the sign was essentially a copy of the Middle Ages' witch's foot or crow's foot, both of which were tied closely to the devil.

The U.S. Supreme Court wasn't as put off by the symbol. In their landmark 1969 decision, *Tinker v. Des Moines Independent Community School District*, the justices ruled that teenage students were allowed to wear peace sign armbands on campus under their First Amendment rights. It was one of a handful of cases ruling in favor of the iconic sign.

Back in England, Holtom's efforts in the antinukes movement offered him little peace. Four years after his sign debuted at the 1958 march, Holtom and his wife divorced. According to one of his daughters, Holtom's focus on disarmament "put considerable financial pressure on his family, which later resulted in family disputes and probably contributed to his later divorce."

Handy Way to Say "Peace"

The **peace sign hand gesture** (the index finger and middle finger raised, palm pointing outward) became the symbol of hippies during the Vietnam War era. Many believe it was a riff on the same gesture representing courage, or V for victory, popularized by Winston Churchill during World War II. Others suggest it was a cheeky twist (literally) by antiestablishment types. The same gesture—but with the palm facing inward—is the British equivalent of flashing the middle finger.

Holtom's peace sign continues to be used by a diverse parties, both political and commercial. As the authors of the book *Peace: The Biography of a Symbol* put it: "Peace may come at a price, but the peace symbol is free."

Rainbows

There was a time when rainbows were seen as a bad news version of FedEx.

The Greek deity Iris, the personification of the arc of color we see in the sky, was a divine messenger and brought intelligence to the mortal world on such downer topics as war and vengeful violence.

Babylonian astronomers in 651 B.C. carefully reported rainbow sightings to their king. Like the Greeks and Egyptians, Babylonians, according to some historians, feared that rather than offering a happy "Rainbow Connection" moment (à la Kermit the Frog, strumming on a banjo), the rainbow could be a harbinger of doom. Aboriginal Australians saw a rainbow as a giant serpent in the sky, and people in such far-flung locales as Hungary, China, Mexico, and Gabon lived in fear of the rainbow.

THE RAINBOW GETS ITS FIRST MENTION IN MESOPOTAMIAN TEXTS DATING BEFORE 2000 B.C.

Rainbows were considered so powerful that pointing or even looking at one was considered a really bad move. "Hungarian folk belief says that a person's finger will wither after pointing at a rainbow, a grim prophecy surpassed by the Chinese text that promises immediate ulceration of the offending hand," according to the encyclopedic book *The Rainbow Bridge: Rainbows in Art, Myth and Science.* (Scandinavia's Norsemen dialed down the fear, believing that the burning rainbow Bifröst was a bridge between the world of gods and earth.)

So how did we get to our far more reassuring—and nonbody-withering—modern conception of the rainbow?

The Judeo-Christian faiths played a role. Rainbows are mentioned a number of times in the

The Song that Almost Never Was

After an initial screening, MGM execs planned to cut the ballad **"Over the Rainbow"** from *The Wizard of Oz* soundtrack because they thought it was too slow. They ultimately decided otherwise, and the piece won the Academy Award in 1940 for best original song. Decades later, the American Film Institute voted it the greatest film song of all time.

Bible, starting with the book of Genesis. Noah, his family, and a menagerie of animals floated in the ark following 40 days and 40 nights of rain, and when the water eventually receded, God created a rainbow. The almighty proclaimed: "I do set my bow in the cloud, and it shall be for a token of a covenant between me and the earth . . . the everlasting covenant between God and every living creature of all flesh that is upon the earth."

With that ringing endorsement (and the rise of Christianity), the rainbow got a pretty sizeable makeover. It began popping up somewhat regularly in early Christian art. For nearly a thousand years, Jesus was often depicted perched on a rainbow. For example, Belgian painter Hans Memling's fifteenth-century work *Last Judgment* portrays Christ seated on a colorful rainbow with his legs dangling over the mortal world.

Memling's painting came toward the end of the rainbow trend, and while artists moved on to new religious iconography, the rainbow retained a secular appeal. Artist Isaac Oliver painted a portrait of Queen Elizabeth I (circa 1603) holding a rainbow. The rainbow even snagged a supporting role in Constantino Brumidi's 1866 *Apotheosis of Washington* mural in the U.S. Capitol's rotunda. (The rainbow is the vehicle for George Washington's ascension to heaven.)

The rainbow continues to play a colorful role in culture. It's been used as a symbol in advertising for nearly everything, including (but certainly not limited to) motels, Ford dealerships, the lottery, vodka, pubs, hair salons, laundry detergent, gay rights, police officers, and worldwide peace.

Musicians have also drawn inspiration from rainbows. Rainbow shout-outs can be heard in countless songs, including those crooned by such all-time superstars as Frank Sinatra ("I've Got the World on a String"), Mick Jagger ("She's a Rainbow"), and, of course, Judy Garland in "Over

Gold and Leprechauns

One of the most popular myths of any kind is the **pot of gold at the end of a rainbow.** Rooted in Irish lore about leprechauns who allegedly guarded the treasure, some claim the story originally came from a twist on a far more reasonable thirteenth-century saying: "One would be as likely to find a pot of gold as to find the end of a rainbow."

the Rainbow." Kermit the Frog even noted the trend in "The Rainbow Connection," with the opening lyric: "Why are there so many songs about rainbows?" I'm not sure of the answer, but for those who may still believe in Hungarian or Chinese folklore, it's nice to know you can enjoy the majesty of rainbows without even having to look at them.

Salutations and Closings

My dearest and most benevolent reader,

Thank you for taking the time to peruse my book.

Yours truly, warmest regards, and hopes for a better tomorrow full of sunshine and rainbows.

The Author

As over-the-top as that salutation and closing (the beginning and sign-off phrases in a letter) may seem, this type of gushing deferential prose was once not only welcome but also expected—and the more obsequious, the better. For example, in 1553, the viceroy of Spanish America Don Luis de Velascio ended a letter to king of Spain Charles I with the following flourish: "Your Sacred Catholic Caesarian Majesty's faithful servant who kisses your Majesty's imperial feet."

Not to be outdone, in the following century, the British Duke of Buckingham often finished notes to England's King James I with the more succinct but every bit as submissive: "Your Majesty's Most Humble Slave and Dog."

Even in the early days of the egalitarian United States, the founding fathers believed it necessary to prostrate themselves in writing. In correspondence following George Washington's election as president of the United States, Thomas Jefferson signed off a letter to Washington with: "Your most obedient and your most humble servant."

"Few things tell us so much about a period in history in so few words," business language expert Walter Macauley said about salutations and closings in a 1988 Associated Press interview. "The way we signed off over the centuries is a window into societal values and etiquette of the times."

For instance, the fawning salutations and closings of early Western letters reflect the supreme importance placed on hierarchy, whether it be class, rank, or relationship.

Fourth-century Roman rhetorician C. Julius Victor explained that "the salutations and signatures of letters . . . are intended to show the discriminations between degrees of friendship and degrees of station." And in the eleventh century, a group of writers from the Italian city of Bologna outlined the elements required in a proper letter's opening and closing. One of the authors, Hugo of Bologna, laid out more than a dozen formal salutations, depending on the writer and the recipient. (He covered everyone from a pope writing to an emperor to a scholar looking for wisdom from a teacher.)

Indeed, times changed. Reflecting the loosening of social rules, by the nineteenth century, many

THE ART OF LETTER–WRITING IS A RELATIVELY NEW PHENOMENON. THE GREEKS AND ROMANS FAVORED PERSONAL EMISSARIES TO DELIVER MESSAGES. THE PROCESS OF PUTTING QUILL TO PARCHMENT DIDN'T BECOME TRENDY UNTIL JUST BEFORE THE DAWN OF THE MEDIEVAL PERIOD.

letter writers were cutting down the depth of these flowery openings and closings, inserting a basic "Dear" at the top and "Yours sincerely" to finish off a dispatch. Then, in the mid–twentieth century, Americans began to rethink these niceties altogether.

"I have always held that business letter salutations and complimentary closes are relics of the Dark Ages," wrote syndicated columnist Frank Colby in 1949. "Both are unnecessary and meaningless, and often ridiculous as in the case of one business man addressing another as 'Dear,' and assuring him that he (the writer) is true to him ('I am yours truly')."

For manners experts, the issue became something of a cottage industry. In 1955, Amy Vanderbilt disagreed with a reader who argued that using "Sincerely" without "yours" wasn't proper style. "It is usually custom that changes rules of etiquette, rather than authorities themselves," Vanderbilt wrote in defense of just "Sincerely." Still, like Hugo of Bologna, Vanderbilt also had a long list of acceptable closings, depending on the letter recipient. Apparently if you're writing to the president, you must say "Respectfully," but if you're dropping a line to the vice president, "Very truly yours" is okay.

In 1976, Abigail Van Buren (Dear Abby) declared "Dear sirs" and "Gentlemen" out of date, and solicited readers for alternatives. She got back everything from "Howdy" to *"Lexitori Salutem"* (Latin for "hail to the reader"). Three years later, the more conservative Judith Martin (better known as Miss Manners) stumped for sticking with "Yours truly" for business and "Sincerely yours" for social letters. By using these, "one avoids the possibility of overcommitment or undercommitment," she explained. In 1983, Ann Landers threw her hands up in the air over this formality, saying, "I don't know who laid down those silly rules, but they are long overdue for revision."

In the modern era of short text messages, emails, and tweets, revision may give way to wholesale elimination of salutations and closings. Like letters themselves, these phrases may soon become artifacts of a forgotten age.

XOXO

In the days of handwritten letters, XOXO was a nice way to tell a loved one "hugs and kisses." Before you sigh about yet another vestige of your youth drifting away, fear not. As any member of Gen Y will tell you—once they're done texting OMG!—XOXO has made the seamless transition into the Internet age. In making the crossover, it's a social media rarity. (Sadly for fans of SWAK, short for "sealed with a kiss," time has not been so kind.)

Though we call it "hugs and kisses," it should really be "kisses and hugs," since the X signifies the kiss and the O represents the hug. Chronologically, the X is also the older symbol. The letter X once carried great religious importance in the Christian faith. Beyond representing the cross, X was the first letter for Christ in Greek (Χριστός).

The letter X was also an easy symbol for illiterates to write. As a result, beginning some 2,000 years ago, it served as a

A RECENT APPLICATION OF Xs AND Os COMES FROM FOOTBALL AND BASKETBALL. COACHES WHO WILL DRAW UP PLAYS WITH THE Xs REPRESENTING DEFENSE AND THE Os OFFENSE. WHILE SPORT'S Xs AND Os REFLECT ONE FORM OF TOUCHY—FEELY INTERACTION, IT'S UNLIKELY TO LEAD TO THE MORE AMOROUS USAGE.

proxy for a signature. Still, a single letter on the dotted line was a bit understated for some ancient parties. At the time, kissing a Bible amplified one's commitment to an oath, so a tradition started wherein a smooch on the X mark added a touch of sincerity to an agreement. With the X tied to an affectionate act, even if it wasn't for an affectionate reason, it was only a matter of time before it

OMG! BFFS?

Word experts believe naming your closest pal your **BFF** (Best Friends Forever) started in 1996 (though some anecdotal evidence places its genesis in the 1980s). Either way, the term reached maturity (or at least its teenage years) when instant messaging, Facebook, and Twitter became everyday tools of communication. In 2010, the venerable *Oxford English Dictionary* added the term to its listings, defining it as "a girl's best friend."

crossed over for loving purposes. But it did take a while. The earliest known use of an X as a kiss in a letter occurred in 1765, according to the *Oxford English Dictionary*.

The story of the O is far less certain. One candidate is that O symbolizes eternity and by extension represents a circle of love. (How this gets us to "hugging" is unclear.) Another option, which takes a diagram approach, is that the roundness of an O appears a bit like an aerial view of two people hugging. Then there's the connection of the X and O in other areas. Tic-tac-toe (originally called "noughts and crosses" by the British) dates back to at least 1864.

Yellow Smiley Face

Smiley—yes, that iridescent yellow-hued happy face has a name—was born from discord. In 1963, State Mutual Life Assurance, a Worcester, Massachusetts, insurance company, was having trouble with a corporate takeover. They'd bought out an Ohio outfit called Guarantee Mutual, and the Midwesterners were not happy with their new bosses.

In a move that would probably be considered naïve nowadays, a vice president at the

Massachusetts company thought an "in-house friendship campaign" would solve the problem. Personally, I would have gone with a round of raises to calm nerves, but instead a graphic designer, Harvey Ball, was hired for the much more cost-effective sum of approximately $45 to create a design that would bring détente.

Ball knew a little something about hostilities. He'd fought in some of the Pacific's fiercest battles on Okinawa during World War II, earning a Bronze Star for his bravery. When it came time for this assignment, Ball kept it simple, drawing the iconic yellow-backed circle with vertically oblong eyes and a beaming closed-mouth smile. (Similar happy faces predated Ball's work, but they didn't feature the combination of the yellow color and the artist's style.) His employers promptly stamped the face on buttons and distributed them to employees. Amazingly, not only were tensions eased, but workers also started hoarding the popular pins.

Entrepreneurs quickly seized on the concept, and by 1972 an astounding 50 million smiley buttons had hit the market. As for Ball, he never filed for a copyright. Despite losing out on millions in royalties, he was the personification of his emblem's upbeat attitude. Even when two men cashed in on his design, pairing it with the phrase, "Have a nice day," Ball's reaction was mild: "I would have gone with, 'Have a great day.'" (See Have a Nice Day, page 338.)

But then he found out about Frenchman Franklin Loufrani. Following French student riots in 1968, Loufrani created a yellow smiley face logo to be included with positive stories in the newspaper *France Soir*. He told *Forbes* magazine he did it "because French people are never happy." In an ironic capitalistic twist, the European Loufrani— rather than the American Ball—was quick to protect his smiley design. Loufrani started a company in 1971 selling the happy face on a wide range of products and, to date, he's secured trademarks for it in more than 100 countries.

While there's been a "Harvey Ball Day" in his hometown of Worcester and the U.S. Postal Service issued a stamp in 1999 based on his design, Ball found his smile decidedly upside down when it came to Loufrani. "He annoys me," seventy-seven-year-old Ball would tell the *Hartford Courant* in 1998. "He's a creep."

In a slightly more diplomatic stance, Loufrani's son Nicholas didn't necessarily dispute Ball's claim to being the first. "If you make a design and you don't do anything with it, and someone else makes the same design and develops it and promotes and markets it, you cannot thirty-five years after say you have rights over the design," he said.

It may not be clear who Smiley's real father is, but if Ball was first, Loufrani received a small dose of karmic payback. In 2009, the French business-man lost a lawsuit against Walmart in an attempt to get the store to stop using a smiley face in its adver-tising. To this day, Smiley remains in America's public domain for all to use.

Ball died in 2001, satisfied that he'd created a smile that arguably could compete with Leonardo da Vinci's *Mona Lisa* as having the world's most famous grin. He proudly claimed: "Never in the his-tory of mankind or art has any single piece of art gotten such widespread favor, pleasure, enjoyment, and nothing has ever been so simply done and so easily understood in art."

Even if it's a bit of an oversell, he no doubt brought smiles to many faces.

Looking Nice

From the beginning of time, people have strived to enhance their appearance. The following are some of the landmark moments in that painstaking effort.

4000 B.C.

Egyptians used *kohl*, a forerunner to **mascara**, on both their eyelashes and eyebrows. The **comb** also dates back to at least this period, with both Africans and Egyptians using a variety of options, including fish bone skeletons.

3500 B.C.

The fashion-conscious folks of the Babylonian city of Ur were the first known to use **lip makeup**. The key ingredient: a white lead base. It would take a while until **lipstick** arrived in metal tubes (circa 1915). **Mirrors** also surfaced around this time, because the Bronze Age allowed artisans to finely polish metals enough to see a reflection. Glass mirrors emerged in Venice 1300 A.D.

3000 B.C.

Egyptians used henna to dye their nails previous to this date, but the first **nail polish** came from China around this time. Ingredients included egg white, vegetable dyes, beeswax, and a gelatin or gum to keep it together. Social rank determined what color someone could apply. Wigs were also commonplace by this time.

1500 B.C.

The Assyrians were out in front

when it came to **hair coloring** and also created the first **curling iron**. Located in modern Iraq, these people were noted hair stylists, who knew how to give a layered cut. The ancient Greeks were also fans of finely coiffed hair, particularly hair coloring. But the first (safe) modern hair coloring formula was developed by French chemist Eugène Schueller in 1909.

100s

The Roman physician Galen came up with the original **cold cream** to keep skin soft and smooth. The formula featured white wax, which was melted into a mixture of olive oil and rose buds.

1500s

Men wore clothes over their upper torso long before this period, but the **shirt** as we know it (hip length so it could be tucked in) was developed in Western Europe around this time as a response to the modern trousers. For women, **high heels**, which had existed in various forms, began their upward fashion trajectory in this century as did the **white wedding dress.**

1600s

The **cosmetic compact** was an outgrowth of a European-wide smallpox epidemic. Those who survived carried small cases containing patches, which were used to cover the scars. Men started donning **neckties** in the 1660s. Roman soldiers had used scarves to keep cool in the heat of the day, but it became a modern fashion accessory, particularly in London, gaining a massive following in the 1700s. (The **bow tie** was popularized by Americans in the 1920s.)

1762

Men have employed makeshift items from shells to flints as **razors** for as long as there have been, well, men. But the first safety razor (rather than the always dangerous straight blade) was devised by French barber Jean Jacques Perret. The T-shaped razor was developed in the U.S. by King Gillette, a man who popularized it in the years leading up to the twentieth century. The **electric razor** was unveiled around 1910. But Jacob Schick revolutionized the instrument, patenting his first electric design in 1923 before it reached the masses eight years later.

1797

Fred Astaire might not have been so suave and Abraham Lincoln so distinguished if not for the **top hat**, a late eighteenth-century creation. A London hat maker named John Etherington is credited by many with the stove pipe lid, while a coterie of French historians say the first top hat was made in Paris a year earlier.

1880s

A salon-style **hair dryer** (those alien helmet-looking things) was invented by Parisian Alexandre Godefroy, its hot air powered by a gas stove. The first electric dryer originated in Germany in 1889, but it wasn't until 1920 that an inventor in Racine, Wisconsin, developed a version efficient enough to be used regularly in salons. Still, it was bulky. Home versions began popping up in the 1970s.

1886

To be accepted among the wealthy, a man's formal evening jacket required long tails until the **tuxedo** came around. The style (sans tails) was first worn by the American elite in Tuxedo Park, New York, and it may have been rejected as odd if not for the fact its first wearer, Pierre Lorillard IV, came from a blue-blood family.

1890

The first **shampoo** was created in Germany. In America, John Breck was one of the early pioneers of scalp products beginning in the 1900s. (Fun fact: The word *shampoo* comes from the Hindu term *champo*, which means "to massage" or "to knead.")

1906

The **perm** was developed in London. What a labor for looks: The treatment took six hours, countless two-pound brass rollers, and borax paste.

1946

Specialized swimming clothes, which existed in the Greco-Roman times and probably earlier, reentered popular culture in the mid-1800s. But the concept was racheted up a few notches when French designer Louis Réard unveiled the first **bikini** on a Paris runway. The suit was named after the location of the first American peacetime nuclear test on the Bikini Atoll in the Pacific Ocean.

1959

Panty hose were seen as a fantastic alternative to the even more cumbersome garter and stocking combo. They were invented in North Carolina by Allen Grant Sr.

Nice Sayings and Songs

Auld Lang Syne

BURNS

It wouldn't be New Year's Eve without "Auld Lang Syne." While one survey claimed that 80 percent of people can't make it all the way through the song (between the arcane lyrics and heavy drinking on New Year's, the percentage must be higher), it's a sentimental melody that is beloved around the world.

Ask any Scotsman and he'll tell you the song's author is Robert Burns. The poet is Scotland's favorite native son, a fact confirmed by a poll that placed Burns just ahead of William Wallace of *Braveheart* fame as the country's all-time greatest historical figure. When people in Scotland refer to "the Bard," they aren't talking about William Shakespeare; they're hailing Burns. In fact, the poet has his own holiday, Burns Day, which is celebrated on his January 25 birthday and is commemorated with a lot of singing and drink. (The dashing Burns would have undoubtedly liked that, since he was a big partier and a bit of a carouser, known to have had numerous love affairs.)

Yet, in spite of his country's undying devotion, Burns's authorship of "Auld Lang Syne" is actually pretty murky, much like a rolling Scottish fog. Most music historians agree Burns adapted the song rather than creating it out of whole cloth.

Burns's first known mention of the tune came in a 1788 letter to one of his patrons, Frances Dunlop. In it, he made no pretenses about his role in its development. "Light be the true on the breast of the heaven-inspired Poet who composed this glorious fragment," Burns wrote. In a letter five years later, he told a friend that he'd modified the song after hearing an old man sing it.

It wasn't uncommon for Burns to mine history for inspiration in his work. "He would take these

New Year's Changes

Many believe the origins of **New Year's resolutions** date back to the Babylonians, but our application of the concept stems from the development of the modern calendar. The year's first month, January, was named after the god Janus, who was the deity of beginnings and endings. To bury the past and look positively to the future, Romans were said to ask opponents for forgiveness at the start of the New Year. This spurred the custom of looking to the start of the year as an opportunity to make positive changes to one's life.

old melodies that he heard in his lifetime and just whistle them to himself during the day," Scottish fiddler and Burns lecturer Alasdair Fraser told NPR in 1999. "And then he would decide that as he was doing that he could add more poetry to them, and then he would become inspired by the melody."

In the case of "Auld Lang Syne," he did make some updates. According to one source, he took three old stanzas and added two more to develop a fully formed piece. That said, the melody, which permeates pop culture in films as diverse as *It's a*

Wonderful Life and *When Harry Met Sally...*, is attributed by some to a Scot's worst nightmare—an Englishman. Composer William Shield, who hailed from northern England, wrote the music as part of his 1782 opera *Rosina*. Still, it's likely that Shield borrowed the tune from earlier composers just like Burns (Scots can take a deep breath—it's possible they could still lay claim to the melody's roots).

"Auld Lang Syne" made its way to the United States in the nineteenth century with Scots-Irish emigrants. But the tune didn't become a New Year's Eve phenomenon until 1929. Credit goes to Canadian bandleader Guy Lombardo, who selected it as part of his December 31 radio and TV specials, which were broadcast for years from New York City throughout North America.

None of this, of course, makes the tune's words any easier to remember. After all, it is practically a New Year's Eve tradition to butcher Burns's lyrics. The song's most famous phrase, "auld lang syne," is literally translated as "old long since," but is typically understood to mean something to the effect of "days gone by." My favorite bewildering line: "And surely ye'll be your pint-stowp!" (It supposedly means something along the lines of "and surely you'll buy your pint cup!")

A Familiar Tune

"**Auld Lang Syne**" has been widely covered by musicians as varied as Jimi Hendrix, Elvis Presley, Mariah Carey, and Billy Joel. Even George M. Cohan quoted it in his 1906 standard "You're a Grand Old Flag." Versions of the tune exist around the world from China to India to Denmark.

Nonetheless, the piece's inherent tenderness has cemented its place as a beloved tradition.

"The song has and enacts a physical warmth," said Robert Crawford, professor at Scotland's University of St. Andrews and a Burns expert. "The way people often join hands or link arms when they sing the last verse is just an embodiment of what the song sings. It's a very useful song."

Break a Leg

L eave it to actors to come up with a phrase so full of mystery that it could be the plotline for a production of its own.

"Break a leg" is certainly a baffling way to wish luck to someone going out onto a stage. (Should I have a heart attack while I'm at it?) We do know its encouraging meaning was used in the United States by the 1920s, but that in the eighteenth century it described something completely different—a woman who had a child out of wedlock. (Crass example: "Did you hear that hussy Miss Johnson broke a leg?")

But beyond that, its origin is all about interpretation. The first candidate is that the phrase relates to the act of bowing. When a woman curtsies, she bends her back leg, or as it could be said in a more creative way, she's breaking that leg. In this theory, the hope was that a good performance would lead to many bows and, hence, many leg bends. As this seems to primarily cover female performers, a variation says when actors performed well, the crowd would throw coins at them as a sort of gratuity. Men on stage in the Elizabethan era (women in that period weren't allowed to tread the boards) would have to bend or, using this line of thinking, break a leg to pick up the change. In the sixteenth century, the phrase "make a leg" was used for taking a bow, and the modern-day version could be a basic tweak on that idiom.

Another option ties into the age-old cliché "don't tempt the gods." A superstitious lot, actors have been known to say the opposite of what they wish in order to avoid jinxing a performance. French performers, for example, say *merde* (an expletive for feces) to each other before going on stage. In this instance, hoping for the worst, like "break a leg," supposedly got you the best.

Then there's the theory that it came from a linguistic misunderstanding. Jewish actors would sometimes say *"hatslakha u'brakha"* (translation: "success and blessing") to each other before going on stage. (Apparently, they weren't as superstitious as the French.) "Because of the intermingling of Jewish and non-Jewish theatrical cultures," explained writer Joan Alpert in a 2011 article, "this Yiddish-inflected Hebrew phrase was corrupted into the phonetically similar German phrase, *"Hals und Beinbruch"* ("break a neck and a leg") which World War I German pilots also used to mean 'good luck.'" Despite positing this possibility, Alpert is not a fan, pointing out that *"hatslakha u'brakha"* wasn't that widely used in Yiddish theater.

Still, more claims abound. There's the notion that "break a leg" reflected a desire to perform like the great Sarah Bernhardt, who late in her career continued to wow audiences even after one leg was amputated. Or it's a reference to curtain rods used on stage, which were known as legs and could break from being frequently opened and closed when actors came out multiple times postperformance to bow for the audience.

Somehow the assassination of Abraham

Va Bene

English isn't the only language with peculiar ways to wish good luck. Italians, for example, say *"in boca al lupo"* (translation: "in the mouth of the wolf") to wish someone good fortune.

Lincoln has been pulled into this one as well. A few have claimed that the phrase refers to the killer John Wilkes Booth, who jumped onto stage at Ford's Theatre after shooting the president. But this one is far-fetched. Booth didn't break his leg in the jump (he did later in his getaway) and none of it was particularily lucky.

I'll be waiting patiently for someone to write a good screenplay that sorts it all out.

Nice Superstitions

FINGERS CROSSED

The most popular tale behind this gesture stretches back to the early days of Christianity, when flaunting religious icons could lead to persecution by the Romans. The holy cross was a particularly meaningful symbol and had to be kept on the hush-hush. So Christians devised a stealthy alternative—wrapping your middle finger around your index finger—as code for the cross. Some believe that because the gesture represented such a powerfully positive message, the finger-cross trickled into secular society as a sign of good luck or protection. (And for the naughty, protection while telling a lie.)

FOUR-LEAF CLOVER

The Druids were the first to collect this once rare plant (the odds of finding one were about 1 in 10,000). The four-leaf clover may have found a special place in early Christian society thanks to its four-point form resembling a cross. During the Middle Ages, it was considered by some to be a witch deterrent. In the 1950s, the lucky find lost a bit of its mojo when biologists developed a seed for a four-leaf variety, making it far easier to produce.

HORSESHOES

The horseshoe's lucky properties took shape by at least the fourth century. Speculation abounds on how it gained its reputation. One credits its similarity to the crescent moon. Primitive cultures believed the moon had great power and the horseshoe was an emblem of it. Another is the respect for iron. An early form of metal, iron was often regarded as magical and, maybe, the horseshoe held a bit of that enchantment. An alternative possibility: Animal worship. Some ancient Europeans did worship horses and, just maybe, the beast's shoe was a relic of those beliefs. A slightly more recent tale goes that St. Dunstan, Archbishop of Canterbury in the tenth century and later patron saint of blacksmiths, once fixed a horseshoe on the devil's foot (causing Satan much pain in the process). In return, the saint extracted a promise from the lord of the underworld to never enter a door with a horseshoe hanging over it.

KNOCK ON WOOD

Whether you're British and you touch it or you're American and you give it a good knock, making contact with wood has a longstanding history as a lucky act. If you're looking to connect with the right wood, consider oak. Cultures as diverse as Native Americans and the Greeks believed oak trees were the earthly dwelling of the deities. The ancient Norse people were partial to the ash tree; in their mythology, Yggdrasill was an ultraholy giant ash tree located at the center of the universe. The Egyptians deemed sycamores sacred. From those early roots,

Christians picked up the habit, imbuing the wood of the holy cross or that of a church door with protective powers. In some Mediterranean countries there's also a tradition of touching metal to avoid bad luck. Apparently, precious shiny substances offer excellent protection because of their value.

RABBIT'S FOOT

Well before monotheism or even Greek and Roman gods blanketed the European continent, locals worshipped animals. Starting before 600 B.C., clans would adopt different creatures as their spiritual ancestors. One theory says that there was a group

that worshipped the hare, a more athletic cousin of the rabbit. People carried a hare's foot as a totem of the sacred beast to bring good luck. Eventually, the cuter rabbit stepped in for the hare as the foot of choice. An alternative explanation is that hares are born with their eyes open, giving them the ability to see the "evil eye" and shoo away bad tidings. The foot offers up some of this power.

WISHBONE

The Etruscans, who lived in modern Italy's Tuscan region some 2,500 years ago, were an advanced yet superstitious civilization. Soothsayers considered birds to be useful in the art of divination. Everything from the bird's entrails to their bones could have meaning. (In fact, the Romans later used the term *auspex*, which meant "one who looks at birds," as the word for a fortune teller.) Apparently, touching the clavicle of a small bird, which we now call the wishbone, could grant wishes. From there, we developed the practice of breaking the wishbone, with a wish being granted to the individual getting the larger piece.

WISHING ON A STAR

Falling stars have long been revered sightings. A popular age-old bit of lore suggests they were the souls of the recently deceased moving on to another world. Why we first started wishing on them, along with the first star in the sky, has been obscured by time. Perhaps, the rarity of seeing a falling star bestowed it with magical properties. (As for wishing on the first star of the evening, it's possible we needed something a little more reliable.) Still, we can be pretty certain that the tradition continues today thanks to the popular nursery rhyme "Star Light, Star Bright." The late nineteenth-century ditty, which includes the lines, "The first star I see tonight; I wish I may, I wish I might," is thought to be an American creation. Disney solidified the starry meaning when the studio included "When You Wish Upon a Star" in its 1940 animated feature *Pinocchio*. The tune won an Academy Award for best originl song.

Carols

Caroling may seem like a quaint Christmas tradition, with happy singers sporting festive outfits going door to door, but its history isn't all decked halls and figgy pudding. Its story is rooted in a tussle between church traditionalists and a more progressive set willing to take a little from the non-Christian world all in the name of a good time.

In the fourth century, the Catholic Church officially decreed December 25 as the day to recognize

Jesus Christ's birth. From the beginning, music was a no-brainer for reveling during the celebration. But with so many popular tunes of the time rooted in pagan religions or bawdy drinking traditions, the church wanted to keep tight control over what was to be on musical offer. To that end, songs were carefully vetted and singing was kept inside churches. Written in Latin and lacking the sing-song merriment of modern carols, many of the hymns were difficult for regular folk to master or enjoy.

Thankfully, St. Francis of Assisi, a man of the people, was bringing accessible music to the streets in the early thirteenth century. Outdoor nativity scenes had been common since at least the tenth century, but St. Francis amped up the outside-the-church celebrations. He taught locals songs in their own language and, while many of these events were more nativity plays than present-day caroling, it led to "a new enthusiasm [among] the singers," according to the book *Stories Behind the Great Traditions of Christmas*.

At around the same time, the pagan practice of wassailing was flourishing. Derived from an Old Norse phrase meaning "be healthy," the word *wassail* was initially used as a drinking toast like we use "cheers" today. The act of wassailing featured

Lover's Performance

A **serenade** is the ultimate form of live musical tribute. (Think Lloyd Dobler holding a boom box above his head outside of Diane Court's house; if you have no clue what I'm talking about, immediately download the timeless 1989 film *Say Anything*.) The word comes from the Italian term *sereno*, which means "calm," and the custom of serenading a woman while singing and playing a string instrument dates to medieval times. The term also reflects a style of upbeat music composed by the likes of Mozart and Tchaikovsky.

groups going house to house singing tunes in the hopes of receiving some nourishment and, ideally, a tipple or more of ale (there were even wassailing bowls used for downing hearty drinks). Keeping with wassailing's pagan rites, singers would often go into orchards and sing to give thanks for apple trees as well. In those instances, appreciation could include a warming spot of hard cider.

The song most closely associated with this practice, "Here We Come-a-Wassailing," inspired such carols as "We Wish You a Merry Christmas," with the request for figgy pudding serving as a remnant of this ritual. Singing about town was not just for pagans. Along with wassailing, the *waits* were another contributor to caroling's heritage. This custom, which lasted from the thirteenth until at least the seventeenth century, starred night watchmen at first (known as "waits") and later minstrels, meandering around neighborhoods singing in return for a little cash.

Indeed, the combination of the two traditions put people in a singing mood. But back in the church, the debate over caroling continued. It was banned by church councils in the early fourteenth century, and even as late as the seventeenth century, the Puritans prohibited the practice. But caroling had its champions. In particular, Martin Luther (1483–1546) embraced the sing-along practice as part of his liberalizing ways. (Geek note: Caroling comes from the Old French term *carol* or *carole*, meaning "joyful song" or a "dance in the round.")

By 1833, caroling at Christmas was a well-established tradition throughout the British Isles. That year, London lawyer William B. Sandys published a successful volume *Christmas Carols, Ancient and Modern*. In the later part of the century, the Salvation Army also added to the custom's growth, playing caroling music on British streets during the Christmas season. This helped average people learn popular song lyrics.

Caroling came full circle in the 1880s when a church in the small southeast English town of Truro welcomed this upbeat style of hymns into its house of worship. Known as *Nine Lessons and Carols*, it was added to the church's Christmas Eve festivities. The service was so popular that in 1918, the BBC began broadcasting a similar ceremony from Cambridge, an event that still airs today.

The Customer Is Always Right

H arry Gordon Selfridge knew firsthand what it felt like to be a mistreated customer.

As a successful executive for the famed Chicago department store Marshall Field's, Selfridge would go on reconnaissance missions to Europe, looking for new ideas to bring back to the Windy City. Once, at a swank store in England, an employee approached Selfridge. "Is Sir intending to buy something?" the man asked in an aristocratic British accent. Selfridge politely responded that he was just browsing, to which the man dropped the refined inflections and barked, "Then 'op it mate!"

Selfridge never forgot that moment, and it likely helped spur one of the business world's most famous nice sayings: "The customer is always right."

At Marshall Field's, Selfridge was known as the ideas man. He would often post pithy notes—mantras for the staff—in the department store's cafeteria. Some examples: "To be satisfied with nothing short of perfection"; "To know both sides of the question"; and "To be courteous; to be a good example; to anticipate requirements." It's not clear whether "the customer is always right" made it onto the board. In fact, some have credited Selfridge's boss, Marshall Field, with inventing the phrase.

IN 1908, THE GREAT SWISS HOTELIER CÈSAR RITZ ALSO OFFERED A SIMILAR SENTIMENT WHEN HE SAID, "LE CLIENT N'A JAMAIS TORT" (TRANSLATION: "THE CUSTOMER IS NEVER WRONG").

But it was Selfridge who made it a cornerstone of his business. After leaving Marshall Field's, Selfridge went on to open one of Britain's first truly grand department stores in 1909. It would make sense that Selfridge made the phrase big, because he did nothing small. His store, which he named after himself, was located in London's shopping epicenter, Oxford Street. Selfridges featured not only fabulous goods but also a library, a barber-shop, a post office, a currency exchange, and a gigantic restaurant boasting its own orchestra, among other amenities.

These over-the-top efforts did not dampen his commitment to detail. Selfridge spent an hour every morning walking through his 6-acre store ensuring that everything was "business as usual" (a phrase coined by one of his employees). His primary goal was to ensure that anyone who entered Selfridges would come back. He did not hire floorwalkers, who were expected to pressure purchasers. Instead, he told his sales assistances to treat consumers "as guests when they come and when they go, whether or not they buy. Get the confidence of the public and you will have no difficulty in getting their patronage." Regardless of when or how Selfridge said it, at his store, the customer was always right. The approach worked. The establishment would be heralded as "the great cathedral of shopping" by French writer Émile Zola, attracting more than one million shoppers in its first week of business.

For a man so dedicated in his professional life, Selfridge was apt to stray in his personal life. Though the department store baron was a married father of four, he was linked to such celebrity hotties as dancer Isadora Duncan and ballerina Anna Pavlova. He also had a fondness for gambling and lavishing gifts on his mistresses. When his wife passed away in 1918, his debauched lifestyle began to impact his work. In the end, the department store's board forced its founder, who by the 1940s owed both the company and the government enormous sums of money, out of the business. He would die in 1947 at age eighty-nine, too broke to afford a headstone for his grave.

As for the customer always being right, Selfridge seemed to reconsider that concept around the time his lifestyle grew out of control. In the same year as his wife's death, Selfridge published a telling book, *The Romance of Capitalism*. "The time has passed," he wrote, "when an irritable customer, no matter who he or she may be, can whether right or wrong, ride rough-shod over the young man or woman behind the counter and demand his or her dismissal."

Eat, Drink, and Be Merry

Most people would nominate William Shakespeare as the most influential writer in the English language. But William Tyndale probably deserves a mention too.

A relative unknown today, Tyndale gave English "eat, drink, and be merry" and scores of other phrases like: "the powers that be"; "the sign of the times"; "salt of the earth"; "pearls before swine"; "the apple of his eye"; and "fight the good fight."

Like Shakespeare, Tyndale worked long ago (his most significant work was published in the 1530s). But unlike Shakespeare, who never ran afoul of the law despite writing in a time when royal censors often came down on subversive work, Tyndale paid dearly for his efforts with the quill.

Tyndale was born around 1495 to a merchant family in Gloucestershire, England. Educated at Oxford University, he'd become a religious scholar, spending a handful of years at Cambridge University. The man's greatest skill was in translation, and he was driven to bring the granddaddy of all texts, the Bible, to the people. He was steered by the belief that if a common "boy that driveth the plough" could read this all-important text, he would be less dependent on the church and its rituals.

This was a dangerous proposition. During Tyndale's lifetime, the Bible's official Latin version was deemed so sacred that those who attempted to translate it into the vernacular were declared heretics. The punishment was death.

Undeterred, Tyndale embarked upon his perilous effort. Betrayed at times by spies, he was forced to flee his native country for continental Europe. In an ironic twist, Britain's King Henry VIII, who was causing his own stir by separating from the Roman

Catholic Church, continued to pursue Tyndale and ultimately had him detained and executed in 1536.

But, before that sad day, Tyndale was able to complete an English translation of the New Testament and a good chunk of the Old Testament. Proving that timing is everything, just a year after Tyndale's death, the British crown decided to endorse a translation. There were numerous efforts, but the one that has resonated the most through the ages is the *King James Bible*, which was published in 1611.

Six committees comprised of fifty-three religious figures and one lay scholar were tasked with the King James translation. So did they sweat it out, deliberating the transformation of every word themselves? The answer appears to be not exactly. Theologians today believe the vast majority of the English language translation of the original Hebrew and Greek in the famed King James volume came directly from Tyndale's volume: 84 percent of the New Testament and 67 percent of the Old Testament, according to one study.

As for Tyndale's phrase "eat, drink, and be merry," it wasn't sanctioning big-time partying. The words appear in two places in the Bible, once in Ecclesiastes and again in Luke. (Many mistake it for the famous line in the book of Isaiah: "Let us eat and drink . . . for tomorrow we shall die.") While much of religious text is down to interpretation, the reference in Luke is considered to be less of an endorsement of those activities and more of a warning about the consequences of constantly living it up. This cautionary sentiment still resonates with many today, but "eat, drink, and be merry" has been broadly co-opted for festive occasions. And with good reason: It can be good for you. A 1996 study found that pleasure seeking is a healthy option under certain circumstances. "If you enjoy what you're doing," said one of the researchers, "the body releases white blood cells, which fight infection. If you feel guilty, you undermine that biological effect."

Alas, while "eat, drink, and be merry" has become the theme for many a party, Tyndale's contribution remains obscure. In 2011, a survey by The Bible Society found that more than 40 percent of people credited "eat, drink, and be merry" to that far more famous influential writer, Shakespeare.

For He's a Jolly Good Fellow

MARIE ANTOINETTE

Marie Antoinette is not known for her stellar reputation. Profligate, vain, occasionally cruel (though, to be fair, the queen likely never actually uttered "Let them eat cake"), she was ultimately beheaded. Essentially, she was one big downer.

But Marie deserves credit for one particularly upbeat achievement: She popularized the tune for the cheerful song "For He's a Jolly Good Fellow." Without Marie, the celebratory ditty that's perfect for so many occasions (and has, appeared in everything from the film classic *Gone With the Wind* to a TV episode of *Star Trek: Deep Space Nine*) would probably never have been.

The familiar melody had been bouncing around a long time before Marie made its acquaintance. The tune likely came to France in the eleventh century and was eventually paired with lyrics about the British Duke of Marlborough in a song called *Marlbrough s'en va-t-en guerre* (translation: "Marlborough goes off to war"). The piece was well known enough to be included in a book of French street songs sometime before 1778.

Nevertheless, the tune was completely unknown to Marie Antoinette when she married the future French king Louis XVI in 1770. As an Austrian princess, Marie knew as much about popular French street music as a modern American teen knows about Gallic songstress Edith Piaf. Marie discovered the "Jolly" tune nearly a decade after her nuptials, when she happened upon a servant cooing it as a lullaby. Immediately a fan, Marie memorized the words and brought it to the king's attention. The song was elevated from a peasant ditty to one worthy of royal court. (When it comes to popularizing music, it's good to be the queen.)

While Marie's legacy would go downhill, the song's melody gained traction. Pierre de Beaumarchais used it in his stage production of *The Marriage of Figaro*, while Ludwig van Beethoven inserted the tune in his *Opus 91*, which is also known as *Wellington's Victory* or the *Battle Symphony*.

How the song made its way to England—where its French words would be replaced with the well-known laudatory lyrics of "Jolly"—is unclear. The tune became a popular way to teach the fundamentals for the harpsichord and violin, so it's possible that a fan of the melody overlaid some English words and the song went viral. But it was certainly an evolutionary process, with lines coming from various sources over time. (The phrase "which nobody can deny" dates back to at least Elizabethan England.)

"Jolly" has enthralled people of all classes ever since. One particular fan was the FBI's longtime director J. Edgar Hoover, who apparently cherished a musical bourbon decanter that played the tune whenever opened. As with Marie Antoinette, Hoover's affinity for the song is a reminder that you don't have to be deemed nice by historians to have some nice taste.

Golden Rule

Opening Day of the Golden Rule Store, Kemmerer, Wyoming, April 14, 1902.

The axiom "Do unto others as you would have them do unto to you" is more than just a foundation of nice behavior—it's an underpinning for moral ethics.

"It functions as a distillation of the wisdom of human experience and of scriptural tradition," Jeffrey Wattles explained in his book *The Golden Rule*. "It serves the needs of educated and uneducated people alike, and stimulates philosophers to codify its meanings in new formulation. Given the equal, basic worth of each individual, the rule implies a requirement of consistency."

Indeed, nearly every culture and every religion has embraced this basic tenet. Greek philosophers like Socrates, Aristotle, and Herodotus helped develop the concept, but it's not the domain of any one group or belief system.

It is unmistakably at the forefront of the Judeo-Christian Bible. The phraseology we typically use for the Golden Rule comes from Luke 6:31 in the New Testament, with a variation also appearing in Matthew 7:12. The Hindu faith has its own version in the *Mahabharata*: "Let no man do to another that which would be repugnant to himself." Same goes for Confucianism: "What you do not wish others to do to you, do not do to them." Ditto for one of the oldest monotheistic religions Zoroastrianism: "That nature alone is good which shall not do unto another whatever is not good for its own self." You can also add Buddhism, Jainism, Islam, and many others to that list, though it's worth noting that different religions emphasize the philosophy to varying degrees.

In the West, we teach the saying to children at a young age. The lesson officially became "golden" in 1674. In a book on physicians and apothecaries, Robert Godfrey referred to the phrase "Do as you

Choice Words

Although the phrase, **"If you don't have anything nice to say, don't say anything at all,"** predates the 1942 animated film *Bambi*, the movie's precocious little bunny, Thumper, popularized the saying (though his version went, "If you can't say anything nice, don't say nothing at all."). In 1998, scientists provided a self-serving reason to follow the axiom. According to a study published in the *Journal of Personality and Social Psychology*, humans often unconsciously apply the negative traits a person says about another to the speaker. Call someone dumb, and your listener may not think you're too smart.

would be done by" as the "Golden Law." Fourteen years later, writer John Goodman penned an 89-page book on the subject, *The Golden Rule, or, The Royal Law of Equity Explained*. (Not surprisingly, the wordy *Royal Law of Equity* didn't quite stick.)

Americans have been particular fans of the sentiment. Beginning in the late nineteenth century, it was used for more than just its basic philosophical meaning. If you were particularly upstanding, you could earn the nickname "Golden Rule." For example, Samuel Milton Jones, the mayor of Toledo, Ohio, from 1897 to 1904 was nicknamed "Golden Rule" Jones for his progressive policies aimed at helping the typically downtrodden average worker. Elsewhere, at least one businessman capitalized on the maxim to great success. J. C. Penney, who would go on to start America's first nationwide department store chain, called his inaugural shop, which opened in Kemmerer, Wyoming, in 1902, the Golden Rule Store. He ultimately opened some thirty-four Golden Rule Stores, before changing the business's trade name to J.C. Penney and Company in 1913.

Yet not everyone has embraced the Golden Rule. While some neuroscientists argue that the reciprocal nature of the philosophy might be inherent to humans, the playwright George Bernard Shaw objected to the Golden Rule's bossy message. "Do not do unto others as you would that they should do unto you," he once wrote. "Their tastes may not be the same." The poet William Blake was equally as pessimistic when he wrote, "He has observ'd the golden rule, / Till he's become the golden fool." As for the most cynical play on the missive, there's the anonymous speaker who quipped: "He who has the gold, rules."

RULES OF CIVILITY

In Johns Hopkins University professor P. M. Forni's 2002 bestseller, *Choosing Civility: The Twenty-Five Rules of Considerate Conduct*, he argues that being civil should be a central part of everyday life and lists twenty-five rules of civility:

1. PAY ATTENTION
2. ACKNOWLEDGE OTHERS
3. THINK THE BEST
4. LISTEN
5. BE INCLUSIVE
6. SPEAK KINDLY
7. DON'T SPEAK ILL
8. ACCEPT AND GIVE PRAISE
9. RESPECT EVEN A SUBTLE "NO"
10. RESPECT OTHERS' OPINIONS
11. MIND YOUR BODY
12. BE AGREEABLE
13. KEEP IT DOWN (AND REDISCOVER SILENCE)
14. RESPECT OTHER PEOPLE'S TIME
15. RESPECT OTHER PEOPLE'S SPACE
16. APOLOGIZE EARNESTLY
17. ASSERT YOURSELF
18. AVOID PERSONAL QUESTIONS
19. CARE FOR YOUR GUESTS
20. BE A CONSIDERATE GUEST
21. THINK TWICE BEFORE ASKING FOR FAVORS
22. REFRAIN FROM IDLE COMPLAINTS
23. ACCEPT AND GIVE CONSTRUCTIVE CRITICISM
24. RESPECT THE ENVIRONMENT &
    BE GENTLE TO ANIMALS
25. DON'T SHIFT RESPONSIBILITY AND BLAME

Happy Birthday to You

The song "Happy Birthday to You" exemplifies two popular American traditions. The first is belting out a joyful tune on the anniversary of someone's birth. The second is lawyering up to protect valuable commerce. Every time you sing the ubiquitous happy birthday song, there is a corporation out there expecting royalties.

The story begins harmlessly enough with sisters Mildred and Patty Hill. The two well-educated women lived in Louisville, Kentucky, and, by 1889, were both successful professionals. Patty, who would later become a professor at Columbia University, worked as a principal at a progressive kindergarten, and Mildred was an accomplished musician (piano and organ) and composer. The pair also collaborated on children's songs, using Patty's kindergarten class as a focus group. "I would take [a song] into school," she'd later say. "If the register was beyond the children, we went back home at night and altered it." They would keep trying until "even the youngest children could learn with perfect ease."

In 1894, they published a collection, *Song Stories for the Kindergarten.* Among the pieces in the book was a little tune called "Good Morning to All." It was the perfect melody for the little ones— each verse was short, words were repeated—and it moved smoothly higher on the register before effortlessly dropping again. Some argue that the music was lifted from other popular songs of the day, but the Hills cleverly copyrighted their work, protecting themselves (at least financially) from such claims.

The tune, like others in the Hills' songbook, could have fallen into obscurity if not for a cultural development taking place at just the right time. The birthday party, particularly for a child, became a popular event starting in the 1870s. Around 1900, the easy-to-croon lyrics of "Good Morning to All" were replaced with the words of "Happy Birthday to You." The new combo proved perfect for these celebrations. Consequently, in the 1910s, the song started popping up in American songbooks. The ditty truly saturated popular culture by the 1930s, with at least two movies (*On the Avenue* and the Oscar-nominated *Stella Dallas*) using the melody in birthday scenes. Between 1933 and 1941, the birthday song was offered up in an estimated 1.5 million singing telegrams.

But the song didn't come free. Thanks to copyright law, those who sing "Happy Birthday to You" are technically required to pay a royalty whenever it is sung in public—whether for commercial purposes or at a family event in the local park. That meant $15,000 to $20,000 a year in royalties were rolling in during the late 1940s and early 1950s. Even Marilyn Monroe should have been required to pay up for the right to famously woo John F. Kennedy with her seductive rendition of "Happy Birthday' Mr. President" at Madison Square Garden in 1962. (It's unlikely that anyone collected.) The value of the song, which is the English language's most publicly performed ditty, continued to skyrocket over the years. By 1996, estimates put the tune's value at just under $2 million a year.

As often happens when there's money to be made, lawyers get involved, and "Happy Birthday to You" was no exception. Its ownership has been the subject of litigation four times, according to an authoritative legal study by law professor Robert Brauneis. While none of those cases ever led to any definitive rulings, Brauneis's work disclosed two key facts (beyond the realization that attorneys were raking in nice fees to litigate these cases). The first is that the Hills may have created the melody, but they probably didn't write the "happy birthday" lyrics (that author has never been identified with certainty). The second is despite that detail, the Hill family held on to the authorship title.

Of course, authorship and ownership are two very different things. The chain of copyright control for "Happy Birthday to You" is complicated, but we do know that since the 1930s, various companies and large corporations have owned at least a piece of it. And you can be sure these businesses take their cut seriously. In 1996, Warner Music Group nearly collected royalties from the Girl Scouts of America for singing "Happy Birthday to You" around the campfire. Mercifully, public pressure

Other Sing-Along Birthday Wishes

Dozens of songs have used the word *birthday* in their title or lyrics. The Beatles' "Birthday," which was written and recorded by the group in a single session, is among the most famous. But Stevie Wonder's "Happy Birthday" may be the most meaningful. Wonder wrote the song in 1981 as part of the campaign for a holiday to commemorate Martin Luther King Jr.'s birth. It must have helped, because in 1986 we began celebrating the civil rights leader on the third Monday in January.

helped scupper the effort. Even a waiter singing the song at a restaurant doesn't fly under the radar. Eateries like Red Lobster, Outback Steakhouse, and Macaroni Grill have all devised their own birthday song to sidestep payments. No doubt, lawyers will continue to listen closely, because under current law, the copyright will remain in private hands until 2030.

Nice Ways to Say NOT—So—Nice Things . . .

The old cliché, "If you don't have anything nice to say, don't say anything at all" (see page 328 for its history) is sometimes a difficult mantra to live up to. Thankfully, Linda Berdoll wrote the book *Very Nice Ways to Say Very Bad Things: An Unusual Book of Euphemisms*. A sampling of her research provides ways to lessen the sting when you just can't hold your tongue.

For those who kiss up, rather than mentioning a certain connection to the rear end, you can try **tuft-hunters**. The term was once a popular slur for social climbers at England's Oxford University. The tuft referred to a special tassel worn on the hats of aristocratic students.

If you want to refer to a woman's "time of the month" in a way that might be even vaguer— and ideally less offensive—**flowers** or **vapors** were popular euphemisms in the Victorian era. You'll probably want to steer clear of another term from that time: **domestic affliction**.

Speaking of behinds, some fun (and less offensive) nicknames for the butt include **ampersand**, **differential**, and the potentially too-obvious **parts behind**. Latin aficionados can deploy the somewhat well-known *gluteus maximus*.

Venereal diseases like gonorrhea and syphilis have drawn a number of relatively benign code names over the years. They've included **bad blood**, **nasty complaint, bone ache**, and **delicate taint**. The most common modern choices, of course, are the **clap** for gonorrhea and the slightly less popular **the pox** for syphilis.

Consuming too much alcohol has always been a source for great terms—**blotto, soused, sauced,** and plain **stinking drunk**, to name a few. But if you want to come across as a bit more erudite, try **bibulous**. While its primary meaning is "highly absorbent," it can also be used for a person who has downed a few too many intoxicating drinks.

To lessen the blow, when observing a lady who isn't very attractive, a soft adjective choice could be **unprepossessing**. It's certainly better than the more obvious **unlovely** or **disagreeable to the eye**. And, if the person also has a sour attitude, rather than calling her a shrew you can go with the more obscure **harridan** or **slattern**.

Have a Nice Day

HAVE A
NICE DAY

menu

ast-food servers say it when handing over French fries. It's printed on novelty napkins along with yellow smiley faces. It's not hard to find T-shirts billboarding the sentiment. "Have a nice day" is a mainstay in everyday conversation. It might not pack the linguistic punch it once provided, but it has been an integral part of the American lexicon since the days of disco.

"I can think of no other phrase or saying which has gained such [a] ubiquitous place in American speech in recent years," wrote renowned syndicated columnist Jack Smith in 1973. "Its function is simply to end some everyday human transaction, social or business, on a note of goodwill."

"Have a nice day" started saturating pop culture in 1970 when brothers Bernard and Murray Spain paired the optimistic slogan with the now iconic yellow smiley face illustration (see Yellow Smiley Face, page 287). The Philadelphia natives were looking for a positive, upbeat message to cut through the dark news enveloping the country (think Vietnam War). At first they went with "Have a happy day," but ultimately shifted to "Have a nice day." The slogan, which has since appeared on every conceivable surface—mostly buttons—was a worldwide hit.

Of course, the brothers were not the first to leverage the sentiment. Long before the saying was slapped on commemorative mugs and beer cozies (and before it became the go-to parting statement of telemarketers and convenience store cashiers around the country), a variation on the phrase "Have a good day" entered the English language in the 1200s. "Nice" took over for "good" in the mid-twentieth century (the expression popped up in the 1949 film *A Letter to Three Wives* starring Kirk

Douglas). While I can't say whether truckers were serious movie fans, big rig drivers started using the optimistic exhortation on citizen-band (aka CB) radios in the 1950s.

Even after it hit the big time, the phrase, like most fads, suffered intense backlash. "The expression has taken the nation by its throat," lamented *New York Times* language maven William Safire in 1979.

In 1988, the Brunswick, Maine, police force banned officers from using the well-worn statement, particularly when giving traffic tickets. It's "nothing short of an absurdly shallow insult," concluded the town's deputy chief Richard Mears.

Among the haters was comedian George Carlin. At least he was able to lighten the mood when riffing on his disgust, and, at the same time, partially explaining why the expression has its detractors. "The problem with 'have a nice day': it puts all the pressure on you," he deadpanned during a 1980s stand-up routine. "Now you've got to go out and somehow manage to have a nice time, all because of some loose-lipped cashier."

Yet, the saying has proved resilient. The rock band Bon Jovi used the phrase for a 2005 song (and album) title. Singer Jon Bon Jovi explained the expression was meant to offer a respectful way to end conversations on touchy subjects like tolerance. So instead of saying, "I hate you," to someone spouting negative ideas, you'd hold your tongue, say, "Have a nice day," and move on. (You rock, Bon Jovi!)

In a more ironic twist, the British group Stereophonics reached number five on the U.K. pop charts in 2001 with "Have a Nice Day," which was allegedly inspired by a grouchy taxicab driver. The phrase, depending on which sources you believe, was used to lampoon the man, society, or both. Whichever is the case, George Carlin would have been proud.

Hip, Hip, Hooray!

We encourage our kids to say it after their Little League games and we use it congratulate our friends. But is "Hip, hip, hooray!" a remnant of oppressive discrimination?

There is a school of thought that suggests that "hip, hip" comes from an early nineteenth-century rallying cry against those of the Jewish faith. In 1819, the Hep Hep Riots, a series of pogroms aimed at Jews in Northern Europe, led to widespread violence. The attackers would shout the strange phrase "hep, hep." Some believe it was a German shepherding expression, while others suggest it had a more erudite (and insidious) background. Supposedly, centuries before, the Crusaders used "hep" as an acronym for the Latin phrase *Hierosolyma est perdita*, which meant "Jerusalem is lost." During the Crusades, it allegedly served as part of a violent slogan against the Jewish people and others.

But the connection between "hep" and "hip" isn't ironclad. A handful of decades after the riots, any sense of a possible connection was already lost to many. "The Europeans, of course, gave voice to the inspiring old 'Hip, hip, hooray!' which no one knows the origin or age or meaning of, but everybody so likes to hear given heartily," an Australia author wrote in 1882. (Geek note: The hip in "hipster" or "hip-hop," likely came from the word *hep* as well. In this case it was a military marching cadence that went "Hep, two, three, four"—the original cool usage probably suggested someone was in step.)

As for "hooray," its history is a little more straightforward. Most agree the term comes from the seventeenth-century sailor salute "huzzah," with the British eventually changing it to "hurrah" and "hurray." According to the *Oxford English Dictionary*, the modern "hooray" spelling launched

Why So Many Cheers?

Nowadays, "Hip, hip, hooray!" is most often heard after an enthusiastic call for **three cheers**. But why do we request three cheers instead of two or four? This is a true linguistic mystery. A 1911 article in the *National Guard Magazine* claimed it had something to do with a three-chord musical salute given to knights going off to the Crusades. Language expert Christine Ammer, author of *The American Heritage Dictionary of Idioms*, disagrees, writing that the three cheers came from the nautical world and first appeared in 1751. Yet, even she can't explain why we insist on three cheers.

in either Australia or New Zealand. (Though some, looking to keep the negative vibe going, believe it stems from a Cossack's menacing shout of attack.)

If "Hip hip, hooray!" did indeed once have horrible connotations, by 1845 it was already a benign, mainstream cheer. That year, the prominent British periodical *Punch* used it in a jaunty poem. At the end of the century, the cheer was hugely popular in America. In 1890, St. John's University included it as part of their college cry: "S-J! S-J! Hip, hip, hooray, hooray!" The musical *Hip! Hip! Hooray!* which featured famed composer John Philip Sousa and his band, was one of the biggest stage spectacles of 1915 and 1916. And, perhaps surprisingly, among its many fans was a Chicago-based Jewish journal *The Reform Advocate*.

Still, the potential connection to anti-Semitism has left some members of the Jewish faith sensitive to the phrase. "Jewish feelings have long been offended by the word[s]," Raymond Apple, the one-time senior rabbi at the Great Synagogue in Sydney, Australia, wrote in 2011. He suggests using the Hebrew words *he'ach, he'ach* (which roughly mean "aha, aha") instead of "hip, hip."

GREAT MINDS
on Nice Manners

Confucius:

The philosopher once wrote, "The superior man is dignified." In regard to a person's "countenance, he is anxious that it should be benign." He also gave advice on listening to and watching carefully what others did. His takeaway: "Considerations for others is the basic of a good life, a good society."

Sir Walter Raleigh:

One of England's great explorers, Raleigh once quipped: "Better were it to be unborn than to be ill bred." Though he took manners seriously, Raleigh certainly had his weak spots. He was once imprisoned by Queen Elizabeth after impregnating and subsequently secretly marrying one of the monarch's ladies-in-waiting. He was later beheaded after being caught in political intrigue.

Benjamin Disraeli:

The talented British prime minister also deliberated on the topic of manners. Included in the book The Wit and Wisdom of Benjamin Disraeli is a section on his favorite manners-related statements. They included: "Nowadays manners are easy and life is hard" and "Manners change with time and circumstances; customs may be observed everywhere."

Ralph Waldo Emerson:

Emerson devoted a whole essay to the topic of manners. Among his conclusions: "Manners aim to facilitate life, to get rid of impediments and bring the man pure to energize. They aid our dealing and conversation as a railway aids traveling, by getting rid of all avoidable obstructions of the road and leaving nothing to be conquered by pure space."

Johann Wolfgang von Goethe:

The German writer and artist claimed, "A man's manners are the mirror in which he shows his portrait."

Benjamin Franklin:

Franklin often touched on manners in his famed Poor Richard's Almanack. He could be stern, with lines like: "Teach your child to hold his tongue; he'll learn fast enough to speak." But he was insightful on the topic of Native Americans: "Savages we call them because their manners differ from ours."

Oscar Wilde:

The writer delivered this manners-inspired joke: "The world was my oyster but I used the wrong fork."

Home, Sweet Home

If there's a needlepoint magazine out there (*Cross Stitch Illustrated*, perhaps?) compiling a list of the art form's ten most popular designs, *Home, Sweet Home* would have to rank near the top. While many primarily know the words thanks to some colorful embroidery framed at Grandma's house, the phrase—and the nineteenth-century song that carries its name—has become a nice way to remind people that where they live is more than just a house.

The song "Home, Sweet Home" was written for the 1823 melodramatic opera *Clari, or the Maid of Milan*, by lyricist John Howard Payne and composer Sir Henry Bishop. Commissioned by a theater in London's Covent Garden, Payne completed his work only to find that another nearby venue was about to embark on a production with a similar plot. He shifted gears and quickly collaborated with Bishop on a number of songs, including "Home, Sweet Home," which appeared in the second act.

The tune would become an American favorite and, by the mid-1800s, no matter what region of the country you came from, it was beloved. Consider this: It was one of the few melodies that soldiers in both the Confederate and Union armies embraced during the Civil War. On the eve of a battle near Murfreesboro, Tennessee, in 1862, musicians from both sides of the hostilities, separated by a mere 700-yard no-man's-land, famously began playing "Home, Sweet Home" in a sort of prebloodshed battle of the bands. Abraham Lincoln loved the song so much that he invited famed Italian opera singer Adelina Patti that year to *his* home, the White House, to perform the tune.

Its popularity lasted. One famous line from the song, "There's no place like home," were the magic words that propelled Dorothy back to her little slice of heaven (aka Kansas) in *The Wizard of Oz*. Judy Garland intersected with "Home, Sweet Home" again, when it was played at a dance in another one of her musicals *Meet Me in St. Louis*.

While the creators of "Home, Sweet Home" fashioned a wonderful melody and memorable turns of phrase, their lives certainly didn't epitomize the ditty. Lyricist Payne was an itinerant soul who never stayed in one place for very long. Born in New York and raised in Boston, Payne became an actor at a young age and traveled the country and the world, often in the name of theater. He lived in Paris, London, and ultimately Africa, where he served as the American consul in Tunis. A humanitarian, he also spent time lobbying for the Cherokees' right to stay on ancestral lands in Georgia. One legend claims that it was homesickness for his family's cottage in East Hampton, New York, that inspired the words to the song.

Payne may never have settled into a picturesque two-story house with a green lawn and white picket fence, but at least he wasn't consumed by multiple home-wrecking dramas. Bishop took that dubious honor. A talented music man, he oversaw the production of more than fifty operas. For his work, he was knighted by Queen Victoria in 1842. Still, his home life was a shambles. Married at a young age, he had three children, but left his wife to tie the knot with

PAYNE SOLD THE RIGHTS TO "HOME, SWEET HOME" AND THE OPERA IT APPEARED IN FOR $100.

a younger and more glamorous lady, singer Anna Riviere. Maybe there were *feng shui* issues in the pair's new abode, because Riviere would later turn around and run off with another man, leaving the famed composer's home none too sweet in the final years of his life.

Put Your Best Foot Forward

Conceptually, the phrase "put your best foot forward" is befuddling. We know it has to do with making a good impression (it's been used in advertising for everything from galoshes to weddings). But which is our "best foot"? And how can putting it forward really make a difference?

The answers may come from the Romans, who had strong opinions on feet and which one was the better of the two. One expert on the phrase, A. Pelzer Wagener, wrote a detailed history of the idiom's history in 1935: "The foot itself, without concern for right or left, is frequently used as symbolical of speed, power, and firmness [in Roman literature]," he wrote. As for which foot was ultimately the best, it was clearly the right one. Romans were often superstitious on this front, with none other than the Emperor Augustus leading the way. The potentate believed so strongly about the varying luck of each foot that he allegedly refused to put on the left sandal before sliding on the right.

Wagener argued the phrase itself came from a famous Latin work, the *Satyricon*. The book, said to be written by the Roman author Gaius Petronius Arbiter, used the Latin expression *pede dextro*. The phrase literally meant "right foot" but it was widely used as a way to wish someone "good luck."

While Wagener's work has an authoritative feel, and the *pede dextro* reference offers a nice sentiment just like putting your best foot forward, there are other theories. Some believe the Roman connection is shaky, in part because the ancient phrase had a different meaning (using "right foot forward" to signal superior fortune) than our modern expression ("presenting oneself in a positive light").

With that in mind, another origin explanation for "put the best foot forward" is far more basic. It began as a metaphor for making a strong first step in a foot race. William Shakespeare was the first English-language author to come up with a similar phrase, writing about putting "the better foot before," in his 1594 play *Titus Andronicus*. About two decades later, author Sir Thomas Overbury refined the idiom when he wrote of "setting the best foot forward" in a poem. Neither writer was referring to luck when they strung those words together, nor did they specify which foot to use.

Still, the authors could have been inspired by *pede dextro*. On the balance, during the period of Shakespeare and Overbury, the right foot remained the favored one. For example, in a 1534 book on husbandry, the author insisted planters step with their right foot first when distributing seeds. Over the years, English brides have been encouraged to step first with the right for luck when entering the church.

However, don't expect anyone nowadays to stump for the right foot. In our modern world, we'll leave it to the individual to choose the best foot.

Sleep Tight, Don't Let the Bedbugs Bite

The cuddle-up invocation "Sleep tight, don't let the bedbugs bite"—which often starts with the wish for a "good night" and ends with hopes that "you wake up bright"—emerged in the late nineteenth century.

One fun origin story, explaining the first part of the phrase "sleep tight," referred to the construction of beds in the early 1800s. Rather than box springs, many mattresses were perched on crisscrossed rope (like a hammock), and sleeping tight meant the rope was pulled taut to give a firm foundation for a good night's sleep.

A more plausible explanation is that the use of *tight* came from a secondary definition of the word used around the same time the phrase took hold. At the beginning of the seventeenth century, according to the *Oxford English Dictionary*, the word *tightly* was defined as "soundly, properly, or vigorously." Sleeping tightly would have been widely understood as shorthand for resting well.

As for the bedbugs, hoping for a night without the vermin taking a bite was a reasonable request. (Of course, it also conveniently rhymed with sleep tight.) Bedbugs are vampires that have plagued humans since at least the ancient Greeks, and likely longer than that. The insects feed exclusively on blood and do their feasting long after dark between midnight and 5 a.m. Scientists believe they got their start sucking blood from bats (the vampire's alter ego) in caves before migrating into beds to dig in on humans. Why infest beds? With sleeping humans, the bedbugs, which painlessly bite their prey, had easy pickings. "Why crawl further than

Other Ways to Sleep

"**Sleep the sleep of the just**," which suggests those with a clear conscience slumber soundly, comes from a 1695 translation of a work penned by French writer Jean-Baptiste Racine. As for advising a person to **"sleep like a log,"** some believe this stems from the obsolete fourteenth-century simile **"sleep like a swine."** Who knew pigs and logs slept so well?

you have to for your next meal?" explained one entomologist.

Still, for most of the second half of the twentieth century, the bedbug phrase was anachronistic. The reason: Chemists found the perfect mixture to ward off these bloodsuckers—DDT. Starting in the 1940s, DDT spray was to bedbugs what a wooden stake is to the heart of a vampire—immediate death. The only problem was that humans and the environment found it devastating as well.

DDT was outlawed for domestic use in the United States in the early 1970s. Even so, for years after the ban, the insects rarely cropped up. But in the mid-1990s, they started making a comeback.

One study concluded that bedbug infestations increased 300 percent between 2000 and 2001. By 2010, the emboldened creatures had branched out from hotels, homes, and college dorms into Laundromats, libraries, movie theaters, and stores.

Some argue chemical companies aren't financially incentivized to come up with a new bedbug repellant unless there are more lucrative agricultural applications. So those wishing to sleep tight will continue to have good reason to hope the bedbugs don't bite for some time to come.

Sugar AND Spice AND Everything Nice

In the battle of the sexes, the centuries-old poem describing girls as being made of "sugar and spice and all things nice," while boys were a combination of "snips and snails and puppy dog tails," had to be an early victory for the ladies.

Yet, ironically, the man who brought this sweet description of little girls into the public eye was far from a protofeminist. Writer Robert Southey (England's Poet Laureate from 1813 to 1843) is credited with popularizing these ingredients, which had previously been part of the oral tradition, by committing them to paper for the first time.

Southey opted to add his own flair to the effort, including an additional ten stanzas to the poem. The additions did not treat the fairer sex nearly as nicely as what he borrowed. He nastily concluded, in his version: "What are some women made of? / Bell metal mouths and leathern lungs / Goose's brains and parrot's tongues."

Lest you think Mr. Southey just had a momentary lapse of gender egalitarianism, he also once told *Jane Eyre* author Charlotte Brontë, "Literature is not the business of a woman's life and it cannot be." In his defense, Southey did end up marrying a successful poet, Caroline Anne Southey, so perhaps his views softened over time.

Happily for future generations—and for stores that like to sell frames, lockets, and other items displaying the "sugar and spice and everything nice" credo—Southey's connection to the phrase didn't stick. Over time, other writers would use the saying in their own work, obscuring Southey's role.

One author in the 1840s added his own ingredients for "young women," writing they were made of "ribbons and laces, and sweet pretty faces." Another nineteenth-century poet followed Southey's cranky lead, saying "old women" came from "bushes and thorns and old cow's horns."

In a lighter take, *The Powerpuff Girls*, an animated series that won two Emmy Awards between 1998 and 2005, provided some additional elements for turning girls into superheroes. The show's main characters, girls with special powers, were made of "8 cups of sugar, a pinch of spice, 1 tablespoon of everything nice" along with an accidental drop of something known as "chemical X."

As for what boys and girls are really made of, it's the same thing: 99 percent is a combination of oxygen, carbon, hydrogen, nitrogen, calcium, and phosphorus. Unfortunately, the other 1 percent is neither sugar nor spice, nor snails and puppy dog tails, for that matter.

NICE Public Places to Go

In the days before we holed up at home with our streaming video, social media, and massive multiplayer online role-playing games, we tried to find activities that got us out of the house. Here are landmark moments from some of our favorite public hangouts:

Circus: Philip Astley, a former English cavalry sergeant major, organized the first circus sometime after 1769. Starting with an equestrian show, he eventually added features such as a strongman, clown, and acrobats. Animals—in the form of two elephants—joined the proceedings by 1816. By then there were circuses throughout Europe.

Concert: While the aristocracy could always muster up a private concert, music for the masses began in London on December 30, 1672. For one shilling, anyone could attend and see singers and musicians perform "very good musick." Egalitarian New Yorkers enjoyed at least forty-six public concerts in the years before the Revolutionary War.

Movie Theater: While films had been shown in makeshift locations since the mid-1880s, the first movie theater was the Cinématographe Lumière in Paris. It opened December 28, 1895, in a former billiard hall. It is thought that the first regular movie house in the U.S. opened its doors in 1896 in New Orleans.

Museum: The first museum opened to the public was Venice's Statuario Pubblico, established in 1596. It remained an attraction for 200 years. Well-to-do locals in Charleston, South Carolina, launched America's first museum in 1772. The building burned down in 1778 (though what remained eventually served as the foundation for the Charleston Museum, which still stands today).

Park: The first public park in the U.S. was the Bowling Green in New York City. Originally a military ground, it opened in 1733. (Boston Common may also stake a claim, but its early uses included other purposes like animal grazing.) The inaugural children's playground is thought to be Washington Park in Chicago, built in 1876.

Sporting Events: Sports as a public spectacle dates back to ancient times, but in the U.S., our favorite teams didn't start luring paying customers until the late nineteenth century. Baseball's Cincinnati Red Stockings were the first professional baseball club, selling some 200,000 tickets during a 12,000-mile tour that began March 15, 1869. Basketball became a pro sport in 1896 in Trenton, New Jersey, while football got its start a year earlier in Pennsylvania.

Swimming Pool: London's *Daily Advertiser* heralded what was likely the first modern public swimming pool in 1742. Advertisements for the 43-foot-long pool promised attendants and warm water cleaned daily. America joined the fad in 1791, when John Coyle opened a pool in Philadelphia.

Zoo: Royalty and the überwealthy have enjoyed private menageries since antiquity, but the first one available for public enjoyment in the modern Western world was established in the Jardin des Plantes in Paris in 1793. The original collection of animals came from varied sources, including traveling sideshows, Versailles's royal menagerie, and the spoils of France's recent battle with the Netherlands.

Nice Characters

Cupid

Would the real Cupid please stand up? For most romantics, it's easy to picture Cupid, complete with a sweet baby face, wings, a bow, and tiny love-inducing, gold-tipped arrows (and, to keep him PG-rated, wearing some cloth diapers).

Sorry, lovers, the original story of Cupid isn't so simple. Ancient poets mention many different Cupids, each one with a variety of godly parents. The earliest tales featuring the steamy deity (Cupid

Attractive Lips

The phrase **"Cupid's bow"** doesn't just refer to the weapon of love wielded by the tiny immortal. It's also a term used to describe the shape of the upper lip, which has a similar curvature to the mythological bow. According to one study, most women believe they look more attractive if they have a full, nicely defined Cupid's bow.

comes from the Latin *cupere*, meaning "to desire") ditches the cutesy cherub for a robust man, who got himself into an R-rated romance.

Around 700 B.C., the Greek poet Hesiod was the first to write about the character we now know as Cupid. Back then, he was called Eros and was one of the four original gods at the time of Earth's creation. Rather than an adorable little mischief maker, Eros was described by Hesiod as "loveliest of all the immortals, who makes . . . men's bodies go limp, mastering their minds and subduing their wills."

This wasn't the guy you'd find on a box of chocolates. "Eros is not cute in the Greek conception," University of Kansas classics professor Tara Welch explained in a 2000 interview. "He's awe inspiring." The potent Eros drove many a god to love, from Pluto, the god of the underworld, to Apollo, the deity of reason.

But the ultrapowerful Cupid eventually deals with *amore* like the rest of us. In a second-century tale penned by Apuleius, the studly god is sent by his mother, Venus, goddess of love, to make Psyche, a beautiful princess, fall madly in love with a hideous monster. (Venus was jealous of Psyche's mortal popularity.) Instead, Cupid falls for the stunning Psyche after being pricked by his own arrow. Drama ensues, including Cupid posing as a monster and Venus requiring Psyche to endure a series of trials. In the end, the pair lives happily ever after.

NOT ONLY HAS THE STORY OF CUPID AND PSYCHE BEEN THE SUBJECT OF GREAT ART, BUT SOCCER'S DAVID BECKHAM (A DEMIGOD IN HIS OWN RIGHT) HAS A TATTOO FEATURING THE PAIR ON HIS LEFT ARM.

As the story of Cupid developed in the Roman era, he began to multiply. Cicero cited three Cupids, all with different parents, and Plato mentioned two. During this period, the depiction of a mischievous winged child or baby began to emerge. "He is represented as amusing himself with childish diversions," according to one nineteenth-century author.

As the god who spreads love, Cupid's connection to Valentine's Day makes sense. But the holiday's indelible tie with Cupid was likely sealed by the greeting cards industry, which cottoned to the sweeter images of Cupid from the very beginning. There are numerous examples of Cupid fronting cards from the first decade of the twentieth century, and it's likely the winged archer made appearances on the earliest cards produced in the second half of the 1800s.

Easter Bunny

All around the world, Easter inspires some head-scratching traditions. In Sweden and parts of Finland, children dress up as Easter witches in the week leading up to the holiday. (The Scandinavians have a myth that sorceresses fly around just before Easter and must be scared off with bonfires.) In Latin America, it's not uncommon to burn the betraying apostle Judas in effigy. This often includes a modern twist: For example, in a 2008 Venezuelan celebration, Judas was depicted as an Exxon employee after litigation with the company didn't go the country's way.

Of all the seemingly baffling Easter traditions, the most well known is the Easter Bunny and the animal's penchant for eggs. This enduring oddity (eggs and rabbits?) is a result of good marketing. And for once, chocolate makers and stuffed animal manufacturers are off the hook. It was early Christian leaders who deserve credit for employing a soft sell as the religion spread in the second century to the Teutonic people in northern Europe.

Rather than try to fight pagan rituals, missionaries either incorporated some indigenous customs or politely overlooked others. There was a practical reason for this. If Christians were celebrating at a time other than a local pagan holiday, nonbelievers might grow angry (Why do they get to party when we don't?). By aligning some holidays and habits with the natives, it caused less of a disturbance.

The Easter Bunny likely emerged from these efforts. The rabbit was originally a hare (they look like our beloved fluffy creatures but are more athletic, a little less cute, and live in fields rather than underground). The hare was the earthly sign of Eostre, the Anglo-Saxon goddess of fertility. At the start of spring, European pagans held festivals to celebrate the deity. When Christians began observing Christ's rebirth around the same time as the Eostre feast, they co-opted the name and, though not officially, accepted the hare as part of the celebration.

Germans immigrating to America in the eighteenth and nineteenth centuries brought the long-eared tradition with them, subbing in little white bunnies, which were more plentiful in the New World. Still, many denominations, like the Puritans and the Presbyterians, saw the rabbit as a frivolous addition, and it wasn't until after the Civil War that the bunny really caught on.

As for the animal's connection to eggs, it probably started in stories passed down in the oral tradition but was bolstered by the written word. A sixteenth-century German author first floated the combo in print with the following puzzling passage: "Do not worry if the bunny escapes you; should we miss his eggs then we shall cook the nest." That practice wouldn't leave too many modern kids happy, but it was a start. Mentions of the pair appear in the following century, when another German book described a hare laying eggs and hiding them in a garden.

Though biologically impossible, the figurative connection between the rabbit and eggs makes sense as the egg, like the bunny, is a lasting symbol of new life. From a practical standpoint, eggs were also often given up during Lent. Accordingly, they were popular gifts when it became permissible to dig in again on Easter. Some claim that coloring eggs grew out of a need for people to do something with all the eggs they'd prohibited themselves from eating. Dyed eggs are still a popular Easter symbol, but chocolate is the treat of choice. In the U.S. alone, more than $2 billion is spent on the confection each Easter season.

NICE HOLIDAYS

2000 B.C.: The earliest known **New Year's** festival occurred in Babylonia, and it was celebrated around what we now know as late March. The Romans shifted the holiday to January 1 around 153 B.C. Still, some cultures didn't buy in. In fact, a January New Year's has only been widely accepted for about four centuries. As for the Times Square ball drop, that didn't come around until 1908.

Fifth century B.C.: Although days honoring the dead are a worldwide phenomenon, our **Halloween** cames from the Celts in Ireland. Called All Hallows Eve, the festival took place on October 31—the day that those who died in the past year congregated in preparation for moving into the afterlife. To keep those not-so-nice souls away, the Celts would dress up as scary witches or demons.

A.D. 493: Likely born in what is today Wales (gasp, *not* Ireland), the future St. Patrick was captured as a teenager and forced to herd sheep in Ireland. He eventually escaped the Emerald Isle and studied at a monastery in Auxerre in modern-day France. Later, he returned to Ireland as a bishop, successfully converting many locals to Catholicism. For his efforts, he is remembered on March 17, which is believed to be the day he died, with **St. Patrick's Day**.

Fifth century: The namesake for **Valentine's Day** had a reputation as a romantic long before he got his own holiday. In 270, Valentine crossed the Roman emperor Claudius II by performing marriages, despite a royal edict banning the practice. (Claudius was worried that married young men wouldn't go to war on behalf of the empire.) Valentine was imprisoned and eventually executed for his efforts. But before his death, he fell in love with a woman to whom he wrote loving letters (hence, valentines). The holiday, originally on February 15, was organized by early Christians as an alternative to the Roman festival Lupercalia.

1863: School children will probably tell you that the first **Thanksgiving** feast occurred in 1621 in Plymouth, Massachusetts, and was a get-together featuring the Pilgrims and Native Americans. But it was a decidedly non–New Englander, Abraham Lincoln, who put the celebration on our permanent calendar. The president was likely swayed by Sarah Josepha Hale, editor of the magazine *Godey's Lady's Book*, who had campaigned to make the meal a national holiday. Originally held on the fourth Thursday in November, it was moved to the third Thursday in 1939. The reason: capitalism. Thanksgiving marked the unofficial start of the Christmas season and merchants wanted more time to sell their holiday wares.

1868: John A. Logan, an Illinois congressman, stumped for a special holiday to be set on May 30. The event was originally known as Decoration Day and its post–Civil War purpose was to laud "comrades who died in defense of their country during the late rebellion." The holiday, which was renamed **Memorial Day** after World War I, was expanded to cover the casualties of all conflicts. It became a national holiday in 1971, when Congress moved it from May 30 to the final Monday in May.

1870: Nearly every American can tell you that **Independence Day** celebrates the signing of the Declaration of Independence on July 4, 1776. But far fewer know that it wasn't until August 2 of that year that the members of the Continental Congress ratified the document, actually putting it into effect. Nevertheless, July 4 was chosen as the important date, though it took until 1870 to become a formal holiday and it wasn't declared a federal government day off until 1941.

1894: The U.S. Congress designated the first Monday in September as a federal holiday called **Labor Day** in 1894, but supporters started picketing for a special day dedicated to America's workers long before that. On September 5, 1882, New York City held the first Labor Day parade. In 1884, the American Federation of Labor began lobbying for the holiday. Three years later, Oregon, Colorado, and New York became the first trailblazing states to recognize the day.

1908: Mother's Day as we know it first occurred on May May 10, 1908 in Grafton, West Virginia. The initial proposal for the holiday, made the year before by Anna Jarvis, a mother, was pretty modest: that the day involve some religious exhortations praising Mom and the distribution of carnations—her mom's favorite flower—to mothers and their children. While the carnation gesture didn't become universal, the sentiment did. Though other cultures had long set aside time for maternal rejoicing (the British, for example, celebrate Mothering Sunday during Lent), President Woodrow Wilson proclaimed a U.S. holiday on May 10, 1914.

1910: The concept of **Father's Day** quickly followed the maternal day of observance. The seeds were first planted in Spokane, Washington, by Sonora Smart Dodd, whose father had reared six children after his wife had died. Backed by local ministers and the YMCA, the occasion was seen as a nice complement to Mother's Day, which had yet to earn official nationwide status. Still, Congress didn't officially give dads their special day until 1972. Originally observed on July 19, it was later moved to the third Sunday in June.

1919: Veteran's Day made its debut on November 11, one year to the day after World War I ended. Known as Armistice Day, solemn public meetings and prayers, along with more upbeat parades, were encouraged. Also a two-minute moment of silence was expected at 11 a.m., the time when the hostilities officially ceased.

1986: Martin Luther King Day did not happen overnight. The first bill aimed at recognizing the civil rights leader was submitted to Congress in 1968, just four days after he was assassinated. It took another eighteen years before it received national holiday status to be observed on the third Monday in January.

Fairy Godmother

Even fairy godmothers need help from a good man every once in a while.

Frenchman Charles Perrault was their greatest benefactor. But before he spruced up their reputations, the ancestors to our fairy godmothers were pretty formidable ladies who often made life hard on humans. For example, the Norns of Norse mythology were female beings who decided the destinies of individuals, and while they often looked kindly on people, sometimes they weren't so nice (they were often blamed for deaths). In Greek mythology, the Fates, known as the Moirai, were a trio of other-worldly women who performed as advertised, charting out mortals' futures. The Greeks believed that they were on hand at the births, prepared to determine each child's path.

Many early folktales featured similar all-seeing women—fairies who were powerful, but not always kind. So why do fairy godmothers give us the warm fuzzies today?

Perrault deseves some credit. A successful member of the bourgeoisie during the reign of the Sun King Louis XIV, Perrault studied law but yearned for the arts. His wealth gave him the freedom to pursue his passion. He authored a number of significant works and became a high-profile member of L'Académie Française, which regulated grammar, spelling, and literature in France.

Although a serious man, Perrault didn't shy away from fantastical stories. In 1696, while in his late sixties, Perrault collected and published a compendium of old folktales for children—known to English speakers as *The Tales of Mother Goose*. Throughout his writing life, Perrault argued that the contributions of contemporary modern writers were greater than those of the ancients. And so it should come as no surprise that he took liberties with many of the yarns, updating them to reflect the values of the Age of Enlightenment.

He brought the fairy godmother (as we now know her) into the modern world with his telling of *Cendrillon*, or *Cinderella*. Similar rags-to-riches fairy-tale love stories had been told in cultures from East Asia to Europe. But Perrault added so many of the touches we know today: the wicked step-sisters; the glass slipper; and, of course, the ultrabenevolent fairy godmother. Who could ever forget that kindly winged sprite who could turn a pumpkin into a coach, a rat into a coachman, mice into powerful horses, and transform Cinderella's tattered dress into a stunning gown? Cinderella's fairy godmother ushered in the age of the kind, loving, helpful, and superpowerful lady friend.

FAIRY—TALE AUTHOR CHARLES PERRAULT WAS CREDITED WITH CONVINCING LOUIS XIV TO INSTALL FORTY FOUNTAINS AT HIS STATELY PALACE AT VERSAILLES REPRESENTING AESOP'S FABLES.

Perrault, whose other tales included *Puss in Boots*, *Little Red Riding Hood*, and *Bluebeard*, didn't let all magical fairies off the hook. In *Sleeping*

Beauty, the king and queen invite a group of fairies to serve as godmothers to their long-desired newborn girl. Another fairy, snubbed by the royal parents, jealously throws a curse on the baby, foretelling her untimely demise. (Luckily, one of the kinder fairies commutes the princess's death sentence; instead of dying, she'll sleep until kissed by a prince.) But *Cinderella* was arguably his most popular. And when Disney, in its 1950 animated version of the story, depicted the title character's fairy godmother as a sweet maternal figure, the fairy godmother's destiny was set on the side of nice for generations to come.

Santa Claus

Everything wasn't always so *ho, ho, ho* for the man we know as Santa Claus.

Born around the year 270, Nicholas lost his parents at a young age and devoted himself to his Christian faith. He became the Bishop of Myra (located in modern Turkey) and was renowned for his generosity and gift giving. Despite his benevolent ways, he was persecuted by the Roman ruler Diocletian. Imprisoned and tortured, Nicholas persevered until Constantine the Great took the throne.

The ruler would ultimately convert to Christianity, and freed Nicholas to return to his good works.

Historians believe the bishop died between 342 and 352. From there, it was a long road to the brightly dressed jolly fat man that we all know from popular culture. Designated a saint before the Catholic Church's official canonization process began in the tenth century, St. Nicholas was in fact a skinny man. Still, some parts of his legend would be recognizable today. For example, he supposedly wore a red bishop's coat and had a long white beard. There are also stories that he left gifts in the shoes of little children. No reindeer, though. He apparently traveled via donkey.

The saint's status grew among Catholics, and Justinian I erected a church in his honor in the sixth century. Around that time, it became customary as part of a feast on December 6 (purportedly the day of his death) to give children small presents left in shoes, just like St. Nick. Instead of cookies, kids left a little hay for his donkey.

But Santa would have never made his global rounds if not for the fine folks of the Netherlands. You see, St. Nick is also one of the patron saints of mariners, and held a special place in the hearts of the seafaring Dutch. In the sixteenth century, as

Santa's Most Famous Reindeer

Rudolph the Red-Nosed Reindeer was a relatively late addition to the Christmas story. He was created by copywriter Robert May in 1939 as a way to get families excited about shopping at Montgomery Ward department stores throughout the U.S. The animal with a special nose quickly took off as 2.4 million copies of his story titled *Rudolph* were distributed nationwide in booklet form. May initially wanted to name his reindeer Rollo but was overruled by Montgomery Ward execs.

leaders of the Protestant Reformation were cutting back on festivals venerating Catholic saints, St. Nicholas—known in Dutch as *Sinterklass*—fell out of favor in many parts of Europe. But the Dutch held on to their beloved saint and all the frivolity that surrounded him.

When Dutch families immigrated to the American colonies beginning in the seventeenth century, they brought the fun of St. Nicholas with them. Under the influence of the English language, his name would transform from Sinterklass to Santa

Claus. Other newcomers to America had different titles for him. The British dubbed him Father Christmas, the Russians called him Uncle Frost (or *Dyet Moroz*), and from the Germans came Kris Kringle. The latter was a mistaken take on the German word *Christkindlein*, which means the "Child in the Manger" or "Little Christ Child."

In the nineteenth century, Santa Claus began to develop his more iconic look. Our current traditions also took shape. Shoes were replaced with stockings (better for holding multiple presents) and the 1823 poem "The Night Before Christmas" put Santa in his flying sleigh and gave him reindeer to power it. American illustrator Thomas Nast, who drew Christmas pictures for *Harper's Weekly* between the 1860s and 1880s, nudged the evolution of St. Nick into a rotund merrymaker. Making his home at the North Pole was a detail likely invented in the 1860s.

Nowadays, Santa is high tech, thanks to a little military assistance. Since the 1950s, the North American Aerospace Defense Command (NORAD) has tracked Santa's Christmas Eve route. Its website receives nearly 9 million visitors annually.

Stork

"Where do babies come from?" Nearly every parent has faced this vexing inquiry. In his typically clinical style, Sigmund Freud described this query as "the oldest and most burning question that confronts immature humanity." For generations, those who wanted to avoid getting into the carnal logistics of the process—there's been the stork.

The idea of a gangly-legged, big-beaked bird ferrying newborns to waiting parents seems like the type of explanation a parent of yore gave in a moment of utter nerve-rattling panic ("Uhhh, let's just say your sister was brought to us by a large winged animal").

And, yet, there is good reason why storks are appropriate players in the story of childbirth. For the family values set, the stork has long represented a domestic ideal. The animals are serially monogamous and have a reputation for both nurturing their young with enthusiasm and taking care of their old. The Roman goddess Juno, who among other duties was connected to fertility and childbirth, was closely associated with storks. As for the bird's respect for the aged, the Romans had *Lex cinconaria* (translation: "Stork's Law"), which required children to provide for their parents "in imitation of the stork."

Farther to the north, Scandinavians tied the storks' familial ways with their tendency to nest on chimneys of dwellings. The combo (good with family and close to home) was probably the root of the whole stork-bringing-a-baby link. Hans Christian Andersen is credited with popularizing the connection. His 1838 story *The Storks* centered on a family of the birds that were being harassed by a group of small children. At the end of the fairy tale, the storks seek revenge. In Andersen's emblematic tough-love style, the birds don't necessarily live up to their gentle reputation.

Oh Mister . . .

The **Sandman,** an otherworldly character who sprinkles sand into the eyes of children to put them to sleep, has been described in folktales—depending on who you read—as either a benign or a bad character. Hans Christian Andersen suggested he was a good guy, who brought nice dreams to good children (bad kids just didn't get dreams). But E.T.A. Hoffmann, writer of the novelette that the ballet *The Nutcracker* is based on, had his sandman steal children's eyes.

"I know the pond in which all the little mortals lie till the stork comes and brings them to their parents," the mother stork said in the fable. "The pretty little babies lie there and dream so sweetly as they never dream afterwards." Her twisted plan: The storks will bring their biggest tormentor a stillborn brother. And for one of their defenders, he would receive both a brother and a sister.

While the part about delivering babies stuck, the darker shades of the tale were thankfully left behind by future storytellers, helping parents everywhere steer clear of yet another awkward explanation.

Tooth Fairy

I f you take a moment to think about the Tooth Fairy—a creature who comes into your children's room late at night to snatch dislodged teeth in return for money—it's pretty weird. The quick explanation from sociologists and psychologists is that this strange ritual began as a way to help children through this painful rite of passage.

But there's got to be further clarification. After all, we don't have fairies descending when kids break bones or are nervous before their first day of school. No, the reason your choppers get this particular attention comes from the historical symbolism surrounding teeth.

For adults, losing them meant bad things. The Bible describes people asking God to bust an enemy's teeth—one the harshest requests one could make. And in some African cultures, a rightful heir to the throne couldn't be crowned if he had a chipped or missing tooth. When it comes to kids, there have also been stories of witches stealing little teeth in order to cast spells on children. With so much riding on these calcified suckers, societies have long held superstitions about how to safely dispose of baby teeth.

In Mexico, this meant giving wee teeth to a mouse (the Cherokee gave them to a beaver); in New Guinea, they were to be buried with an ancestor; in Vietnam, a tooth from the upper row was thrown over the roof of a house, while a lower one was tossed on the ground in the hope that a rat would take it away. The most committed ritual: Parents in the Spreewald region of Germany would actually swallow their children's baby teeth.

Unlike these ancient acts, the Tooth Fairy is a comparatively new concept. It got its start in the United States at the beginning of the twentieth century. Researchers aren't certain who invented the fairy, but by the second decade of the 1900s, some American newspapers were endorsing the character as a way to con kids into letting their parents pull out wobbly baby incisors and molars.

"Many a refractory child will allow a loose tooth to be removed if he knows about the tooth fairy," *The Fort Wayne* (Indiana) *Journal Gazette* wrote in 1917. "If he takes his little tooth and puts it under the pillow when he goes to bed, the tooth fairy will come in the night and take it away and in its place will leave some little gift. It is nice for mothers to visit the 5-cent counter and lay in a supply of articles to be used on such occasions."

Despite the paper's advice and some early literary efforts (a short children's play, *The Tooth Fairy*, debuted in 1927), the tooth-taking sprite didn't really catch on until the 1950s. With the post–World War II bump in disposable income, presents or a bit of money was an affordable extravagance.

The price per tooth has been contemplated by adults ever since. In fact, beginning in the 1970s, Rosemary Wells, who was a dental school lecturerand longtime curator of The Tooth Fairy Museum in Deerfield, Illinois, tracked the rise in cost of baby teeth for decades (see chart).

Toothy Fairy Prices
A Look at the Rise in Cost of Baby Teeth

1900: 12 cents	**1991:** $1
1956: 19 cents	**1997:** $1.50
1966: 30 cents	**2009:** $1.88
1981: 66 cents	**2010:** $3

Sources: *Chicago Tribune, New York Daily News, Lancaster* (Pennsylvania) *Intelligencer Journal, Sacramento Bee*

Still, this financial exchange does not sit well with everyone. "The tooth fairy is modeled after the exchange ritual of our capitalistic society," folklore author Tad Tuleja told the *Chicago Tribune* in 1991. "Children learned to take an item, even a part of their body, and exchange for coins."

But the far less grumpy Wells, who died in 2001, had a more upbeat take on the oddest of all fairies: "The tooth fairy's job is to conduct a rite of passage that helps the child move to the next stage of life," she said.

Appendix

Further Reading

While it's not likely that there is another volume as nice-centric as this one, many books have touched on topics discussed in these pages. If you're searching for more information, check out the following sources:

Adamson, Melitta Weiss, and Francine Segan, eds. *Entertaining from Ancient Rome to the Super Bowl: An Encyclopedia*. Westport, CT: Greenwood, 2008.

Ammer, Christine. *The Facts on File Dictionary of Clichés*. 3rd ed. New York: Facts on File, 2011.

Bremner, Robert H. *Giving: Charity and Philanthropy in History*. New Brunswick, NJ: Transaction, 2000.

Elias, Norbert. *The History of Manners*. New York: Urizen Books, 1978.

Hendrickson, Robert. *The Facts on File Encyclopedia of Words and Phrase Origins*. 4th ed. New York: Facts on File, 2008.

Kane, Joseph Nathan, Steven Anzovin, and Janet Podell. *Famous First Facts*. 6th ed. New York: H. W. Wilson, 2006.

Leeming, David Adams, and Marion Sader, eds. *Storytelling Encyclopedia*. Westport, CT: Greenwood, 1997.

Lundmark, Torbjörn. *Tales of Hi and Bye: Greeting and Parting Rituals Around the World*. Cambridge: Cambridge University Press, 2009.

Morris, Desmond, Peter Collett, Peter Marsh, and Marie O'Shaughnessy. *Gestures*. New York: Stein and Day, 1979.

Opie, Iona, and Peter Opie, eds. *The Oxford Dictionary of Nursery Rhymes*. New York: Oxford University Press, 1997.

Panati, Charles. *Panati's Extraordinary Origins of Everyday Things*. New York: Perennial Library, 1987.

Patrick, Bethanne Kelly. *An Uncommon History of Common Courtesy*. Washington, DC: National Geographic, 2011.

Patrick, Bethanne, and John Thompson. *An Uncommon History of Common Things*. Washington, DC: National Geographic, 2009.

Post, Emily. *Etiquette in Society, in Business, in Politics, and at Home*. New York: Funk & Wagnalls, 1922.

Radford, Edwin, and Mona A. Radford. *Encyclopedia of Superstitions*. New York: Philosophical Library, 1949.

Robertson, Patrick. *Robertson's Book of Firsts: Who Did What for the First Time*. New York: Bloomsbury, 2011.

Tuleja, Tad. *Curious Customs: The Stories Behind 296 Popular American Rituals*. New York: Harmony, 1987.

Visser, Margaret. *The Gift of Thanks: The Roots and Rituals of Gratitude*. Boston, MA: Houghton Mifflin Harcourt, 2009.

Visser, Margaret. *The Rituals of Dinner: The Origins, Evolution, Eccentricities, and Meaning of Table Manners*. New York: Grove, 1991.

Notes

For easier reading, I did not include citations for quoted remarks in the text of this book. But it wouldn't be nice if I didn't give credit where credit is due. So the following notes provide source information on all quotes used. They are listed by page number in the book. Unless indicated otherwise, definitions in the book came from the online version of the *Oxford English Dictionary* at www.oed.com. Any omitted documentation was truly inadvertent. You'll find citations for various sidebars, charts, lists, and timelines at the end of the list.

INTRODUCTION

ix "If you ever want . . . doubt and pessimism." Gabe Habash, "The Worst Word in the English Language is 'Nice,'" *Publishers Weekly*, October 19, 2011, blogs.publishersweekly.com/blogs/PWxyz/?p=7386&utm_source=Publishers+Weekly%27s+PW+Daily&utm_campaign=b0240b9b4f-UA-15906914-1&utm_medium=email.

x "I know what . . . a lot of character." George Carlin, accessed December 5, 2012, www.youtube.com/watch?v=7vmknnXoOJk.

NICE HANDIWORK

APPLAUSE

7 "an appropriate way . . . something good has occurred." Marcel Berlins, "Can Applause Really Replace the Minute's Silence?" *The Guardian*, September 11, 2007: www.guardian.co.uk/comment isfree/2007/sep/12/comment.comment2.

BLOWING A KISS

8 "lifting the hand." James Hastings, ed., *Encyclopaedia of Religion and Ethics* (New York: Charles Scribner's Sons, 1922), 757.

9, 10 "slavish," "those solemnities that . . . they were holy things," and "The secret . . . to the informal" Desmond Morris, Peter Collett, Peter Marsh, and Marie O'Shaughnessy, *Gestures* (New York: Stein and Day, 1979), 4, 7.

FIST BUMP

12 "With its restraint . . . rapturous high-five," and "an aroused emotional . . . or fear," Stephan Talty, "Noticed: A Bump and No Shake," *The New York Times*, November 25, 2001, 9.

15 "the fist bump . . . the world," Amy Argetsinger and Roxanne Roberts, "The First Couple: Giving a Big Bump to Authenticity," *The Washington Post*, June 5, 2008, www.washingtonpost.com/ wp-dyn/content/article/2008/06/04/AR2008060404521.html.

15 "'Hezbollah' . . . fist-jabbing." Christopher Beam, "Pounds," *Slate*, June 4, 2008, www.slate.com/blogs/trailhead/2008/06/04/ pounds.html.

15 "It captures what . . . silly things." M. J. Stephey, "A Brief History of the Fist Bump," *TIME*, June 5, 2008, www.time.com/time/ nation/article/0,8599,1812102,00.html.

HANDSHAKE

17 "The origin . . . weapons in reserve." Mary Holland, "Handshakes Follow When Leaders Have Respect for Each Other," *Irish Times*, September 10, 1998, 16.

18 "a firm exhortation to burn all discord in the fire of love." Jan Bremmer and Herman Roodenburg, eds., *A Cultural History of Gesture: From Antiquity to the Present Day* (Cambridge: Polity Press, 1991), 174.

18 "in rather poor . . . receiving a rebuke," Torbjörn Lundmark, *Tales of Hi and Bye: Greeting and Parting Rituals Around the World* (Cambridge: Cambridge University Press, 2009), 60.

18 "firm . . . but not weak." Chris Moncrieff, "To Shake or Not to Shake," *Press Association*, March 6, 2012.

19 "Hand, hand . . . or your scum!" Chris Emery, "A Hands-Off Approach," *Baltimore Sun*, July 5, 2007, 1C.

HANDS JOINED IN PRAYER
20 "looked upon . . . token of trouble." Lucy M. Mitchell, *A History of Ancient Sculpture* (New York: Dodd, Mead, 1883), 552.

HIGH FIVE
23, 25 "one of the most contagious . . . matter, American life" and "I thought, yeah and jump so high," Jon Mooallem, "The History and Mystery of the High Five," *ESPN The Magazine*, July 29, 2011, espn.go.com/espn/story/_/id/6813042/who-invented-high-five.

HOLDING HANDS
30 "Hand-holding is . . . demonstration about coupledom," Stephanie Rosenbloom, "A Simple Show of Hands," *The New York Times*, October 5, 2006, www.nytimes.com/2006/10/05/fashion/05hands.html?pagewanted=all.

30 "holding hands . . . starlight." Associated Press, "Clark Gable is Divine, Della Carroll Coos," *Spokesman-Review* (Washington), November 28, 1935, 5.

31 "eyeball to eyeball," accessed December 5, 2012, www.beatlesinterviews.org/dba02with.html.

32 "disorderly conduct . . . offensive condition" John Nolan (Associated Press), "Judge Clears Men for Holding Hands: Freedom of Association Cited," *Register-Guard* (Eugene, Oregon), October 26, 1990, 6A.

I-L-Y SIGN
34 "Its popularity rose . . . decals with the sign I-L-Y." Author e-mail correspondence with Benjamin Bahan, March 20, 2012.

35 "By the time . . . it has become." Cathryn Carroll and Catherine Hoffpauir Fischer, *Orchid of the Bayou: A Deaf Woman Faces Blindness* (Washington, DC: Gallaudet University Press, 2001), 121.

OKAY SIGN
36 "an uncomplaining . . . 'OK' spoken aloud." Allan Metcalf, *OK: The Improbable Story of America's Greatest Word* (New York: Oxford University Press, 2011), 4.

37 "a graceful gesture . . . relate, distinguish or approve." Desmond Morris, Peter Collett, Peter Marsh, and Marie O'Shaughnessy, *Gestures* (New York: Stein and Day, 1979), 103.

SALUTE
43 "The men are . . . bow as they pass." U.S. Army Quartermaster Center and School, "Historical Vignettes," accessed December 5, 2012, www.qmmuseum.lee.army.mil/history/vignettes/respect1 .html.

44 "The American Patriotic . . . and our Country!" and "One Country! . . . One Flag!" Marc Leepson, *Flag: An American Biography* (New York: St. Martin's Griffin, 2006), 164.

44 "juvenile . . . in dignity." "Columbus and the Pledge," *Wisconsin State Journal*, October 15, 1992, 13A.

SHAKA SIGN (HANG LOOSE)
47 "One of his jobs . . . the way was clear." June Watanabe, "Wherever It Came From, Shaka Sign Part of Hawaii," *Honolulu Star-Bulletin*

(Hawaii), March 31, 2002, archives.starbulletin.com/2002/03/31/ news/kokualine.html. 48 "shark eye . . . plausible explanation." June Watanabe, "Interesting Stories Pour in on the Shaka Sign's Origin," *Honolulu Star-Bulletin* (Hawaii), April 21, 2002, archives.star bulletin.com/2002/04/21/news/kokualine.html.

49 "I think it . . . world of goodness," Treena Shapiro, "Could the Shaka Become a Sign of Peace?" *Honolulu Star-Bulletin* (Hawaii), July 9, 1999, archives.starbulletin.com/1999/07/09/news/story8 .html.

THUMBS-UP
51–53 "This made sense . . . be visible to all," "disfavor or disgrace," "an expression importing . . . of praise," and "first class." Desmond Morris, Peter Collett, Peter Marsh, and Marie O'Shaughnessy, *Gestures* (New York: Stein and Day, 1979), 187, 189, 191, 192.

53 "Here's my thumb on it." Nancy Armstrong and Melissa Wagner, *Field Guide to Gestures: How to Identify and Interpret Virtually Every Gesture Known to Man* (Philadelphia: Quirk Books, 2003), 53.

WAVE
55 "People such as . . . there to wave." *Onion*, March 5, 2008, www .youtube.com/watch?v=n5pkDB7zEeo.

56 "the president is . . . such an image." Dan Amira, "President Obama Waving Grudgingly," *New York*, February 22, 2011, nymag .com/daily/intel/2011/02/president_obama_waving_grudgin.html.

56 "Why well to do . . . a moving train." *Daily World* (Lawrence, Kansas), October 11, 1892, 2.

OTHER NICE PHYSICAL GESTURES
BOWING
63 "a sign of . . . testimony of submission." Juliet Lapidos, "How Ceremonious You Are!" *Slate*, November 17, 2009, www.slate.com/

articles/news_and_politics/explainer/2009/11/how_ceremonious_
you_are.html.

64 "Daily, across America . . . physical act of bowing." Andi Young,
The Sacred Art of Bowing: Preparing to Practice (Woodstock, VT:
SkyLight Paths, 2003), 14.

COVERING A YAWN
66 "There is no excuse . . . while yawning." Abigail Van Buren,
"Dear Abby," *Register-Guard* (Eugene, Oregon), August 16, 1963,
12A.

HELPING AN ELDERLY WOMAN CROSS THE STREET
70–71 "a bit," "to help . . . cross the street." Robert Baden-Powell,
Scouting for Boys: The Original 1908 Edition (New York: Oxford
University Press, 2004), 23.

72 "Woodward had the disarming . . . across the street," Colin
Powell with Joseph E. Persico, *My American Journey* (New York:
Ballantine, 1995), 407.

HUGGING
74 "There seems to . . . well as he should." David Streitfeld,
"Celebrations Embracing a Holiday for Huggers," *The Washington
Post*, June 16, 1986, C5.

74 "Infant Hugging and Comforting Device," "cloth hugging" and
"adjustable arm portions," "U.S. Patent Issued on March 1 for 'Infant
Hugging and Comforting Device,'" *U.S. Fed News*, March 3, 2011.

75 "inappropriate behavior." "Australian School Bans Hugs
Between Preteen Boys, Girls to Set Example for Younger Students,"
Toronto Star, October 20, 2009, 1.

75 "Touching and physical . . . happening all day." Sarah Kershaw,
"For Teenagers, Hello Means 'How About a Hug?'" *The New
York Times*, May 27, 2009, www.nytimes.com/2009/05/28/
style/28hugs.html?_r=2&em.

75, 76 "hugging is certainly . . . it a success," and "object to hugging . . . cold while hugging," Mark Twain, *Wit and Humor of the Age* (Chicago: Star Publishing, 1883), 52.

KISSING
78, 80 "Fighting the tongue," and "lewd . . . behavior," Joanne Wannan, *Kisstory: A Sweet and Sexy Look at the History of Kissing* (Philadelphia: Running Press, 2010), 17, 44.

79, 80 "sniffing," "setting mouth to mouth" and "The Romans . . . chief exports." Joshua Foer, "The Kiss of Life," *The New York Times*, Feburary 14, 2006. www.nytimes.com/2006/02/14/opinion/14foer .html?ex=1297573200.

80 "Under the emperors . . . great themselves." *The Mirror of Literature, Amusement and Instruction* (London: J. Limbird, 1803), 207.

NODDING
85–86 "These signs are . . . when we disapprove, "Anglo-Saxons . . . instinctive." Charles Darwin, *The Expression of the Emotions in Man and Animals* (New York: D. Appleton, 1913), 272, 273.

OPENING A DOOR FOR A LADY
89, 90 "a paternalistic . . . them affectionately," and "if gallantry begets . . . workplaces and marriages." Jenna Goudreau, "Is Chivalry Sexist?" *Forbes*, June 28, 2011, www.forbes.com/sites/ jennagoudreau/2011/06/28/is-chivalry-sexist/.

90 "Men who hold . . . feminists claim." "Men who hold open doors for women are SEXIST not chivalrous, feminists claim," *Daily Mail* (UK), June 15, 2011, www.dailymail.co.uk/news/ article-2003821/Feminists-claim-men-hold-open-doors-women- SEXIST-chivalrous.html#ixzz1Q7gpsMgF%.

90 "Whether a man . . . removes awkwardness." Peggy Post, Anna Post, Lizzie Post, and Daniel Post Senning, *Emily Post's Etiquette, 18th Edition* (New York: William Morrow, 2011), 372.

SMILING

91, 92, 93, 94 "a miraculous . . . of art," "widely celebrated," "the slave . . . smile," "belonged to . . . tax collectors," "entirely contrary . . . conceal them, " and "I could heartily . . . while you live." Angus Trumble, *A Brief History of the Smile* (New York: Basic Books, 2004), 22, 24, xxiii, 6, 74.

TIP OF THE HAT

98 "novel device . . . in any manner." "Patent Curiosities," *Popular Mechanics*, April 1910, 602.

99 "Lifting the hat . . . strangers only," "In lifting . . . his courtesy," Emily Post, *Etiquette in Society, in Business, in Politics and at Home* (New York: Funk & Wagnalls, 1923), 23.

WINKING

102 "If, after . . . some homely girl." Clifton Fadiman, ed., *Fifty Years* (New York: Borzoi Books, 1965), 891.

102 "winking is for . . . all about context." Maegan Carberry, "Opening Eyes to the Art of Winking," *Chicago Tribune*, June 28, 2004, articles.chicagotribune.com/2004-06-28/news/0406290001 _1_winking-alice-kindness.

103 "Although the ads . . . Christian beliefs," "'Winking Jesus' advert banned for being 'disrespectful,'" *London Evening Standard*, September 7, 2011, www.standard.co.uk/news/winking-jesus-advert-banned-for-being-disrespectful-6440827.html.

103 "I have not slept a wink," R. W. Criswell, *The New Shakespeare and Other Travesties*, 3rd ed. (New York: The American News Co., 1882), 84.

103–104 "to shut . . . the eyelids," Noah Webster, *An American Dictionary of the English Language*, 3rd ed. (New York: S. Converse, 1830), 929.

104 "active connivance," and "not only . . . purposely asleep," Charles John Smith, *Synonyms Discriminated: A Dictionary of Synonymous Words in the English Language* (New York: Henry Holt, 1889), 175.

NICE WORDS TO SAY
AMEN
108 "Amen to that" William Shakespeare (Michael Neill, ed.), *The Oxford Shakespeare: Othello: The Moor of Venice* (Oxford: Oxford University Press, 2006), 253.

BLESS YOU
111 "plague of the groin," George C. Kohn, ed., *Encyclopedia of Plague and Pestilence: From Ancient Times to the Present*, 3rd ed. (New York: Facts on File, 2008) 323.

111, 112 "puts a healthy . . . to get," "May the . . . nothing," "divine favor" and "God help you." Leslie K. Arnovick, *Diachronic Pragmatics: Seven Case Studies in English Illocutionary Development* (Philadelphia: John Benjamins , 1999), 128, 129.

111 "physiologic response . . . of the nose," Pamela Georgeson, "Why Do We Sneeze?" *Scientific American*, April 17, 2000, www.scientificamerican.com/article.cfm?id=why-do-we-sneeze.

112, 113 "health," "healthiness," "healthiness is better than illness," "may you live 100 years," Bethanne Patrick and John Thompson, *An Uncommon History of Common Things* (Washington, DC: National Geographic Society, 2009), 74.

COMPLIMENTS
118, 116 "What seems like . . . wishful-thinking speech," and "in great houses . . . and principalities." Richard Stengel, *You're Too Kind: A Brief History of Flattery* (New York: Simon & Schuster, 2000), 63, 105.

117 "I can live . . . compliment." Albert Bigelow Paine, *Mark Twain: a Biography, Volume 4* (New York: Harper and Brothers, 1912), 1334.

CONGRATULATIONS

119 "the civility of envy," Julie Coleman, *A History of Cant and Slang Dictionaries: Volume III: 1859–1936* (New York: Oxford University Press, 2009), 4.

119 "sincere . . . congrats," Charles R. King, ed., *The Life and Correspondence of Rufus King: Volume IV* (New York: G. P. Putnam's Sons, 1897), 444.

EULOGY

123 "Praise famous . . . generation." Abe Aamidor, "A Great Send-Off," *Indianapolis Star*, March 17, 2002, J2.

124 "He was one . . . in your conversation." Cyrus M. Copeland, ed., *Farewell, Godspeed: The Greatest Eulogies of Our Time* (New York: Harmony Books, 2003), 152.

EXCUSE ME (PARDON ME)

129–130 "The expressions . . . one's own awkwardness," and "a social tabu . . . your pardon." Emily Post, "Good Taste Today," *Reading Eagle* (Reading, Pennsylvania), January 13, 1937, 9.

130 "NEVER SAY," and "must *not*," Emily Post, *Etiquette in Society, in Business, in Politics and at Home* (New York: Funk & Wagnalls, 1923), 60, 23.

130–131 "I can only answer . . . bad taste." Emily Post, "'Pardon Me' Is Bad Taste," *Spokesman-Review* (Spokane, Washington), December 2, 1941, 9.

131 "virtually interchangeable." Ann Landers, "When His Business Is Bad Dad Gives Kids 'Business,'" *St. Petersburg Times* (Florida), February 23, 1961, 3D.

131 "sounds a tad . . . '*pardonnez-moi*,'" and "Today . . . Richard Nixon." Abigail Van Buren, "Wrong Birth Sign Made Starry-Eyed Woman Blink," *Sarasota Journal* (Florida), April 19, 1982, 9A.

GOOD-BYE
134 "They think . . . familiarity graciously." Torbjörn Lundmark, *Tales of Hi and Bye: Greeting and Parting Rituals Around the World* (Cambridge: Cambridge University Press, 2009), 214.

HELLO
136 "a new word . . . tags," Robert Siegel and Linda Wertheimer, *NPR All Things Considered*, March 19, 1999.

138 "When the first . . . soul-satisfying word—Hello!" "Origin of the Telephone 'Hello,'" *Telephony: An Illustrated Monthly Telephone Journal*, January 1905 (9:6), 492.

MR./MRS./MS.
141–142 "The use of Ms. . . . in a name." Wendy Atkins-Sayer, "Naming Women: The Emergence of 'Ms.' as a Liberatory Title," *Women and Language*, March 22, 2005 (28:1), 8.

142 "We still teach . . . rigid rules." Bethanne Patrick, *An Uncommon History of Common Courtesy* (Washington, DC: National Geographic Society, 2011), 35.

PLEASE
143 "The stiffness and curtness . . . six letters," John R. Tunis, "What a Difference If—," *Rotarian*, November 1937, 19.

143 "Please sir . . . more," Charles Dickens, *The Adventures of Oliver Twist* (London, England: Chapman & Hall, 1866) 13.

145 "There are some people . . . exercise discretion." "Forget Please When in Philadelphia," *The American Telephone Journal*, July 6, 1907 (16:11), 174.

145 "No doubt . . . the right number," "Concerning 'Number, Please?'" *Telephony: An Illustrated Monthly Telephone Journal*, October 1907 (14:4), 223.

145 "wherever . . . introduced." "Telephone Courtesy," *Electrical Review*, December 18, 1908, 1050.

146 "Its cost . . . who receives it," "Costs Millions Annually But 'Please' Pays," *American Stationer and Office Outfitter*, February 14, 1920, 32.

146 "please stand clear . . . 'thank yous.'" James Ruttenberg, "TA Switches Track, 'Please' Is Back," *New York Daily News*, March 30, 1999, articles.nydailynews.com/1999-03-30/news/18100573_1_al-o-leary-announcements-subway.

SAYING GRACE
152 "a natural piety . . . Supreme being," Henry Lancelot Dixon, *'Saying Grace' Historically Considered* (Oxford, England: James Parker and Co., 1903), 8.

SORRY
155–156 "The commonplace phrase . . . by the other," Nicholas Tavuchis, *Mea Culpa: A Sociology of Apology and Reconciliation* (Stanford, CA: Stanford University Press, 1991), 19.

156 "This imperious . . . form of wimpishness." Marilyn Gardner, "Knowing When to Say 'I'm Sorry,'" *Christian Science Monitor*, May 11, 1990, 14.

157 "the year . . . apology." Andrew Brown, "Apologising for History," *The Independent* (UK), July 2, 1997, 20.

157 "Indeed I did . . . regret that." Claire Suddath, "Top 10 Apologies: *TIME*, September 10, 2010, www.time.com/time/specials/packages/article/0,28804,1913028_1913030_2016537,00.html.

THANK YOU
159 "Thanking is . . . offend no one," "In giving thanks . . . to give thanks," and "thanks as neither . . . ironic subversion," Margaret Visser, *The Gift of Thanks: The Roots and Rituals of Gratitude* (New York: HarperCollins, 2008), 63, 235, 50.

TOASTING
165 "The gallants . . . before toasting," "filthy and . . . drinking healths," and "I never fare . . . is drunk." London Globe, "Origin of Toasting," *Gazette* (Montreal), September 17, 1903, 10.

YOU'RE WELCOME
169 "You're supposed . . . some one," "The transaction . . . on either side," and "You're welcome will eventually . . . be obsolete." Maria Tucker, "Here's the Problem: 'No problem' is Replacing 'You're Welcome,'" *McClatchy Newspapers*, January 29, 2009, www .mcclatchydc.com/2009/01/29/61012/heres-the-problem-no-problem-is.html.

170 "As if decreed . . . talent and money." William Safire, "On Language: At the Pleasure," *The New York Times*, May 13, 2007, www.nytimes.com/2007/05/13/magazine/13wwln-safire-t .html?_r=2.

NICE OFFERINGS
ANNIVERSARY GIFTS (WEDDING)
176 "partly in congratulation . . . into the grave." Robert Thorne, *Fugitive Facts: An Epitome of General Information* (New York: A. L. Burt, 1889), 446.

178 "After the ninth . . . were necessary." "Wedding Anniversary List Keyed to Modern Family Life," *Oak Leaves* (Oak Park, Illinois), June 24, 1948, 78.

179 "Silver is always serious," Emily Post, *Etiquette in Society, in Business, in Politics and at Home* (New York: Funk & Wagnalls, 1923), 379.

BIRTHDAY CAKE
182 "a striking . . . birthday cake," John A. Selbie, ed., *Encyclopedia of Religion and Ethics* (New York: Charles Scribner's Sons, 1914), 565.

185 "a cake constructed . . . birthday cake," Andrew F. Smith, ed., *The Oxford Companion to American Food and Drink* (New York: Oxford University Press, 2007), 52.

BOX OF CHOCOLATES
187 "the first specially . . . design," Patrick Robertson, *Robertson's Book of Firsts: Who Did What for the First Time*, Kindle Edition (New York: Bloomsbury, 2011).

189 "Let me say . . . of chocolates." Winston Groom, *Forrest Gump* (New York: Doubleday, 1986), 1.

BREAD, SALT, AND WINE
191 "Bread! . . . reign forever." Michael Willian, *The Essential It's a Wonderful Life: A Scene-By-Scene Guide to the Classic Film* (Chicago: Chicago Review Press, 2006), 54.

192 "The bread . . . and happiness." Sandra Choron and Harry Choron, *Planet Wedding: A Nuptial-Pedia* (Boston: Houghton Mifflin Harcourt, 2010), 31.

192 "Wine is . . . and wealth," "Former factory gets a new use," *Leicester Mercury* (UK), July 19, 1999, 4.

CHARITY
194 "no action . . . and unjust," "Some gifts . . . other to take," and "unreclaimably poor," Robert H. Bremner, *Giving: Charity and Philanthropy in History* (New Brunswick, NJ: Transaction, 2000), 7, 9, 159.

196 "The best philanthropy . . . called charity." Peter Frumkin, *Strategic Giving: The Art and Science of Philanthropy* (Chicago: University of Chicago Press, 2006), 8.

CHICKEN SOUP
199 "soup of fat hens," Victoria R. Rumble, *Soup Through the Ages: A Culinary History with Period Recipes* (Jefferson, NC: McFarland, 2009), 67.

200 "chicken soup . . . essential drug" Abraham Ohry and Jenni Tsafrir, "Is Chicken Soup an Essential Drug?" *Canadian Medical Association Journal*, December 14, 1999 (161:12), www.cmaj.ca/content/161/12/1532.full.

FLOWERS
203 "return of affection," A Lady, *Flora's Dictionary* (Baltimore: Fielding Lucas, 1832).

204 "say that . . . with grace." Mandy Kirby and Vanessa Diffenbaugh, *A Victorian Flower Dictionary: The Language of Flowers Companion* (New York: Ballantine, 2011), 7.

GREETING CARD
211, 212 "men and women . . . produced in that context," "The rooms are . . . and dressmaker," and "Surely a . . . the gods!" Barry Shank, *A Token of My Affection: Greeting Cards and American Business Culture* (New York: Columbia University Press, 2004), 21, 63, 65.

MAY BASKET
215 "The job now in hand . . . hunt for flowers," Louisa May Alcott, *Jack and Jill: A Village Story* (Boston: Roberts Brothers, 1888), 224.

216 "To do it right . . . but not too fast." "May basket tradition lives on—in memories and deliveries," *Lincoln Journal Star* (Nebraska), May 1, 2011, journalstar.com/news/local/article_e876dafd-ccf7-5a1e-b96b-8b25a8921150.html.

MINT ON YOUR HOTEL PILLOW
219 "The chocolate has . . . a treat." Jennifer Tung, "Hotel Turndown Treats: No More Chocolates on the Pillow," *The New York Times*, September 11, 2005, travel2.nytimes.com/2005/09/11/travel/11next.html.

PARTY FAVORS
220 "celebrated with . . . returned wealthy," William Langhorn, ed., *Plutarch's Lives* (New York: John W. Lovell, 1889), 562.

221 "inspired by . . . or prosperity," Melitta Weiss Adamson and Francine Segan, eds., *Entertaining from Ancient Rome to the Super Bowl: An Encyclopedia* (Westport, CT: Greenwood Press, 2008), 394.

TIPPING
224 "Though I confess . . . to withhold," Ralph Waldo Emerson, *Selected Essays* (Chicago: Book Production Industries, 2005), 36.

225 "offensively . . . fawning for favors," and "patron saint . . . crusade." Kerry Segrave, *Tipping: An American Social History of Gratuities* (Jefferson, NC: McFarland & Co., 1998), 23, 21.

225–226 "Americans are . . . they ponied up." Steve Dublanica, *Keep the Change: A Clueless Tipper's Quest to Become the Guru of the Gratuity* (New York: HarperCollins, 2010), 23.

WEDDING AND ENGAGEMENT RINGS
229 "having no worth . . . the giver," George Frederick Kunz, *Rings for the Finger* (Philadelphia: J. B. Lippincott, 1917), 103.

WRAPPING PAPER
238 "packages . . . in paper," Patrick Robertson, *Robertson's Book of Firsts: Who Did What for the First Time* Kindle Edition (New York: Bloomsbury, 2011).

239 "Good taste . . . business," Eric Pace, "J. C. Hall, Hallmark Founder, is Dead," *The New York Times*, October 30, 1982, 1:35.

NICE IMAGES AND WRITING

DOVES
244 "When we malign . . . foul houses." Peter Watkins and Jonathan Stockland, *Winged Wonders: A Celebration of Birds in Human History* (New York: BlueBridge, 2007), 26.

FAIRY TALES
251 "Over time these . . . of generations." Richard Gray, "Fairy Tales Have Ancient Origin," *Daily Telegraph* (UK), September

5, 2009, www.telegraph.co.uk/science/science-news/6142964/
Fairy-tales-have-ancient-origin.html.

251, 252 "Tehrani has bought . . . real world" and "Anyone who . . .
always have had." Lynda Hurst, "Red Riding Hood's Not out of the
Woods Yet," *Toronto Sun*, September 13, 2009, Insight 1.

HEART SYMBOL
256–257 "The shape we . . . male dominance." Eve Ensler, Gloria
Steinem (Foreword), *The Vagina Monologues: The V-Day Edition*
(New York: Villard Books, 1996), xiv.

NURSERY RHYMES
259–260 "'unsavoury' material . . . body snatching." David Adams
Leeming and Marion Sader, eds., *Storytelling Encyclopedia*
(Phoenix: Oryx Press, 1997), 335.

260 "adult . . . joviality," "grown-ups . . . miniature," and "guardian spirit." Iona and Peter Opie, *The Oxford Dictionary of Nursery
Rhymes* (New York: Oxford University Press, 1997), 3, 4, 323.

OBITUARIES
264 "Weary of reading . . . he died." John Ingold, "Frank Obituary
for Man Who Loved Booze, Women and Fords Finds Life in
Cyberspace," *Denver Post*, April 13, 2012, www.denverpost
.com/breakingnews/ci_20391232/frank-obituary-man-who-
loved-booze-women-and.

264, 265, 266 "having left behind . . . years together," "elo-
quent . . . defender," and "Readers . . . live people." Nigel Starck,
"Posthumous Parallel and Parallax: The Obituary Revival on Three
Continents," *Journalism Studies* 2008 (6:3), 268, 271, 272.

266, 267 "dwelling in . . . half dead," "He would listen . . . was sin-
gular," and "It turned me . . . of person." Marilyn Johnson, *The Dead
Beat: Lost Souls, Lucky Stiffs, and Perverse Pleasures of Obituaries*
(New York: HarperCollins, 2007), 47, 97, 100.

NOTES
......

PEACE SYMBOL
270, 271, 272 "The face of . . . crossed himself," "stuck into . . . Field of Remembrance," "put considerable . . . his later divorce," "be remembered . . . be based," and "Peace may . . . is free." Ken Kolsbun with Michael S. Sweeney, *Peace: The Biography of a Symbol* (Washington, DC: National Geographic Society, 2008), 50, 36, 52, 170.

271 "I was in . . . circle round it." Rose Zgodzinski, "A Man and His Symbol," *Globe and Mail* (Canada), April 12, 2008, A20.

272 "footprint . . . chicken." Paul Farhl, "For 50 Years This Has Been the Symbol Of Peace. Far Out." *The Washington Post*, April 4, 2008, C01.

RAINBOWS
275 "Hungarian folk . . . offending hand," Raymond L. Lee Jr. and Alistair B. Fraser, *The Rainbow Bridge: Rainbows in Art, Myth, and Science* (University Park: The Pennsylvania State University Press, 2001), 28.

276 "I do set . . . the earth." Adam Clarke (commentary), *The Holy Bible* (New York: B. Waugh and T. Mason, 1833), 78.

278 "One would . . . of a rainbow." Leland Gregory, *Stupid History: Tales of Stupidity, Strangeness, and Mythconceptions Throughout the Ages* (Kansas City, MO: Andrews McMeel, 2007), 99.

SALUTATIONS AND CLOSINGS
260 "Your Sacred Catholic . . . imperial feet," James Lockhart and Enrique Otte, eds., *Letters and People of the Spanish Indies, Sixteenth Century* (Cambridge: Cambridge University Press, 1976), 194.

280 "Your Majesty's . . . and Dog," *Letters of the Duke and Duchess of Buckingham* (Edinburgh: Thomas G. Stevenson, 1834), xxii.

280 "Your most . . . servant," Henry Stephens Randall, *The Life of Thomas Jefferson: In Three Volumes*, Vol. 1 (New York: Derby & Jackson, 1858), 555.

280 "Few things . . . of the times." "Ways to Close Letter Show Social Changes Over Years," *Gazette* (Schenectady, New York), April 18, 1988, 15.

281 "the salutations . . . degrees of station," James J. Murphy, *Rhetoric in the Middle Ages* (Berkeley: University of California Press, 1974), 196.

282 "I have always . . . ('I am yours truly.')." Frank Colby, "Take My Word for It," *Pittsburgh Post-Gazette*, December 28, 1949, 17.

282 "It is usually . . . themselves," Amy Vanderbilt, "Etiquette Rules Concerning Letter Closings Are Less Rigid," *Toledo Blade* (Ohio), July 11, 1955, 13.

283 "one avoids . . . undercommitment," Judith Martin, "When are Sexual Advances Considered Polite Behavior?" *St. Petersburg Times* (Florida), August 15, 1979, 2D.

283 "I don't know . . . for revision." Ann Landers, "Letter Salutations Overdue for Revision," *Press-Courier* (Oxnard, California), April 28, 1983, 6.

YELLOW SMILEY FACE
288 "in-house . . . campaign," Ellen Barry (*The Boston Globe*), "'Smiley face' designer gets stamp of approval," *Salina Journal* (Kansas), October 7, 1999, A3.

289 "I would . . . great day," "He annoys . . . creep," and "If you . . . over the design," Matthew Kauffman, "Creator of 'Smiley Face' Icon Not Laughing Now," *Hartford Courant*, October 14, 1998, E4.

289 "because French . . . happy." Parmy Olson, "Scott's Wal-Mart in Trademark Clash Over Smiley Face," *Forbes*, May 8,

2006, www.forbes.com/2006/05/08/walmart-smiley-trademark-cx_po_0508autofacescan08.html.

290 "Never in . . . understood in art." Associated Press, "Boston Man Frowns On Smiley Battle," *Post-Standard* (Syracuse, New York), July 7, 1998, A8.

NICE SAYINGS AND SONGS
AULD LANG SYNE
298 "Light be the . . . glorious fragment," "'Auld Lang Syne,'" *The Burns Encyclopedia*, accessed December 5, 2012, www.robertburns .org/encyclopedia/AuldLangSyne.5.shtml. 298 "He would . . . by the melody." Bob Edwards, "Fiddler Alasdair Fraser on the Origins of 'Auld Lang Syne,'" *NPR Morning Edition*, December 31, 1999.

301 "The song . . . very useful song." Jeffrey Lee Puckett, "Auld Lang 'Syne' of the Times: Lyrics are Familiar yet Baffling," *Courier-Journal* (Louisville, Kentucky), December 27, 2010, "Scene."

BREAK A LEG
304 "Because of the . . . 'good luck.'" Joan Alpert, "Never Say Good Luck," *Jewish World*, July 1, 2011 (36:4), 24.

CAROLS
311 "a new enthusiasm . . . singers," Ace Collins, *Stories Behind the Great Traditions of Christmas* (Grand Rapids, MI: Zondervan, 2003), 47.

THE CUSTOMER IS ALWAYS RIGHT
315 "Is Sir . . . 'op it mate!'" "To be . . . anticipate requirements." "as guests . . . getting their patronage." Lindy Woodhead, *Shopping, Seduction & Mr Selfridge* (London: Profile Books, 2008), 6, 36, 35.

317 "the great cathedral of shopping," Suzy Menkes, "Harry Selfridge: The 'Showman of Shopping,'" *The New York Times*, October 30, 2007, www.nytimes.com/2007/10/29/style/29iht-FSELF.1.8092028.html.

318 "The time . . . her dismissal." Harry Gordon Selfridge, *The Romance of Commerce* (New York: John Lane, 1918), 372.

EAT, DRINK, AND BE MERRY
320 "boy . . . plough," Fran Rees, *William Tyndale: Bible Translator and Martyr* (Minneapolis: Compass Point Books, 2006), 87.

322 "Let us eat . . . shall die" John N. Oswalt, *The NIV Application Commentary: Isaiah* (Grand Rapids, MI: Zondervan, 2003), 260.

322 "If you enjoy . . . biological effect." "Eat, Drink and Don't Be Sorry," *European Magazine*, November 14, 1996, 8.

GOLDEN RULE
326–327 "It functions as . . . requirement of consistency." Jeffrey Wattles, *The Golden Rule* (New York: Oxford University Press, 1996), 186.

327 "Let no man . . . to himself." "What you do . . . to them." and "That nature alone . . . its own self." Jeffrey Wattles, *Journal of Religious Ethics*, Spring 1987 (15:1), 106.

329 "Do not do . . . unto you," W. H. Auden and Louis Kronenberger, *The Viking Book of Aphororisms* (New York: Viking Press, 1966) 140.

329 "He has observed . . . golden fool." William Blake, *The Selected Poems of William Blake* (Ware, England: Wordsworth Editions, 1994), 170.

329 "He who . . . rules." Robert Hendrickson, *The Facts on File Encyclopedia of Word and Phrase Origins*, 4th ed. (New York: Checkmark Books, 2008), 353.

HAPPY BIRTHDAY TO YOU
332 "I would take . . . perfect ease." Robert Brauneis, "Copyright and the World's Most Popular Song," *GWU Legal Studies Research Paper No. 1111624*, October 14, 2010, 11.

HAVE A NICE DAY

338–339 "I can think . . . note of goodwill." Jack Smith, "The Inescapable 'Nice Day,'" *Tuscaloosa News* (Alabama), March 30, 1973, 4.

340 "The expression . . . throat," William Safire (*The New York Times*), "'Have a nice day'—America's Favorite Farewell is Driving Folks Crazy," *Lakeland Ledger* (Florida), July 8, 1979, 16A.

340 "The problem . . . loose-lipped cashier," George Carlin, Accessed December 5, 2012, www.youtube.com/watch?v=7vmknnXoOJk.

HIP, HIP, HOORAY

343 "The Europeans . . . given heartily," William Sowden, *The Northern Territory as it Is* (Adelaide, Australia: W. K. Thomas, 1882), 25.

344 "S-J! S-J! . . . Hooray!" "College Cries," *Christian Union (New Outlook)*, September 11, 1890 (42:11), 349.

345 "Jewish feelings . . . word[s]," Raymond Apple, *Let's Ask the Rabbi* (Milton Keynes: AuthorHouse UK, 2011), 123.

PUT YOUR BEST FOOT FORWARD

353 "The foot itself . . . [in Roman literature]," A. Pelzer Wagener, "On 'Putting the Best Foot Forward,'" *Transactions and Proceedings of the American Philological Association*, 1935, 66:75.

354 "setting . . . foot forward" James A. H. Murphy and Henry Bradley, eds., *A New English Dictionary on Historical Principles*, Vol. IV (Oxford, England: Clarendon Press, 1901), 402.

SLEEP TIGHT, DON'T LET THE BEDBUGS BITE

356–357 "Why crawl . . . next meal?" Terry Gross, "Good Night, Sleep Tight, Don't Let the Bedbugs Bite," *NPR Fresh Air*, September 8, 2010, www.npr.org/templates/story/story.php?storyId=129701363.

SUGAR AND SPICE AND EVERYTHING NICE

360, 361 "What are some . . . parrot's tongues." and "young women . . . old cow's horns." Iona and Peter Opie, *The Oxford Dictionary of Nursery Rhymes* (New York: Oxford University Press, 1997), 117.

360 "Literature is . . . cannot be." Carroll Smith-Rosenberg, "Their Writing Was Suspect," *The New York Times*, January 22, 1984, 7:16.

361 "8 cups . . . Chemical X." "The Rowdyruff Boys," *The Powerpuff Girls*, Season 1, Episode 12. Accessed December 4, 2012, www.you tube.com/watch?v=SVyiONoSN98&feature=related.

NICE CHARACTERS

CUPID

368 "loveliest of all . . . their wills." and "Eros . . . awe inspiring," Roger Martin, "Cupid aka Eros, Has Long History," Kansas University Research and Public Service, February 11, 2000, www .news.ku.edu/2000/00N/FebNews/Feb11/cupid.html.

369–370 "He is represented . . . diversions," John Lemprière, *A Classical Dictionary Containing a Copious Account of All the Proper Names Mentioned in Ancient Authors*, 11th ed. (London: T. Cadell and W. Davies, 1820), 225.

EASTER BUNNY

373 "Do not worry . . . cook the nest." Frank Whelan, "Roll Out the Rabbit, We'll Have a Basket of Eggs," *Morning Call* (Allentown, Pennsylvania), April 19, 1987, articles.mcall.com/1987-04-19/ features/2580451_1_easter-bunny-rabbit.

STORK

387 "the oldest . . . immature humanity." Pamela Thurschwell, *Sigmund Freud* (New York: Routledge, 2000), 49.

388 "to furnish . . . the stork." George Crabb, *Universal Technological Dictionary*, Vol. I (London: Baldwin, Cradock and Joy, 1823).

389 "I know . . . never dream afterwards." Hans Christian Andersen, *The Storks* (1838), hca.gilead.org.il/storks.html.

TOOTH FAIRY
392 "Many a refractory . . . such occasions." "Odds and Ends," *Fort Wayne Journal-Gazette* (Indiana), January 1, 1914, 14.

393 "The tooth fairy is . . . exchange for coins." and "The tooth fairy's job . . . stage of life," Linda Mae Carlstone, "Deerfield Resident Follows The Tooth Fairy's Tracks," *Chicago Tribune*, May 29, 1991, articles.chicagotribune.com/1991-05-29/news/ 9102170843_1_tooth-fairy-rosemary-wells.

NICE SIDEBARS, CHARTS, LISTS, AND TIME LINES
AWARENESS RIBBONS
248 "Crosses took almost . . . nearly as far." Jesse Green, "The Year of the Ribbon," *The New York Times*, May 3, 1992, www.nytimes.com/1992/05/03/style/the-year-of-the-ribbon .html?pagewanted=all&src=pm.

MEMORABLE PASSAGES FROM EULOGIES
125–128 First nine quotes from Cyrus M. Copeland, ed., *Farewell, Godspeed: The Greatest Eulogies of Our Time* (New York: Harmony Books, 2003), 28 (Anthony), 286–287 (Twain), 180 (Einstein), 115 (Rockefeller), 61 (Roosevelt), 48 (Keller), 81 (Benny), 75 (Ball), and 19 (Versace).

128 Reagan quote from *Memorial Services in the Congress of the United States and Tributes in Eulogy of Ronald Reagan, Late a President of the United States* (Washington DC: Government Printing Office, 2005), xxxi.

EXTRA CREDIT
172 "With your smiling . . . hunkey dorey." George Christy, *Christy's Bones and Banjo Melodist* (New York: Dick & Fitzgerald, 1862), 54.

172 "All the display of the 'ticker,'" "The Sights and Sightseers," *The New York Times*, "TLC Treatment . . . a children's clinic." Ian Fleming, *Goldfinger* (New York: Penguin, 2002), 255, 264.

NICE THOUGHTS ABOUT KISSING
82, 83 Bergman, Hope, Cummings quotes from Anthony St. Peter, *The Greatest Quotations of All Time* (Bloomington, IN: Xlibris, 2010), 377.

82 Bierce quote from William Cane, *The Book of Kisses* (New York: St. Martin's Press, 1993), 14.

82 Einstein quote from Alice Calaprice, ed., *The Ultimate Quotable Einstein* (Princeton, NJ: Princeton University Press, 2011), 482.

82, 83 Warhol, Fields quotes from Tomima Edmark, *Kissing: Everything You Ever Wanted to Know* (New York: Fireside, 1991), 22, 23.

83 Holmes quote from Lana Citron, *A Compendium of Kisses* (Toronto, Canada: Harlequin, 2010), 28.

GREAT MINDS ON NICE MANNERS
346 Confucius quotes from Bethanne Patrick, *An Uncommon History of Common Courtesy* (Washington, DC: National Geographic Society, 2011), 290, 291, 292.

346 Raleigh quote from Charles Noel Douglas, ed., *Forty Thousand Quotations: Prose and Poetical* (London: George G. Harrap, 1917), 1134.

346 Disraeli quote from Benjamin Disraeli, *Wit and Wisdom of Benjamin Disraeli, Earl of Beaconsfield* (London: Longmans, Green, 1886), 208.

347 Emerson quote from Ralph Waldo Emerson, Eva March Tappan, ed., *Selected Essays and Poems* (Boston: Allyn and Bacon, 1898), 70.

347 Goethe quote from Calvin Thomas (special writer), *The German Classics: Masterpieces of German Literature*, Vol. II (New York: German Publication Society, 1913), 376.

347 Franklin quote on savages from Benjamin Franklin, *Poor Richard's Almanack* (New York: H. M. Caldwell, 1900), 62. Franklin quote on children from Lilless McPherson Shilling and Linda K. Fuller, *Dictionary of Quotations in Communications* (Westport, CT: Greenwood Press, 1997), 45.

347 Wilde quote from June Hines Moore, *The Etiquette Advantage: Rules for the Business Professional* (Nashville, TN: B&H Publishing Group, 1998) 121.

NICE PUBLIC PLACES TO GO
362 "very good musick," Patrick Robertson, *Robertson's Book of Firsts: Who Did What for the First Time*, Kindle Edition (New York: Bloomsbury, 2011).

HOLIDAYS
376 "comrades who died in . . . rebellion." *Journal of the Fifty-Second National Encampment: Grand Army of the Republic*, August 18–24, 1918, 239.

Photo Credits

Acknowledgments

N ice can be found in a broad variety of sources. Most notably, I looked at books of all kinds as well as newspaper and magazine articles, scientific studies, and patents, and I also did interviews (and even watched some YouTube videos). I must express appreciation to each and every author and researcher who came before me and touched on this topic, as well as those experts who took time to correspond with me on various elements of nice.

Closer to home, thank you to my family, beginning with my wife, Jennifer, and my kids, Miller and Becca, for their steadfast patience and kindness. Much gratitude goes to both my dad, Lionel, and my brother, Michael, whose breadth and depth of knowledge I so respect and whose suggestions and help on this book were priceless. As always, words cannot express my appreciation to Dan Snierson, who is an amazing friend and my go-to guy for reading a draft of anything I've written. Of course, praise goes to my editor at Workman, Maisie Tivnan, whose enthusiasm and expert eye were essential with this effort. Last, but certainly not least, a big thanks goes to my mom, Gloria, who has taught me so very much about what constitutes nice in this world.

About the Author

J osh Chetwynd is a journalist, broadcaster, and author. He's worked as a staff reporter for *USA Today*, the *Hollywood Reporter*, and *US News & World Report*, and his writing has also appeared in such publications as *The Wall Street Journal*, *The Times* (of London), the *Harvard Negotiation Law Review*, and *Variety*. In addition, he's been a broadcaster for BBC Radio, among other outlets. His previous books include *The Secret History of Balls: The Stories Behind the Things We Love to Catch, Whack, Throw, Kick, Bounce and Bat* and *How the Hot Dog Found Its Bun: Accidental Discoveries and Unexpected Inspirations that Shape What We Eat and Drink*. Though he doesn't always succeed, he tries to do something nice on a daily basis.